ADVANCE PRAISE FOR PAOLO MANCOSU'S

Moscow Has Ears Everywhere: New Investigations on Pasternak and Ivinskaya

Paolo Mancosu's richly documented and profoundly moving account of some of the most dramatic episodes in the cultural life of the Cold War period is a major contribution to Pasternak scholarship and Russian studies.

—**Lazar Fleishman**, Stanford University

Paolo Mancosu's new book is a treat for the specialist and the general reader. Mancosu has unearthed an enormous amount of new documentary evidence that sheds a completely new light on a story we thought we knew well: Pasternak's persecution following the Nobel Prize award, the arrests of Olga Ivinskaya and Irina Emelianova, and their subsequent release. Mancosu unveils the surprising twists of the story and weaves a rich tapestry describing the political, literary, and private relations among the protagonists. Most important, he gives us insights into their inner lives—the lives of outstanding and ordinary people enmeshed in the cruel hostility of the Cold War. It is a splendid achievement.

—**Anna Sergeeva-Klyatis**, Moscow State University

Professor Mancosu's book investigates the post–Nobel Prize events in Pasternak's life and the repercussions of his confrontation with Soviet power on his beloved Olga Ivinskaya and her daughter Irina Emelianova. It represents a quantum leap in our understanding of those events, both on account of the impressive number of unknown archival sources Mancosu brought to light as well as for the thorough and careful interpretation of those tragic events. Mancosu's first-rate study is a must read for anyone interested in the relationship between literature and politics during the Cold War.

—**Fedor Poljakov**, University of Vienna

MOSCOW HAS EARS EVERYWHERE

MOSCOW HAS EARS EVERYWHERE

NEW INVESTIGATIONS ON PASTERNAK AND IVINSKAYA

Paolo Mancosu

HOOVER INSTITUTION PRESS
Stanford University Stanford, California

With its eminent scholars and world-renowned library and archives, the Hoover Institution seeks to improve the human condition by advancing ideas that promote economic opportunity and prosperity, while securing and safeguarding peace for America and all mankind. The views expressed in its publications are entirely those of the authors and do not necessarily reflect the views of the staff, officers, or Board of Overseers of the Hoover Institution.

www.hoover.org

Hoover Institution Press Publication No. 698

Hoover Institution at Leland Stanford Junior University,
Stanford, California 94305-6003

First printing 2019
25 24 23 22 21 20 19 7 6 5 4 3 2 1

Manufactured in the United States of America

The paper used in this publication meets the minimum Requirements of the American National Standard for Information Sciences—Permanence of Paper for Printed Library Materials, ANSI/NISO Z39.48-1992. ∞

Cataloging-in-Publication Data is available from the Library of Congress.
ISBN: 978-0-8179-2244-3 (cloth. : alk. paper)
ISBN: 978-0-8179-2246-7 (epub)
ISBN: 978-0-8179-2247-4 (mobi)
ISBN: 978-0-8179-2248-1 (PDF)

Contents

Illustrations

Preface

Doctor Zhivago has been slow in disclosing its mysteries. Only recently have the archives begun to reveal the full complexity of the *Zhivago* affair. The documents of the Central Committee of the CPSU (*Le dossier* 1994; Afiani and Tomilina 2001), the *Zhivago* files recently declassified by the CIA (www.foia.cia.gov/collection/doctor-zhivago; Finn and Couvée 2014; Mancosu 2016), and vast holdings in the Feltrinelli archives (Feltrinelli 1999; Mancosu 2013), to name just a few of the major troves of new information, are telling a story that defies belief.

Of all the events related to the *Zhivago* affair, one stands out as having so far resisted closer scrutiny. I am referring to the events that followed Pasternak's death and that led to the arrests of Pasternak's lover and literary assistant, Olga Ivinskaya, and her daughter, Irina Emelianova. This neglect is especially surprising in light of the wide publicity and international visibility generated by the arrests and sentences of Olga and Irina.

The present book consists of three chapters and a documentary appendix, which stem from three long articles I recently published on the Ivinskaya case. It is not an attempt to tell the story of Boris Pasternak and Olga Ivinskaya, a story already recounted first by Olga Ivinskaya herself (Ivinskaya 1978), then by her daughter, Irina Emelianova (Emelianova 2002), and by more recent authors. Rather, my goal is to present hitherto unknown material that enriches, complements, and at times debunks previous accounts. Given the novelty of the material I am presenting, the book will consist of three chapters (chapters 1 to 3) that analyze and put the new documents in context, followed by a large selection of the documents in the appendix. In the original articles from which the chapters originate (Mancosu and Borokhov 2017; Mancosu 2018a; Mancosu 2018b), the documents were also presented in the original language.

Here the documents will be presented only in English translation. Other changes have been made to the original articles to eliminate repetition and ensure a smooth transition between chapters. In addition, I have updated the bibliography, and appropriately modified the narrative, to include references to articles that have appeared since my original articles were written. From the point of view of content, the major change is reflected in section 2.2, which improves the account given in the corresponding section in Mancosu 2018a. A little asymmetry has been preserved in the presentation of the documents, in that the first twenty letters, from 1956 to May 1960, are each accompanied by a commentary that supplements what is said in the main text. This is because those letters often refer to events not treated in the main text and thus require additional context. Also documents 41 and 46 have an individual commentary. By contrast, the context of the remaining letters, dating from June to September 1960, is sufficiently clarified by what is said in the main text. But before I move to a more detailed description of the chapters and the documents, let me give a quick biographical sketch of Olga Ivinskaya.

Olga Vsevolodovna Ivinskaya was born on June 16, 1912, in Tambov. In 1915, her family moved to Moscow. She studied at the Editorial Workers Institute in Moscow, from which she graduated in 1936. In that same year, she married Ivan Emelianov, with whom she had a daughter, Irina Emelianova, born in 1939. In the same year, Ivan committed suicide by hanging himself. In 1941 Olga married Aleksandr Vinogradov. They had a son, Dmitriĭ, born in 1942, who will appear in our story under Mitia. Vinogradov died after an illness in 1945. Olga worked as a literary editor, and she met Pasternak in 1946 in the editorial offices of *Novy mir*, where she was in charge of new authors.[1] Her memoir, *A Captive of Time* (1978), begins with this period. She became romantically involved with Pasternak in 1947 and soon left *Novy mir*. Upon leaving *Novy mir* in 1947, she earned her living translating and editing while helping Pasternak and benefiting from his support. In 1949, she was arrested and was sent to a labor camp the following year, from which she came back, obviously scarred, in 1953, after Stalin's death. The reasons for her arrest remain unclear, but interrogators grilled her about Pasternak's alleged anti-Soviet feelings and contacts with the officials of the British embassy in Moscow. I refer the reader to the memoir of Irina Emelianova, her daughter, for

1. Olga also wrote poems. On Olga's literary work see Ivinskaya 1999, especially the long introduction by Irina Emelianova.

lengthy passages from those interrogations (Emelianova 1997, 2002). Be that as it may, it is clear that Pasternak felt she had been arrested because of him. In a letter to Renate Schweitzer dated May 7, 1958, Pasternak wrote:

> She was put in jail on my account, as the person considered by the secret police to be closest to me, and they hoped that by means of a grueling interrogation and threats they could extract enough evidence from her to put me on trial. I owe my life and the fact that they did not touch me in these years to her heroism and endurance. (Ivinskaya 1978, 109; for the German original, see Schweitzer 1963, 43)

Pasternak also told Schweitzer, in the same letter, that Olga was the inspiration for Lara in *Doctor Zhivago* ("Sie ist die Lara des Werkes"). Upon her return from the camp in 1953, Olga not only resumed her love relationship with Pasternak but also became his assistant and was put in charge of the delicate negotiations with Soviet authorities both during the *Zhivago* crisis in 1957 and during Pasternak's persecution after receiving the Nobel Prize in Literature in October 1958. After 1959, and especially in 1960, she also played a more important role, on Pasternak's behalf, in maintaining epistolary—and at times personal—relations with several Western publishers (for instance, Giangiacomo Feltrinelli) or other Westerners who were helping Pasternak in his literary endeavors and finances (for instance, Jacqueline de Proyart, Sergio d'Angelo, Heinz Schewe, and Gerd Ruge).

While her devotion to Pasternak is beyond question, her conduct was not always transparent. But one must keep in mind that the Soviet authorities exploited her fears. Olga was by Pasternak's side before, during, and after the *Zhivago* affair. She found herself at the center of complex editorial and financial interactions for which she paid dearly.

Doctor Zhivago was published in 1957 by the Italian Communist publisher Giangiacomo Feltrinelli. The battle over the publication was fierce, as Feltrinelli resisted pressure from the Central Committee of the CPSU through the Soviet Writers' Union and the top brass of the Italian Communist Party.[2] Pasternak was also pressured to withdraw consent for the publication, but the book appeared in Italian in November 1957 to Pasternak's delight. The 1957 Italian publication led, in 1958, to the book's

2. As a consequence of such pressure and of the disciplinary trial to which he was subjected by the PCI at the end of 1957, Feltrinelli did not renew his membership in the PCI (Mancosu 2013, 96–102).

appearance in several foreign languages and the original Russian (in the West). The success of the book was enormous, in part on account of the Cold War atmosphere in which it appeared.

After receiving the Nobel Prize on October 23, 1958, Pasternak lost his means of subsistence and was forced to draw on the royalties that were accumulating abroad.[3] Ivinskaya often received the money on Pasternak's behalf. The Soviet authorities were aware of this but did not do anything about it until Pasternak died on May 30, 1960. After he died, however, they took revenge on Olga and her daughter. Olga was arrested on August 16, 1960, and soon afterward her daughter, Irina, was also arrested. They were convicted of smuggling money and sentenced to eight years and three years of labor camp, respectively. After much international pressure and behind-the-scenes contacts between Feltrinelli and Soviet authorities, Irina and Olga were freed in 1962 and 1964, respectively.

The above short summary will allow me to present now the first three chapters of the book in more detail.

In chapter 1 we go back to the year 1956, when Boris Pasternak gave a typescript of *Doctor Zhivago* to Sergio d'Angelo, thereby starting the *Zhivago* saga. Going back to Pasternak's and Ivinskaya's relations with Sergio d'Angelo, which is the main focus of chapter 1, is instrumental for a thorough comprehension of all the events that were to follow on at least two counts. First, Sergio d'Angelo was at the center of the financial arrangements that would lead to disaster. Second, Ivinskaya's role in the *Zhivago* saga emerges with particular sharpness in her contacts with Sergio d'Angelo, starting in 1957 and lasting until her arrest in August 1960. It is to be kept in mind that though Ivinskaya entertained epistolary contacts in 1959 and 1960 with other protagonists of the *Zhivago* saga, including Giangiacomo Feltrinelli, Jacqueline de Proyart, and Hélène Peltier, she developed a personal friendship with Sergio d'Angelo, and this gives particular importance to the correspondence between d'Angelo, on the one side, and Pasternak and Ivinskaya on the other. Indeed, Ivinskaya had met d'Angelo in May 1957, whereas she had not met many of the other correspondents (Proyart, Feltrinelli, etc.).

To put chapter 1 in context, let me emphasize the following. In the last three decades, there has been a steady stream of publications on

3. This was a consequence, as we shall see, of his having been expelled from the Soviet Writers' Union.

Pasternak's contacts with people in the West who played an important role in his life and career. Among the most prominent, one can cite the publication of the correspondence with Feltrinelli (Feltrinelli 1999; Elena and Evgeniĭ Pasternak 2001a, 2001b; Mancosu 2013), Jacqueline de Proyart (Elena and Evgeniĭ Pasternak 1992; Boris Pasternak 1994), Hélène Peltier-Zamoyska (Elena and Evgeniĭ Pasternak 1997; Boris Pasternak 1994), Kurt Wolff (Boris Pasternak 2010a), and his parents and sisters (Boris Pasternak 2010b, 2004). Given the central role played by d'Angelo in the *Zhivago* affair, the publication of his correspondence with Pasternak and Olga Ivinskaya fills an important gap in the story and provides an excellent *fil rouge* for following the developments leading to the events described in chapters 2 and 3.

D'Angelo recently donated all the documents in his possession that relate to his involvement in the *Zhivago* affair to the Hoover Institution Library and Archives at Stanford University. These documents include unpublished autograph letters by Pasternak and by Olga Ivinskaya, drafts of d'Angelo's letters to them, the notebook where he noted the news of the impending publication of *Zhivago*, and many other important items. By complementing the documents in d'Angelo's archive with those found at the Feltrinelli archives in Milan, I was able to reconstruct the correspondence as it is presented in chapter 1 and in the documentary appendix (documents 1–23, 41, 46).

D'Angelo's role in the story goes well beyond his having been the agent who delivered the typescript of *Doctor Zhivago* to Feltrinelli. He remained very close to Pasternak and to Olga Ivinskaya during his stay in Moscow and kept up these contacts even after he went back to Italy in December 1957. During 1959 and 1960, he was instrumental in the scheme, approved by Pasternak, to deliver some of the *Zhivago* royalties to Pasternak. This was done through couriers—usually, but not exclusively, members of the Italian Communist Party visiting Moscow.

The last delivery of rubles, on August 1, 1960 (two months after Pasternak's death on May 30, 1960), was ill-fated, because it gave the Soviets an excuse to prosecute Olga and Irina and send them to a labor camp. Chapter 1 recounts this part of the story. D'Angelo also reappears in later chapters, for in the years 1961–62 he took part in an international campaign on behalf of the two women by writing several articles, an open letter to Alekseĭ Surkov—Pasternak's archenemy in the Soviet Writers' Union—and a private letter to Nikita Khrushchev.

D'Angelo left the Soviet Union in December 1957, but he kept alive the contact with Pasternak and Ivinskaya through his friend Giuseppe ("Pino") Garritano and his wife, Mirella, who had moved to Moscow in the summer of 1957 and would play an important role as the link between d'Angelo (and thus Feltrinelli) and Pasternak (and Ivinskaya). Using hitherto unpublished archival correspondence, chapter 2 reconstructs some crucial events from 1960 that ended with the arrest of Olga, in August 1960, and of Irina, in September of the same year (see documents 29–50). Many of these events involve a document that came to be known as "Pasternak's will," in reality a power of attorney that Pasternak had signed on April 15, 1960, on behalf of Olga Ivinskaya. The document was entrusted to Giuseppe Garritano and his wife for safe delivery to Giangiacomo Feltrinelli, Pasternak's publisher in Italy, but it disappeared in mysterious circumstances in June 1960. The reconstruction shows, among other things, how Olga Ivinskaya tried to restore the document using a blank sheet of paper with Pasternak's signature on it and demonstrates that the original was intercepted by the KGB.

Finally, chapter 3 describes the Ivinskaya campaign in the West. As already mentioned, in the aftermath of Boris Pasternak's death, Olga and Irina were sentenced to eight years and three years of labor camp, respectively. The heavy sentences became a cause célèbre in the West. The accounts of the "Ivinskaya case" have hitherto been restricted to public accounts of the events, as they played out in the international press. However, most of the "Ivinskaya case" was carried out in the West as a hidden campaign aimed at persuading the Soviet authorities to revoke or soften the sentences for Olga and Irina while at the same time allowing the authorities to save face. Using hitherto untapped archival sources, I reconstruct in this chapter the behind-the-scenes efforts that characterized one of the major literary-political confrontations between the West and the USSR during the Cold War.

This is the story of a time dominated by the Cold War, and of the individuals who lived and suffered through it. The documents that constitute the documentary part of this book are therefore an irreplaceable testimonial, as well as a significant step forward in the understanding of this central part of the context of the *Zhivago* affair.

Editorial conventions. For the transliteration of Russian names into English I followed the conventions described in the transliteration table in Mancosu 2013, a slightly modified form of the Library of Congress transliteration table. The spelling given in original English sources has been preserved in the citations in the main text. Thus, in my text one will find Alekseĭ Surkov, whereas in the citations of original English sources the first name will often appear as Alexei (ditto for Tvardovskiĭ and Tvardovsky). In citations that were originally in languages other than English I have followed the official transliteration. An exception to this transliteration policy has been made for a few names of journals or persons, most notably *Novy mir* (rather than *Nov'iĭ mir*), Olga Ivinskaya (rather than Ol'ga Ivinskaia), and Andreĭ Gromyko (rather than Andreĭ Grom'iko).

Acknowledgments

The idea of writing a book centered on Ivinskaya goes back to conversations I had with Carlo Feltrinelli at the time of preparing *Inside the Zhivago Storm* for publication. I am very grateful to Carlo Feltrinelli for having given me access to the trove of documents preserved at the archives of the Feltrinelli Foundation and of the Publishing House Feltrinelli. Those documents, which constitute a great part of the documentary evidence contained in this book, convinced me that there was an important and beautiful story to be told and drove me to complete it with materials from other archives. But even more importantly, I am grateful to Carlo for having turned a publishing project into a human adventure the likes of which I will probably never experience again.

As soon as I finished *Inside the Zhivago Storm* I got in touch with Sergio d'Angelo, who soon after decided to donate his Pasternak and Ivinskaya materials to the Hoover Institution Library and Archives at Stanford University. It was d'Angelo who asked me whether I would consider editing his correspondence with Pasternak and Ivinskaya. Based on the documents found in the Feltrinelli archives in Milan and those donated by d'Angelo to the Hoover Institution, the project was successful, and its results constitute chapter 1. Its contents were published originally as Mancosu and Borokhov 2017. I am grateful to Pavel Borokhov for his contribution to that article and to Lazar Fleishman for his help in revising the article and publishing it in the volume *Novoe o Pasternakach*. Both of them have my boundless gratitude for having helped me in innumerable ways since the beginning of my work on Pasternak and *Doctor Zhivago*. I would like to thank Sergio d'Angelo for long conversations and extensive email exchanges on the material contained in this book. Materials from the Sergio d'Angelo Papers at Hoover Institution Library and Archives are cited by kind permission of Sergio d'Angelo and the director of the archives, Eric Wakin. I owe special thanks to Eric Wakin and to Linda Bernard for their terrific support during my visits to the Hoover Institution Library and Archives. That support resulted in three books (Mancosu 2015, 2016, and the present book), and I hope the books will serve as a token of my appreciation for all they have done for me.

It is also a pleasure to thank Mme Irina Emelianova for having generously granted permission to publish her mother's letters and for her epistolary remarks to the author. In addition, she provided me with scans of several pictures, some of which are included in this book and are published with her kind permission.

The majority of the materials that make up chapter 2 come from the Feltrinelli archives. Once again, I thank Carlo Feltrinelli for permission to cite from the Feltrinelli archives. Chapter 2 came out originally as Mancosu 2018a; I thank Fedor Poljakov, editor of the journal in which the essay appeared, for his careful reading of the essay.

The material presented in chapter 3 originates from a variety of archives. I owe a debt of gratitude to many people, in addition to those already thanked, who made possible this reconstruction of the Ivinskaya case.

Helen Othen, Madeleine Katkov, and Tanya Joyce, daughters of George Katkov, have been enormously supportive and encouraging. They gave me exclusive use of their father's materials and permission to cite from his letters and memos.

I am grateful to Georges Nivat for permission to cite from his letters to Katkov, Peltier, Berlin, Hayward, and Feltrinelli.

I am indebted to the librarian of St Antony's College, Richard Ramage, for his generous support and help. In addition, he facilitated permission from the governing body of St Antony's College for the use of the materials from the Max Hayward Papers.

I thank Henry Hardy for his help with the Isaiah Berlin excerpts and the Isaiah Berlin Trust (Wolfson College, Oxford) for permission to cite.

The letters from the Bertrand Russell Archive (McMaster University Library) are cited with the kind permission of the archive. I thank Rick Stapleton and Ken Blackwell for their kind assistance.

I am grateful to the archivist of the Collins Archives (Glasgow), Dawn Sinclair, for granting permission to cite. Materials from the Peltier archive in Sylvanès are cited by kind permission from André Gouzes. For permission to cite from the Heinz Schewe Papers, I am grateful to Rainer Laabs, head of corporate archive at Axel Springer SE (Berlin).

Chapter 3 came out originally as Mancosu 2018b; I thank Anna Sergeeva-Klyatis for having included the essay in the special issue on Pasternak she edited for *Russian Literature*.

Finally, I would like to thank Elena Vladimirovna Pasternak, Petia Pasternak, Elena Leonidovna Pasternak, Ann Pasternak Slater, Nicolas Pasternak Slater, Inge Feltrinelli, Anna Koznova, Katherine Dunlop, Daniel Isaacson, Kassandra Isaacson, Leonid Grigorovich, Irina Barsel, Irina Erisanova, Lora Soroka, Vincent Giroud, Andrea Gullotta, Marco Bertozzi, Marcello d'Agostino, Savina Scavo, Giuseppe Campanella, Maria Roberta Perugini, Alessandra Piras, Luciano Marrocu, Jacqueline de Proyart, Boris Mansurov, Valeria Paniccia, Stefano Garzonio, Ciro de Florio, Giulia de Florio, Graciela Acedo, Nino Kirtadze, Francesca d'Angelo, Fabio Sozio, Giovanna Bosmans, Jonathan Raspe, Sophie Dandelet, Anna Muza, and Irina Paperno. They have helped me in more ways than I can list here.

The illustrations contained in this book are published with the kind help and permission of Carlo Feltrinelli, Sergio d'Angelo, Irina Emelianova, Valeria Paniccia, Madeleine Katkov, Helen Katkov, and the governing board of St Antony's College.

For the translations from Russian, I am grateful to Alexey Strekalov, Paul Borokhov, and Yana Zlochistaya. The translations from German are due to Jarrett Dury-Agri. I also thank Elena Russo and Rebecca Loescher for assistance with the translations from French. All other translations are mine, unless otherwise stated.

I am delighted to express my gratitude to the Alexander von Humboldt Foundation for a Humboldt Prize Award that gave me the time I needed to finish this book.

Finally, last but not least, I dedicate this book to Elena, *Lara moei knigi.*

Munich, May 25, 2018

Chronology of Events

May 20, 1956. Pasternak gives Sergio d'Angelo the typescript of *Doctor Zhivago.*

November 15, 1957. *Doctor Zhivago* is published in Italian by Feltrinelli, first publication worldwide. The book goes on sale on November 22.

September 1958. The pirate edition of the Russian text of *Doctor Zhivago* appears in Holland and is distributed at the Brussels World's Fair.

September 5, 1958. The American edition of *Doctor Zhivago* is published by Pantheon.

October 23, 1958. The Swedish Academy awards Pasternak the Nobel Prize for literature.

October 25, 1958. Pasternak sends a telegram to Stockholm: "Immensely thankful, touched, proud, astonished, abashed." The Soviet Writers' Union attacks Pasternak, calling him a "Judas" and a "traitor."

October 26, 1958. *Pravda* attacks Pasternak as a reactionary and bourgeois intellectual; Pasternak should reject the Nobel Prize if there is "a spark of Soviet dignity in him."

October 28, 1958. The Soviet Writers' Union expels Pasternak.

October 29, 1958. Pasternak renounces the Nobel Prize. Vladimir Semichastn'iĭ, chief of the Young Communist League, attacks Pasternak, describing him as worse than a "pig."

November 1, 1958. Pasternak writes a letter to Khrushchev asking to be allowed to remain in Russia.

November 6, 1958. Pasternak publishes a public apology in *Pravda.*

February 2, 1959. First authorized edition of the Russian text of *Doctor Zhivago* published by Michigan under permission from Feltrinelli.

February 11, 1959. The *Daily Mail* publishes "The Nobel Prize," a poem by Pasternak that angers the Soviet authorities.

March 14, 1959. Pasternak is interrogated by R. Rudenko, the public prosecutor of the USSR, and accused of crimes against the state.

May 30, 1960. Pasternak dies in Peredelkino.

Abbreviations and Archives

Abbreviations

BL Bodleian Library
CC Central Committee
CPSU Communist Party of the Soviet Union
PCI Italian Communist Party

Archives

Canada

Bertrand Russell Archive, McMaster University (BRA)

France

Hélène Peltier (Zamoyska) Archive, Sylvanès

Germany

Heinz Schewe Papers, Corporate Archive at Axel Springer SE, Berlin

Italy

Archivio Giangiacomo Feltrinelli Editore, Milan (AGFE)
Fondo Carlo Feltrinelli, Feltrinelli Editore, Milan
Fondo Giangiacomo Feltrinelli, Milan (FoGF)

Russia

Pasternak Family Papers, Moscow
Russian State Archive of Contemporary History, Moscow (RGANI)
Russian State Archive of Literature and Art, Moscow (RGALI)
State Archive of the Russian Federation, Moscow (GARF)

United Kingdom

Collins Archives, Glasgow
George Katkov Papers, Oxford (GKP)

Isaiah Berlin Manuscripts Collection, Bodleian Library, Oxford (IBMC, MS. Berlin)

Max Hayward Papers, St Antony's College, Oxford (MHP)

United States

Kurt and Helen Wolff Papers, Beinecke Rare Book and Manuscript Library, Yale University

Nicolas Nabokov Papers, Harry Ransom Center, University of Texas at Austin

Pasternak Family Papers, Hoover Institution Library and Archives, Stanford (PFP, HILA); includes the Pasternak Trust Archive, previously at Oxford

Sergio d'Angelo Papers, Hoover Institution Library and Archives, Stanford (SdAP, HILA)

CIA documents related to *Doctor Zhivago* are available online at www.foia.cia.gov/collection/doctor-zhivago.

CHAPTER ONE

"Just Be Careful, Remember How Frightening Everything Is for Us"

The Problem of the *Zhivago* Royalties

1.1. D'Angelo receives the typescript of *Doctor Zhivago*

The facts concerning how Pasternak handed a typescript of *Doctor Zhivago* to Sergio d'Angelo for possible publication in Italy with Feltrinelli are now well known, so I will limit myself to a bare summary of the facts. In March 1956, Sergio d'Angelo, a member of the Italian Communist Party, left his job as director of the Communist Bookstore Rinascita in Rome and settled in Moscow as a member of the Italian section of Radio Moscow. In Italy, he had already been acquainted with Giangiacomo Feltrinelli, who in 1955 had founded the publishing house Giangiacomo Feltrinelli Editore.[1] Indeed, d'Angelo had already translated and written prefaces for some of Feltrinelli's books. In an unpublished letter to Valerio Riva, d'Angelo pointed out that Feltrinelli had approached him before leaving for Moscow with the proposal of acting as literary scout for works that might be of interest to the publishing house.[2] D'Angelo accepted, and in

1. On Feltrinelli, see Feltrinelli 1999 and Mancosu 2013.

2. This account is based on comments that d'Angelo sent to Valerio Riva addressing Riva and Zveteremich's projected volume on the *Zhivago* affair (the book was never published). In one of the comments d'Angelo wrote: "To be honest, the initiative for my role as consultant originated from Feltrinelli during a conversation at the bookstore Rinascita. At that time I was meeting rather frequently with Feltrinelli both as a bookseller as well as a collaborator of his first forays into publishing. I translated and wrote the prefaces for Hume's *Natural History of Religion* and for Estol's *Pancho Villa*" (SdAP, HILA; original in Italian).

late April he read a news bulletin at Radio Moscow stating that Pasternak had completed a novel titled *Doctor Zhivago* whose publication was imminent.[3] He informed the publishing house in Milan and was asked to contact Pasternak with a view to obtaining the proofs or a manuscript of the novel. On May 20, 1956, d'Angelo met Pasternak, who gave him the typescript of *Doctor Zhivago*. After one week, d'Angelo flew to Berlin, where he delivered the typescript to Feltrinelli. During this time d'Angelo became friends with Pasternak. His friendship with Olga Ivinskaya began in May 1957. For all of 1957, he was the privileged link between Pasternak and Feltrinelli. There are two letters from Pasternak to d'Angelo written in 1957 (see documents 1 and 2 in the appendix), and both contain, among other things, information that Pasternak wished d'Angelo to convey to Feltrinelli the pressure put on Pasternak by the Soviets to halt the publication of *Doctor Zhivago*.

In a letter dated November 25, 1957, ten days after the publication of the Italian *Zhivago*, Pasternak wrote to Feltrinelli:

> I have a big request for you. Nothing of the sort could have been accomplished without Sergio d'Angelo's assistance; he acted in this as our indefatigable guardian angel. Although help of this higher sort cannot be measured in pecuniary terms, please do me the favor of compensating him for his innumerable losses, for the time and energy he spent, in the following way. Set aside from the sum that you designate for me in the future a considerable portion for d'Angelo's benefit, one that you and he will find suitable, and double it. (For the full letter, see Mancosu 2013, 258; original in French)

This letter was written one month before d'Angelo's last visit to Olga and Pasternak before returning to Italy. We have a receipt dated December 24, 1957, in which Olga states she has received from d'Angelo the sum of 12,800 rubles (see document 3). D'Angelo had in fact suggested to Feltrinelli (through the Italian translator Pietro Zveteremich) that he could give some rubles to Pasternak and be paid back in liras upon his return to Italy at the end of 1957.

This was the first of what became a long list of financial transactions meant to provide Pasternak with some of the royalties for *Doctor Zhivago*.

3. D'Angelo wrote in a notebook he kept at the time: "Boris Pasternak (translator of Shakespeare). Very debated poet (impressionist). He has just finished writing 'Doct. Zhivago,' a novel in diary form that encompasses 3/4 of the century and ends with the second world war" (original in Italian). The notebook is now preserved in the SdAP, HILA.

Indeed, it is fair to say that these financial transactions constitute one of the most important topics of conversation in the correspondence from 1959 and 1960. To understand how these issues emerged, it is worth rereading some lines that Pasternak wrote to Feltrinelli on November 2, 1957, only two weeks before the Italian publication of *Doctor Zhivago*:

> Do not worry on my account about the money. Let us postpone the financial issues (there are none for me) to the times when there will be a more sensitive and humane order, when again in the twentieth century it will be possible to correspond and to travel. My trust in you is boundless. I am certain that you will be able to look after what you have earmarked for me. Only if trouble were to strike, if they deprived me of my salary and my means of subsistence were cut off (the case would be extraordinary and there is nothing to suggest that)—, well then, in that case I will try to find a way to inform you and to take advantage of your offers through Sergio who, in accordance with his name, is a true angel and unsparingly devotes his time and his person to this annoying business. (Mancosu 2013, 251; original in French)

And trouble did eventually strike, which led to Pasternak's need to take advantage of the offer of financial help. D'Angelo left the Soviet Union at the very end of 1957, after making sure that communication between Pasternak and Feltrinelli (and himself) would not be interrupted. The new link became d'Angelo's friend Giuseppe Garritano.

1.2. D'Angelo leaves the Soviet Union, and the Garritanos enter the picture

Giuseppe ("Pino") Garritano arrived in Moscow as a correspondent of the Communist daily *l'Unità* in the middle of 1957. He was also a correspondent for *Vie Nuove*. He was accompanied by his wife, Mirella, employed at Radio Moscow, who would also play an important role in the story. D'Angelo and Garritano had known each other at the publishing house Rinascita and were thus in close contact during the period during which they overlapped in Moscow.[4] D'Angelo describes Garritano as "extremely

4. D'Angelo recounts the following with reference to the summer of 1957: "Among those who have just arrived in the capital, there is my old friend, Pino Garritano, along with his wife, Mirella, and their five- or six-year-old daughter. Pino and I actually worked together at the ICP publishing house. A native of Calabria (or better yet, of "Graecia Magna"), he is an extremely cultured,

cultured" and "stubborn." Irina Emelianova (Olga Ivinskaya's daughter) describes him in her memoirs as shy and frightened on account of the various (illicit) tasks he had to fulfill on behalf of d'Angelo and Pasternak, which included carrying letters and other items between Italy and the Soviet Union (Emelianova 2002, 91–92). For instance, Irina Emelianova vividly recalls a conversation she had with Garritano on October 24, 1958 (the day after the awarding of the Nobel Prize to Pasternak), in the public garden near the Belarusian station. Garritano, who "looked worried," informed Irina that Boris had been awarded the Nobel Prize. On that occasion, he gave her a Torpedo typewriter that had been sent from Italy for Olga and Pasternak.[5] This typewriter had been requested in a letter from Olga datable to the summer of 1958 (document 4). The same letter refers to Giuseppe Garritano's role in enabling the transfer of money. And as we shall see, the Garritanos delivered quite a bit of money to Pasternak. Indeed, in an interview given for a documentary by Valeria Paniccia,[6] Giuseppe Garritano said that Pasternak gave him some receipts that he handed over directly to Feltrinelli. Some of these receipts have been published in Mancosu 2013. The Garritanos would be involved in the spring of 1960 in an event that was to have important consequences and to which I will return below.

1.3. After the Italian publication

We have already seen Pasternak's relaxed attitude toward money.[7] He was aware of the complications of trying to transfer royalties officially from

capable gentleman, and also very stubborn. While in Moscow, he will act as a correspondent for the magazine Vie Nuove, as well as a deputy correspondent for l'Unità, for a period of more than two years" (d'Angelo 2006, 97).

5. Emelianova's recollection of her meeting with Garritano on October 24, 1958, is found on p. 93 of her memoir, *Légendes de la rue Potapov* (Emelianova 2002; original in French). The Torpedo typewriter figures also in a similar account given by Olga Ivinskaya in *A Captive of Time* (not surprisingly, as this was one of the objects mentioned at the trial; see Ivinskaya 1978, 222). However, Irina adds some color to the description of Garritano: "The sad and blemished face of Giuseppe, a pudgy man with a face shaped like a pear and melancholic eyes, which reminded one of Alberto Sordi, showed both uneasiness and an unusual gravity." The unusual gravity was due to worries about possible consequences of the Nobel Prize.

6. Valeria Paniccia, *Il caso Pasternak*, Rai educational, http://www.lastoriasiamonoi.rai.it/puntate/il-caso-pasternak/963/default.aspx.

7. Indeed, too relaxed perhaps since Pasternak also promised royalties over which he had no control to Jacqueline de Proyart and Hélène Peltier, thereby wronging Feltrinelli.

abroad and did not seem to need the money. This situation continued in 1958. An interesting letter from Gerd Ruge to Kurt Wolff sheds light on the official reaction (or lack thereof) to the Italian publication of *Zhivago* and Pasternak's financial situation.[8] Gerd Ruge (b. 1928) was a foreign correspondent in Moscow for the German television broadcaster NRD from 1956 until 1959. He would become involved with Pasternak both as the author of a book published in 1958 (Ruge 1958) and by helping Pasternak with some financial transactions.[9] On August 15, 1958, he wrote to Wolff:

> The publication of his novel abroad has not, until today, given rise to any official Soviet reaction. The fact that the State Publishing House for Literature does not provide him with any new translation work and does not pay what is owed to him for previous publications is more a sign of the uncertainty of the people in charge at the Publishing House than the effect of an official decision at the highest levels. However, Pasternak at the moment does not seem to find himself in financial need. He obviously cannot receive any money from abroad, Feltrinelli has been unable in any case to send anything officially, and Pasternak, understandably, does not want to receive anything through means that are not completely legal. He does not seem at the moment to be pressed by financial worries. (FoGF, Fascicolo "Pantheon books (Boris Pasternak)" (1957–1959), 1.2.1–b.18, fasc. 190; original in German)

From this letter it emerges that two months before the Nobel Prize, Pasternak's financial situation was still relatively unproblematic. It is true that he (and Ivinskaya) were receiving some financial help from the West, as confirmed in a letter from Olga Ivinskaya to Sergio d'Angelo (see document 4). The letter is datable to around the end of June or beginning of July 1958. Ivinskaya wrote: "Now regarding the settlements—after you, there have been 4! But I see that settling there, in Moscow, is hard for your friend (G.). Please think about how to make this simpler and increase the

8. The loss of this letter is lamented in the volume *Boris Pasternak—Kurt Wolff: Im Meer der Hingabe* (Boris Pasternak 2010a). I was able to locate a copy of it during my research at the Fondo Giangiacomo Feltrinelli. Kurt Wolff often sent Feltrinelli copies of letters by Pasternak or related to Pasternak.

9. One should also remark that his wife, Elizabeth Ruge, worked in publishing and kept in contact with Pasternak's sisters in Oxford, conveying information about their brother that she received from Gerd Ruge. See PFP, HILA, Josephine Pasternak papers (under "Ruge, Elizabeth"). There are also many letters from Elizabeth Ruge to Boris Pasternak in the Pasternak Family Papers in Moscow.

amount of a single dose. That would be better for B.L., and you will likely be able to come up with a way to get it done and then actually deliver on it."[10] We still have some of the receipts for payments in 1958, with sums ranging from 1,000 rubles to 10,000 rubles. But this state of things was to be radically altered by the Nobel Prize.

1.4. The Nobel Prize, the persecution, and the first financial problems

Pasternak was awarded the Nobel Prize on October 23, 1958. Forced to renounce the prize, he was vilified in the Soviet press, expelled from the Soviet Writers' Union, and threatened with exile.[11] Pasternak wrote a letter to Khrushchev begging not to be exiled, but the measure that had the most tangible financial consequence was his expulsion from the Soviet Writers' Union. This was tantamount to eliminating Pasternak's livelihood, exactly the scenario that Pasternak had hypothetically described to Feltrinelli in November 1957.

Of course, the Soviets were working hard to convey the opposite impression. There is a letter to Feltrinelli from Georg Svensson at Bonniers (publisher of *Doctor Zhivago* in Sweden) dated October 31, 1958. It says:

Dear Mr. Feltrinelli,

We just got your cable in which you want us to recommend the Swedish Academy not to accept Pasternak's refusal to receive the Nobel prize. The Academy met yesterday and then sent Pasternak the following cable: "L'Academie suedoise vient de recevoir votre refus en regrettant profondement. Avec sympathie et respect." This will mean that no prize money will be paid to Pasternak but will go back to the foundation. Officially, however, Pasternak will be regarded as 1958 Nobel prize winner of literature and will always in the records of the Swedish Academy be mentioned as such. Should the situation change so that Pasternak one day would accept his prize,

10. The letter is cited in Mancosu 2013, 263–64, although an improvement in the transcription of the letter accounts for some differences between the translation originally published there and the one published here. The letter is published here in its entirety as document 4.

11. The events are well known and documented in several sources. See, among others, Conquest 1961b; Afiani and Tomilina 2001; *Le dossier* 1994; de Mallac 1981; Barnes 1998; Fleishman 1990; Evgeniĭ Pasternak 1988, 1990, 1997; Elena and Evgeniĭ Pasternak 2004; Mancosu 2013; and Finn and Couvée 2014. See also the chronological table in this book.

he will always get the medal and the diploma, but the prize money only if he changes his mind before the 10th of December, which is the prize giving day.

Another thing that might interest you to know is in today's paper. The chairman of the Swedish Authors' Association, Mr. Stellan Arvidson, yesterday called upon the Russian chargé d'affaires in Stockholm, Mr. Voinov, to hand over a letter from the association to the Sovjet Authors' Association. Voinov then assured Arvidson that no harm will come to Pasternak, that he might stay in his house, that he will not be deprived of any civil rights nor any economic. He will be able to go on writing and translating as before and may also receive fees and royalties including the foreign editions of Doktor Zjivago, all according to Voinov. But I am personally a bit doubtful about the last point. (Kurt and Helen Wolff Papers at Yale, YCGL MSS 16, Box 46, folder 1479)

As we shall see, Svensson could have been even more skeptical than he was. That Pasternak feared immediate consequences for his livelihood is confirmed by his reaction to a letter from Hélène Peltier offering material assistance. Replying to the offer in a letter to Proyart, Pasternak wrote on November 28, 1958: "I received Hélène's letters, her offer of material assistance (it is not at all ridiculous, she has guessed a lot)" (Boris Pasternak 1994, 129; for Peltier's letter see Elena and Evgeniĭ Pasternak 1997). Pasternak was no longer paid the royalties owed to him in the Soviet Union and was no longer given translation work. Without an income, he quickly found himself in need of money.

But reports about a worsening of Pasternak's financial situation antedate the Nobel Prize crisis. For instance, Nicolas Nabokov wrote to Feltrinelli on July 25, 1958, in worried terms about Pasternak's income:

On the other hand, I received some news concerning Pasternak that is worrying me somewhat. I was told that upon his return to Peredelkino after his release from the hospital, in a healthier state, he found a very worrisome financial situation. They have cut by half the royalties he was receiving for the translations he did for the theater of the USSR and for which he receives no new requests for translations. Moreover, Pasternak receives not even a single cent of the royalties for the sale of the Italian edition of his book. In other words, he receives not even a single cent from abroad. I wonder whether you could do something about this matter. I am sure that if you were able to send him his European royalties one way or another, this would help his financial situation. (Nicolas Nabokov to G. Feltrinelli, July 25, 1958, original in French; Nicolas Nabokov Papers, Harry Ransom Center, University of Texas at Austin)

But despite these letters, in general very little was known in the West about Pasternak's financial situation in 1958.

The best source for Pasternak's situation in early 1959 is a letter from Ruge to Manya Harari, datable to mid-March 1959:

Dear Mrs. Harari,

first I have to apologize for not writing earlier. But I was very busy, and there was very little concerning your original question which I could have told you. As David Floyd was returning to London at about that time, I felt sure that he would inform you on his conversation with B.P [Pasternak]. There are some ideas, however, which I would like to think about.

B.P. feels that no money from abroad should be transferred to him, as this might raise a new campaign,—being paid by the West, etc. He would like to be able to earn his living in his own country by translating. Since ca. January 1958 B.P. has received no royalties for his work. Money due to him for earlier translations has not been paid. New translations, which had been ordered (like the Slowarzkij [Słowacki] drama [*Maria Stuart*]) have been accepted, but the publishing house—in this case Goslitizdat—has not paid the usual 60% of the agreed fee, nor is it expected that the Polish play will be published. The new publication of the collected dramas of Shakespeare—prepared by Iskusstvo—will most probably not contain the Pasternak-Translations. B.P. has again not received the 60% of the basic payment due to him, which are normally paid on delivery of the translations, with the other 40% paid on publication. From what I hear, the publishing house has prepared all the necessary bookkeeping actions, but decided to send the whole question up to the cultural section of the Central Committee of the CPSU, where it now rests. NO decision has been coming on this issue,—and probably the question of whether to pay B.P. the money due to him rests there altogether. B.P. feels that he still has enough money to last him some time and that he should not try to get money from abroad as long as the situation is not really unbearable.

I have not seen him after the unhappy incident created by Tony Brown [This indicates that the report concerns conversations at the end of January/beginning of February 1959. —PM]. B.P. left for Tiflis, as you probably know. He telephoned me before he left, and I have no doubt whatsoever that he went entirely of his own free will. He was not sent away from the vicinity of Moscow. As a matter of fact, he had been planning to go to the Caucasus for some time, his decision may only have come earlier than originally planned because B.P. was afraid of the great number of journalists coming with Macmillan. B.P. feels very well, he likes Tiflis very much, as he always did, and the neuralgic pain, of which he complained during the last six months, has ceased altogether. I do not know whether he is back in Peredyelkino by now, but he had prolonged his sojourn in Tiflis already when I left Moscow in the first days of March.

Some of his friends did feel that his decision to leave Peredyelkino was not very wise. This is hard to decide. B.P. himself has not more of an idea how his position is than anybody else in the world. I saw his feeling change from deep pessimism during one visit to optimism and hopefulness a week later. Sometimes he feels that the Soviet authorities are trying to starve him out, at other times he thinks that the development may take a turn towards the better. To me, and to many of his Russian friends, it looks as if nothing at all is happening at the higher levels. Which would mean starving or living on the charity of friends, however, in some 6 to 10 months, I believe. These friends believe that it would be dangerous to let the affair die down altogether in the West, because that would influence the Soviet authorities towards solving the problem by just doing nothing until Pasternak money runs out.

I personally think—and such close friends of Pasternak's as "Lara" [Ivinskaya] are of the same opinion—that a letter to Khrushtshov [*sic*] signed by a number of well known western writers might help to influence the decision on Pasternak's future. Of course, this letter should not look like a maneuver of the cold war, but be a responsible and carefully edited document. I do not know whether one could make some Indian writers to join,—a little bit of colour is worth a lot in Moscow nowadays. But I want to stress that the whole affair should be handled very quietly, no crusade.

Well, these are some of the thoughts about B.P. Kurt Wolff informed me that you were trying to do something for B.P.,[12] and I felt that the little information I have might help you. Please be careful about using what I wrote about the attitude of the publishing houses. In general form it can do no harm, but it must not look as if we were too well informed, I think. Your sincerely, Gerd Ruge (Collins Archives, Glasgow)

Ruge reported similar information to Viktor Frank, who sent Manya Harari a summary of Ruge's letter on March 18, 1959.

Meanwhile, royalties were accumulating in the West, and the Nobel Prize led a vortex of initiatives that are closely related to the issue of royalties. Late January and February 1959 constitute a pivotal moment in the *Zhivago* affair. The US State Department was interested in acquiring all

12. The initiative to do something for Pasternak seems to have originated with Marjorie Villiers and Manya Harari, of Harvill Press. Villiers speaks about it in a letter to Helen Wolff dated March 3, 1959, and describes how Isaiah Berlin had refused to join the effort. The letter is cited at length in Mancosu 2016, section 17.

the translation rights for a huge variety of Asian languages, and Feltrinelli exploited this to get a visa to visit the United States. Feltrinelli was away from February to May on a trip to Cuba, Mexico, and the United States, which included talks with representatives from the State Department for language rights to *Zhivago* for several foreign languages.[13]

Back in Milan, Feltrinelli's lawyer, Antonio Tesone, was left to deal with a very complex question that had just arisen. In late January Jacqueline de Proyart had written to Feltrinelli informing him of an extensive power of attorney that gave her control of Pasternak's literary affairs outside the Soviet Union. This had immediate financial consequences, for it affected the contracts that Feltrinelli had signed with many publishers for Pasternak's *Autobiography*. The full story of Pasternak's delegation of rights to Proyart and the resulting confusion in interactions with Feltrinelli have been recounted at length (Mancosu 2013). Here I would like to emphasize that it was the Nobel Prize that led to the new state of things. This much is clearly stated in a letter from Proyart to the novel's Danish translator, Ivan Malinovski. The letter reads:

> Given that Pasternak has entrusted me with the handling of his interests beyond the borders of the USSR, and given that these interests are becoming more and more important as a result of the success of his novel, of the award of the Nobel Prize, and of the future edition of his verses preceded or not by the Autobiography, I must take a closer look at what publishers are doing on his behalf. . . .
>
> I hope to see Feltrinelli very soon and to speak with him about this matter. I do not know what arrangements have been made between him and Gyldendal concerning the royalties to be credited to the author with regard to the novel. Perhaps you know about this? If it had been agreed to credit these royalties to Feltrinelli on Boris Leonidovich's [Pasternak's] account, could you ask Gyldendal for me to hold off for the moment on the next payment they plan to make (if they were planning to do it in January), and this in the best interest of Pasternak. For to change all the money in the world into liras to then change them again into rubles seems to me to be a bad transaction. Having said that, I still do not know what arrangements Feltrinelli has made for the handling of all these royalties, which are now turning into a fortune. Last year, it had been agreed, according to Pasternak's wishes, that he [Feltrinelli] would be in charge

13. See post "*Doctor Zhivago*, the CIA, and Feltrinelli's visa to the USA," on *Inside the Zhivago Storm*, zhivagostorm.org.

of dispatching them in order not to complicate the author's situation in the USSR. But things have changed since then! (FoGF, "Gyldendal, Danimarca," 1.2.1–b.15, fasc. 142; original in French)

The reader can well imagine how Feltrinelli reacted when he was informed that Proyart was sending around letters of this sort questioning both the contracts and the financial arrangements that Feltrinelli had made with other publishers (see the letter from Feltrinelli to Proyart in Mancosu 2013, 280–86).

The Soviets had also started looking into the royalties. While there was no temptation to let Pasternak accept the Nobel Prize so that the cash prize itself could be put into the coffers of the USSR, things were less clear-cut with the royalties from sales of the book in the West. The documents that constitute the dossier of the Pasternak case in the Central Committee of the CPSU reveal a more hesitant attitude. On January 20, 1959, Dmitriĭ Polikarpov, the director of the Department of Culture of the USSR, sent the Central Committee of the CPSU the following memo.

January 20, 1959
To the Central Committee

The Soviet Embassy in Sweden (comrade Gusev) informs us to have learned from the Swedish Press that the Italian publisher Feltrinelli has received large sums for the edition of Doctor Zhivago. According to the magazine Dagens Nyheter, Feltrinelli declared that up to December 1958, 900,000 dollars had been deposited as royalties for Doctor Zhivago in a special bank account opened in Switzerland for Pasternak ($360,000 originating from England and 440,000 from other countries).

According to our ambassador, these sums could be used by anti-Soviet organizations for the creation of a fund with hostile aims toward the USSR. Taking this possibility into account, the embassy proposes to put pressure on Pasternak to have these honorariums sent to the International Peace Council.

The Department of Culture deems that the question must be submitted to Pasternak.

Given that he is no longer a member of the Soviet Writers' Union, one would have to assign this task to the All-Union Commission for the Protection of Authors' Rights.

We request your agreement.

D. Polikarpov, Director of the Department of Culture
V. Baskakov, Administrative Controller (Afiani and Tomilina 2001, 179–80; *Le dossier* 1994, 147–48; original in Russian)

Meanwhile, as we have seen, payment of Soviet royalties owed to Pasternak had stopped, and Pasternak sent a letter to the chairman of the All-Union Commission for the Protection of Authors' Rights (G. Khessin).

January 11, 1959
Dear Grigoriĭ Borissovich!

I would be grateful if you could shed light on the reasons why I still have not received two payments that are due to me:

1) that of the editions Tbilisi Zaria Vostoka, for a work which appeared in spring Stikhi o Gruzii: Gruzinskie poety as well as for my translations of Chikovani and Lenidze [Leonidze] and others, published in different anthologies. Altogether, a sum of 21,000 rubles (before tax) as confirmed by a letter from October by Bebutov, the editor in chief of this publishing house. I enclose the letter as evidence. I had asked that a part of this sum, 5,000 rubles, be sent to O. Ivinskaya, and the rest deposited on my savings account;

2) the deposit of the sum that is owed to me by the State Publishing House, according to contract no. 10876 of 17-10-58. The work defined in this contract (translation in verse of a drama by Słowacki) has been brought to completion and delivered about a month and a half ago.

I also remind you that I asked you in oral conversation to please let me know if one is planning to give me work and to pay me as an income the salary that I need to live, according to what one keeps saying in official declarations, which for the moment have remained without any effect. If this were not the case, I would find myself forced to find other means of subsistence, which I mentioned to you (exchange of "procurations" with Hemingway, Laxness, Remarque, Mauriac and others).

Respectfully,
Boris Pasternak (Afiani and Tomilina 2001, 240–41; *Le dossier* 1994, 160–61; original in Russian)

The letter was sent to the Central Committee with a cover letter by D. Polikarpov.

January 22, 1959
To the Central Committee

Please take note of a letter addressed by Boris Pasternak to the All-Union Commission for the Protection of Authors' Rights. In the last sentence he makes it clear that if he is not paid his royalties and if one does not provide him with work he will authorize the bourgeois writers mentioned in the letter to receive, abroad, the sums that are owed him, while he will receive here those that are owed to them for the publication of their works in our country.

D. Polikarpov
Director of the Department of Culture (Afiani and Tomilina 2001, 239–40; *Le dossier* 1994, 160; original in Russian)

It is thus clear that despite the official declarations by the Soviets, according to which Pasternak was not facing any hardship, the reality was that his means of subsistence had been effectively blocked. The situation was not to improve. In a letter to d'Angelo, undated but likely from late March or early April (document 7), Ivinskaya mentioned that the State Publishing House had been informally instructed not to publish anything by Pasternak. No payments for the Słowacki translation had been received, and the same was true for the other translations.

It is in this context that on January 30, 1959, Pasternak gave an interview to Anthony Brown of the *Daily Mail.* On this occasion, Pasternak gave Brown a poem with instructions to send it to Proyart (Brown was residing in Paris during that period). Brown published the poem, titled "The Nobel Prize,"[14] leading to another major crisis with the Soviet authorities, which culminated in the interrogation of Boris Pasternak on March 14, 1959, led by the general prosecutor of the USSR, Roman Rudenko, who accused Pasternak of state treason and threatened to prosecute him (see Afiani and Tomilina 2001, 187–93; *Le dossier* 1994, 177–80).[15] But the reason for

14. Brown published the poem in the first of three articles he published on Pasternak. The article containing the poem was published on February 11. The events connected to the interview and Brown's publication of the poem are the subject of Koznova 2017 and 2018.

15. Pasternak was also asked to avoid contact with foreigners. But both Pasternak and Ivinskaya continued to meet and correspond with foreigners, which led to a renewed warning, as indicated by this KGB document recently published in the original Russian (Koznova 2017, 24):

> PROTOCOL
>
> On July 25, 1959, citizen IVINSKAYA Olga Vsevolodovna, born 1912, Russian, no political party affiliation, living at 9/11 Potapov pereulok, apartment 18, Moscow, was called in to talk to Deputy Prosecutor General of the USSR P. I. Kudryatsev.
>
> In the course of conversation O. V. Ivinskaya was warned that her interactions with foreigners showing—out of beliefs related to the hostile activities against the USSR—an interest in B. L. Pasternak are NOT DESIRED and NOT COMPATIBLE with promises given by B. L. Pasternak on March 14 of this year to the Prosecutor General of the USSR and can lead to serious consequences for both O. V. Ivinskaya and B. L. Pasternak.
>
> Citizen O. V. Ivinskaya stated during the course of conversation that she understood this warning and that she promises to cease all communication with the referenced foreigners.

mentioning this interview with Brown, reported in articles in the *Daily Mail* on February 11 and 12, 1959, is that in it Pasternak complained about his impending financial difficulties. As we shall see in section 1.5, this complaint was to spur Sergio d'Angelo into action.

1.5. Using some of the royalties abroad

Already at the end of January 1959, Pasternak decided to make use of a part of his royalties to make presents to several of his friends in the West. He wrote two letters, one to Proyart and one to Feltrinelli, specifying the names and the amounts involved. The letter to Feltrinelli, dated February 2, 1959, touches on Pasternak's financial situation and more general issues related to it.

> To conclude this endless letter, I will speak about the money and address some requests to you. I believe that the entire sum is kept somewhere under your safeguard. I am infinitely grateful to you, and I would like to kindly ask to allow this arrangement to remain and continue further in the same form. My lack of curiosity in knowing the total amount and the other details should not surprise you, nor should it offend you as a kind of seeming indifference. I am honestly not keen to know it, since I dare not and do not have the right and the possibility to actually think about it. I believe that only in the hypothetical case they were to starve me would I decide to accept an official transfer from beyond the border. The financial authorities would consent to this deposit of foreign currency, but the rest of my life would be poisoned by the perpetual accusation of treacherously supporting myself with foreign and depraved sources. But I would like to begin collecting this money in a different way. I would like to make, with

---

I confirm the correctness of the events described in this protocol and have been warned about the consequences of divulging this conversation:

[*signed*]
/Ivinskaya O. V./

Conversation undertaken by: Deputy Prosecutor General of the USSR
[*signed*]
/P. Kudryatsev/
July 25, 1959

Protocol prepared by
[*signed*]
/N. Krasnopevtsev/

your help and permission, some small monetary presents through transfers to some people. Here is the list (of the names and the amounts).

Please transfer

1) Ten thousand dollars ($10,000) to my younger sister Mrs. Lydia Slater, 20 Park Town Oxford England.
2) Ten thousand dollars to my older sister Josephine Pasternak (using the address of my younger sister, if her address cannot be found)
3) Ten thousand dollars to Mrs. J. de Proyart, 21 rue Fresnel, Paris XVI
4) Ten thousand dollars to Mrs. Hélène Peltier-Zamoyska, Maison St- Jean par St Clar-de-Rivière Haute Garonne, France.
5) Five thousand dollars to Mr. Michel Aucouturier
6) Five thousand dollars to Mr. Martinez [*Added in the margin*: Their address can be obtained from Mme de Proyart]
7) Five thousand dollars to the Italian translator Pietro Zveteremich, Mr. Feltrinelli knows the address himself.
8) Ten thousand dollars ($10,000) to Mr. Sergio d'Angelo, Via Pietro d'Assisi, 11, Rome
9) Two thousand dollars ($2,000) to Mr. Garritano, to be paid to him in Italy and not at his temporary address in Moscow
10) Five thousand dollars ($5,000) to Max Hayward
11) Five thousand dollars ($5,000) to Mrs. Harari [*Added in the margin*: Two English translators. Their addresses to be obtained through Collins]
12) Five thousand dollars to the Danish translator Ivan Malinovski in Copenhagen, using the address of the Gyldendal Publishers.
13) Five thousand dollars to Reinhold v. Walter through S. Fischer-Verlag
14) Five thousand dollars to Mr. Karl Theens, director of a museum, Stuttgart-Degerloch, Albstrasse 17 Deutschland
15) Five thousand dollars to Mrs. Renate Schweitzer, Berlin W30, Marbürgerstr. 16
16) Five thousand dollars to John Harris 3, Park Road, Dartington, Totnes, Devon, England
17) Ten thousand dollars to Gerd Ruge in Germany

I finish the letter in haste. A thousand thanks.

Yours, B. Pasternak (Mancosu 2013, 272–78; original in French)

This letter to Feltrinelli passed through Proyart and never reached Feltrinelli. However, a different letter, sent to Proyart together with the one just mentioned, also had the list of beneficiaries and the amounts Pasternak intended them to receive. The actual transfer for these gifts took quite a long time and was brought to completion only toward the end of 1959, although a few people, like Sergio d'Angelo, received their presents around July. There were several reasons for the delay. The first is that when Giuseppe Garritano discovered that his name had been put on the list of recipients for a monetary gift from Pasternak, he panicked[16] and asked that his name be removed (he did not, however, reject the gift). At some point after the February 2 letter, Olga wrote to d'Angelo:

Dear Sergio,

A personal request to you: please hold the list in which B.L. specifies the people to whom he wants to make small gifts. This needs to be done to make sure we don't let friends down. A new list will be sent at the first opportunity. (See document 6; original in Russian)

It appears from the subsequent correspondence that d'Angelo had not been sent the original list. Ivinskaya also sent instructions to Proyart to wait for a new list. Knowing full well that the letter sent in February had not reached Feltrinelli, Pasternak came back to the issue on April 4 and wrote to Feltrinelli:

P.S. (very important) In my letter addressed to you that has disappeared there was a list, enumerating the amounts and the people to whom I wanted to transfer these amounts in the form of gifts (among them, ten thousand dollars to Sergio d'Angelo, ten thousand, which I now raise to fifteen thousand, to Gerd Ruge, etc. etc.). The copy of this list reached Mme de Proyart safely and is in her hands. Dear friend, do not hinder and do not delay this provision. I want this donation to the several people named in the list to be made as soon as possible. Mr. Sergio d'Angelo is offering material assistance for whatever extreme circumstance might arise in which I would not know which way to turn. If need be, I will be forced to resort to his offer, but on this matter, one will have to seek advice from Madame de Proyart according to the attestation here enclosed, without your getting worried about this business. B.P. (Mancosu 2013, 301–4; original in French)

The attestation enclosed in the letter was a power of attorney for Proyart that gave her full control of Pasternak's royalties, thereby extending the

16. Most likely because he did not want Soviet or Italian comrades to know that he was assisting Pasternak.

previous power of attorney she had received in 1958 (see Mancosu 2013, 305–6).

We know from a letter Pasternak sent to Proyart on March 30, 1959, that Ruge had lent Pasternak $7,500, which explains why Pasternak raised the donation to Ruge (see Boris Pasternak 1994, 153).[17] Of course, the information about the gifts had also reached d'Angelo through Garritano.

A further reason for the delay in payments was the complex and litigious relation between Feltrinelli and Proyart (traces of which are amply found in d'Angelo's letters), which was rooted in conflicting instructions and wishes expressed by Pasternak. Moreover, as Feltrinelli explained to Pasternak in December 1959, he had received from Proyart the relevant document authorizing payments (at this stage the financial control of the royalties resided with her on account of Pasternak's instructions) only in September, and in some cases it took time to locate the people to whom the transfer had to be made, and once they were located, some of them took time to decide on the best way to receive the gift so as not to incur taxation. But eventually, Pasternak's desire in this connection was fulfilled by the end of November.

Now back to early February 1959.

1.6. D'Angelo's proposal

As we have seen, in an interview published in the *Daily Mail* on February 11 and 12, 1959, Pasternak lamented his quickly deteriorating financial situation. This led d'Angelo to write to Pasternak (on February 23, 1959) in the following terms:

I read what you told the "Daily Mail" correspondent about the difficult financial situation in which you might find yourself in a few months. But, if you choose to follow my advice, it will not happen. It is well known that Feltrinelli is in possession of a sum of money that belongs to you from royalties (from Italy and other countries). I do not

17. As becomes clear from the indictment against Ivinskaya and Emelianova, this happened in February 1959 (the indictment, published here as document 50, speaks of 12,000 rubles, which Emelianova received from Gerd Ruge on behalf of Ivinskaya and Pasternak). What seems incorrect in the indictment is that Ruge was delivering money originating from Pantheon Press through Kurt Wolff. If that had been the case, it would not be understandable why Pasternak felt he had to pay Ruge back.

know exactly how large a sum, but it is big. I think it would be impossible to send you the money through official channels. But I assure you that it can be sent unofficially (and it will be completely safe).

Why have you only received small change to this day? Unfortunately, I must say that Feltrinelli has not devoted any effort to this problem. One needs to take the initiative to take advantage of unofficial channels. And not only is he not the kind of person to take the initiative, but he doesn't allow me to take the appropriate actions. I can't say what his reasons for this are. In fact, I did not want to write about this delicate topic. Recently, I attempted to explain it indirectly through our friend, but I'm afraid that the only result was an unpleasant misunderstanding.

After reading the declarations of the correspondent of the "Daily Mail," I asked my English friend to talk with your sisters and ask them to write you a letter about this question. I do not yet know whether he has met with them and whether they will carry out my request.

But now, because an Italian journalist, my friend, is leaving for Moscow tomorrow, I decided to send you a personal letter.

And here is my recommendation to you: write to Feltrinelli in French or English (and to me, for my information), that you have decided to grant into my hands the sum that belongs to you, adding only that you wish to charge me with looking out for your interests.

In this case, I can pledge to send you the money in parts and in significant transfers (and, I repeat, completely safely).

Of course, I would take on legal responsibility for the deposit [*vklad*], which would always remain under your control or the control of your authorized agents.

It is a pity to talk about these things, but I hope you will understand that I am doing this with kind intentions. In any case, I entreat you to answer through our friend as quickly as possible. (AGFE, CP, "Olga Ivinskaya–Sergio D'Angelo (1959–1960)," b. 1, fasc. 7; original in Russian; see document 5)

The letter reveals that Feltrinelli and d'Angelo had discussed the issue of payments to Pasternak and that Feltrinelli had stopped d'Angelo from taking any initiative. Perhaps he did not trust the channels used by d'Angelo (having broken with the PCI, Feltrinelli might have felt unsure about using Communist couriers such as the Garritanos), and we will see that he soon found a new way to reach Pasternak, through the "bourgeois" journalist for *Die Welt*, Heinz Schewe. The difference of opinion between Feltrinelli and d'Angelo did not stop d'Angelo from taking the initiative, and there is enough evidence that negative comments about Feltrinelli's attitude with respect to the royalties were being conveyed not only directly from d'Angelo, as in this letter, but also by the Garritanos (as this letter already makes clear) and by later couriers in 1960, such as the Benedettis. One can detect here the beginning of a friction that will explode in 1965 in the court battle between d'Angelo and Feltrinelli for Pasternak's royalties.

In a personal email communication, d'Angelo has confirmed that "our friend" referred to Giuseppe Garritano, that his English friend was the lawyer William Middleton,[18] and that the Italian journalist who was leaving for Moscow was Leo Paladini. There is in fact an extant letter from Middleton to Lydia Pasternak Slater concerning this matter. From the letter, dated March 24, 1959, it is clear that Lydia had disapproved of the proposal made by d'Angelo. Middleton wrote to her:

As arranged, I reported our interview to my friend, Dr. d'Angelo. He has now asked me to express to you his sincerest apologies for any inconvenience which he might have caused and, in view of the difficulties which you envisaged, does not propose to pursue his original plan. (SdAP, HILA)

Pasternak replied to d'Angelo's proposal on April 6, 1959.

Dear Sergio, I thank you for the letter. We always think of you in the most friendly and grateful terms. Since the last time we saw each other, so many unexpected and important things have come to pass. Many conjectures that I had made at the time, whether verbally or in the form of precarious and hypothetical, non–legally formalized wishes, concerning literary translations, editions, etc., have been overtaken by reality, which outpaced our boldest assumptions. Everything has developed and become more complicated, not only in a bad sense but even more so in a good sense. Although the danger with which they threatened me most recently is without exaggeration fatal, it is dwarfed by the things of immortal order that have been achieved alongside it.

---

18. William Middleton (1923–2010) spent his professional life in England but grew up in Italy. He was the son of a British citizen who had moved first to Germany and then to Italy. His mother was Italian. He was a high school friend of Sergio d'Angelo, and they studied together for the final high school examination. They also shared the experience of the first years of World War II. After the end of the conflict, William Middleton opted to keep British citizenship and moved to London. He and d'Angelo remained friends, and Middleton played an important role in d'Angelo's contacts with England concerning the *Zhivago* affair. For instance, Middleton served as intermediary in d'Angelo's contacts with Max Hayward in 1962, when d'Angelo was trying to help Olga Ivinskaya and Irina Emelianova (see chapter 3).

> I thank you for the help that you are offering me. My current situation is uncertain. They have offered an official transfer of funds to me, but I do not know whether this is a concealed trap to destroy me all the more certainly, for so great is the constant desire to ruin me that I do not see anything except this desire in their attitude toward me. All the while with complaint, as if they were preparing something good for me but ran out of time, while I again spoiled everything, and so reconciliation is impossible yet again—just think, what cheap despicable behavior! And so I have not yet decided anything on how to respond to their offer for transferring the funds officially. So, perhaps, I will resort to your willingness to help as a last resort. I'll say this, try this possibility *even now, without waiting for dire straits.*
>
> But I cannot give you a general power of attorney for all of my funds, because I have already given it much earlier to Mme de Proyart. Plus, you do not need such a power of attorney. Appeal to her for advice on your own. If she approves your measure (and she is a friend of mine just like you are and similarly cares about me), she will set aside for you for your kind objective a sufficiently large sum (let us say, if with my previous requests and allocations I have not drained the reserve below the means for covering this amount), let us say up to one hundred thousand dollars ($100,000). Draw from it, then, *without giving an account* (I am not allowed to correspond about this matter) and with some benefit to yourself, for I would not want your efforts and your time to go for naught.
>
> Above, I had mentioned the monetary requests that I have already addressed to Mme de Proyart, in this way reducing the initial amount of the fund. Among these requests, I sent her a list of people to whom I wished to extend monetary gifts. In this list, I assigned ten thousand dollars to you, just as for my sisters; forgive me that it is so little. This has nothing to do with your current suggestion. For the financial support that you want to provide for me, there will be a different source, which I have described above. Thus, this money ($10,000) is yours no matter what, even if you were to have a falling out with me and forget to think about me. I also asked that two thousand dollars be assigned to Garritano. (Mancosu 2013, 309–11; see document 8; original in Russian)

As already pointed out, the threats Pasternak refers to were connected to the aftermath of the publication of the poem "The Nobel Prize" in the *Daily Mail*, which ended in a new scandal in the USSR. Concerning the official proposal of the transfer of funds, the context can be explained as follows.

On April 1, 1959, Pasternak had written a letter to the director of the Department of Culture of the Central Committee, D. Polikarpov, asking advice concerning a recent exchange he had with the Iniurkollegiia, the juridical consulting entity that dealt with the interests of Soviet citizens and organizations abroad (see Afiani and Tomilina 2001, 252; *Le dossier* 1994, 184–85). Pasternak had been informed by Iniurkollegiia that the Norwegian embassy had proposed to receive, on Pasternak's behalf, royalties due to him that had accumulated in a Norwegian bank. In addition, Iniurkollegiia also informed Pasternak that he could receive money due to him that had been deposited in a Swiss bank. In his letter to Polikarpov, Pasternak stated that it was well known to the authorities that he had made no attempt to gain access to any of his royalties from *Doctor Zhivago*. However, he also pointed out that the publication of his books and payments due to him for translations in the USSR were blocked by the authorities. Since Iniurkollegiia had proposed that he access this money officially, Pasternak continued, he was thinking about doing so. Pasternak proposed to donate a part of these funds to Litfond (an official fund for helping writers) to help aging writers. He then asked Polikarpov for advice on whether there would be any objection to his receiving the money, as he would not want to do anything that was contrary to the interests of the state. Polikarpov wrote to the Central Committee on April 16 (see Afiani and Tomilina 2001, 250–51; *Le dossier* 1994, 183–84), stating in no uncertain terms that Pasternak should decline to receive this money and asking authorization to inform Pasternak to that effect. Pasternak was thus informed, and on April 24, he wrote to Iniurkollegiia (see Afiani and Tomilina 2001, 253; *Le dossier* 1994, 185) stating that he refused the transfer of the money kept in his name in Norwegian and Swiss banks about which he had been informed. Meanwhile, Pasternak had also discussed the issue at length in letters to Proyart, first on March 30 (see Boris Pasternak 1994, 146–47), where he informed her of his plan to have the Norwegian money transferred and to split it between his wife, Zinaida, and his lover, Olga Ivinskaya. He asked Proyart not to mention this plan; in this letter he did not mention donating a part of the money to Litfond. In a later letter, dated April 17 (Boris Pasternak 1994, 160), Pasternak claimed that the state was trying to bring about a "reconciliation" with him by appropriating all his money abroad and that he would do everything to limit this plan to the Norwegian and Swiss accounts. Already at the outset, Pasternak was very suspicious about the Iniurkollegiia proposal, which he thought was a trap. Acting on d'Angelo's proposal, Pasternak, in the letter of April 6, suggested the transfer of a large sum ($100,000). Pasternak wrote a letter for

Proyart, introducing d'Angelo and his proposal, which d'Angelo delivered personally to her (the letter, also dated April 6, 1959, is published in Boris Pasternak 1994, 154–55). The consequences of this idea were ill-fated. On account of the problems between Feltrinelli and Proyart (see d'Angelo 2006, 153–66), it took until March 1960 for d'Angelo to get the money for the operation, and only a small part of the money was transferred before Pasternak died (May 30, 1960). A much larger payment reached Olga Ivinskaya after Pasternak's death, and that payment was singled out by Feltrinelli and Heinz Schewe as what caused the sentencing of Olga Ivinskaya and Irina Emelianova to the labor camps (see chapter 2; d'Angelo 2006, 175–224).

1.7. Heinz Schewe

In November 1958, Feltrinelli met Axel Springer (1912–1983), the publisher of many important German magazines, including *Die Welt*. This connection was soon to affect the *Zhivago* story. Just a few months after meeting Feltrinelli, Springer wrote to the foreign correspondent for *Die Welt* in the Soviet Union, Heinz Schewe, to bring about a connection between him and Feltrinelli.[19]

Schewe left a touching memoir of his friendship with Pasternak and Ivinskaya (Schewe 1974). His role as middleman between Pasternak, Ivinskaya, and Feltrinelli placed him in the midst of a very dangerous affair. In an article from the 1980s titled "I Almost Landed in Siberia," he wrote:

> For him I broke the laws of the state. For him I smuggled a hundred thousand rubles across the border. It was his money. He had earned it in the West with his books. They never caught me. But at the time I always had a leg in Siberia. I was lucky. I was spared Vorkuta. . . . I also brought out a manuscript. It was the draft of a play. It was to be called "The Blind Beauty."[20]

---

19. The letter from Springer to Schewe, dated February 10, 1959, is preserved in the Heinz Schewe Papers in Berlin.

20. The article, published in German, is "Beinahe wäre ich in Sibirien gelandet," *Springer Aktuell*. It is preserved in the Heinz Schewe Papers in Berlin. I was unable to find the precise date of publication.

Briefly recounting Schewe's role in the events, I will emphasize the financial aspects of the story. This is a limitation of my treatment, for what makes Schewe's letters truly remarkable are the comments about the mood of the Soviet officials with respect to Pasternak, Ivinskaya, and Emelianova.[21]

Schewe's article, mentioned above, was written much later than his book *Pasternak privat* (1974), where he still claimed that he had no idea what was in the packets given to him by Feltrinelli. But his correspondence with Feltrinelli leaves no doubt that at the time he was fully aware of the risky business he had engaged in. Since most of his actions, including the delivery of money to Pasternak and Olga, were probably well known to the KGB, this has also led to conflicting interpretations about Schewe.[22] Was he just lucky, as he claims in the article just cited, or was he, as d'Angelo has often suggested, a man of the Soviets? After all, any journalist of the "bourgeois press" would have been expelled from the Soviet Union for much less, but Schewe managed to marry a Russian woman and stay in the USSR until 1968. My personal point of view, after having read all his correspondence from the time and followed his actions until after Olga and Irina were freed, is that while he certainly had protection and contacts in high places, he was not playing a double game. I hasten to add, though, that maintaining those kinds of contacts in high places always comes with a certain degree of compromise. However, this compromise was not exploited to damage Pasternak and Olga but rather to shield them.[23]

We now need to come back to February 1959, when Axel Springer put Schewe and Feltrinelli in touch. Already on February 16, 1959, Feltrinelli wrote to Pasternak announcing that he hoped the difficulty of getting in touch experienced in the previous months could be solved by the new channel of communication (meaning Heinz Schewe). It is unclear why the d'Angelo–Garritano connections had become problematic for Feltrinelli,

---

21. This limitation will be overcome in chapters 2 and 3, which will address the period from Pasternak's death to the arrests of Ivinskaya and Emelianova and the Ivinskaya case in the West, respectively.

22. Schewe's role in providing financial assistance to Pasternak was known to the KGB. See chapter 2, note 24.

23. It is also possible that he was protected precisely so that Ivinskaya could be "caught" and convicted. But short of finding new evidence in former Soviet archives, we are left without a precise answer.

but obviously something had happened and Feltrinelli was looking for a new way to reach Pasternak. These were the months after the Nobel Prize, and it is possible that the Italian Communists who had been acting as liaisons were under pressure or that Feltrinelli, now no longer a member of the PCI, simply mistrusted the connection.[24] In addition, the Garritanos had never been a model of efficiency. We know from a complaint raised by Pasternak in a letter to Proyart (dated September 17, 1958) that in one case it took six months for Mirella Garritano to deliver one of Pasternak's letters ("L'italienne bizarre qui laisse mes lettres moisir pendant six mois!"; see Boris Pasternak 1994, 128).

Schewe entered the scene when the conflict between Feltrinelli and Proyart had already exploded, and he became Feltrinelli's trusted emissary throughout 1959 and 1960, until Pasternak's death and beyond. Feltrinelli was delighted with Schewe. In a letter to Axel Springer dated August 25, 1959, he defined Schewe as a "postillon d'amour" and extended through Springer an invitation for Schewe to visit him in Italy, an invitation that Schewe eventually accepted.

On February 21, 1959, Feltrinelli sent the first packet for Pasternak ("Three red envelopes and a white one"). Due to a number of unfavorable circumstances, this packet reached Schewe only on May 19, 1959. On the same day, in a letter to Feltrinelli, Schewe explained why it had taken so long for him to receive the package, which had come through another Italian journalist, Vero Roberti, correspondent with the *Corriere della Sera* in Moscow between June 1956 and July 1960 (Roberti met Pasternak in October 1958).[25] The letters contained in this first packet were the begin-

---

24. Incidentally, in October 1958 d'Angelo decided not to renew his membership in the PCI. In the SdAP, HILA, there is a copy of the letter, dated October 8, 1958, that d'Angelo sent to the "Federazione del PCI" in Rome explaining his decision not to renew his membership in the PCI, of which he had been a member since 1944.

25. Roberti was involved in other aspects of the *Zhivago* affair. Feltrinelli was a diffident man, but he introduced Roberti in a note to Schewe that suggests Roberti's deeper involvement in the story. The note, dated May 6, 1959, reads: "Dear Mr. Schewe, it has been easier to reach you through a different way, by means of an Italian friend. This friend soon leaves Moscow again. Should Pasternak's reply already have reached you before Roberti's departure then you can give it to him for me. Should Roberti no longer be in Moscow or should he stay for too long a time then please send Pasternak's reply to Dr. Axel Springer by means of the German consulate. Many thanks. Giangiacomo Feltrinelli, Milan 6 May 1959" (original in German). Copies of the original letter are found in the AGFE in Milan and in the Heinz Schewe Papers in Berlin. Roberti definitely helped Pasternak in 1960. In his book *Mosca sotto pelle* (Rome: Volpe) published in 1968, Roberti devotes an entire chapter to the Pasternak case and at one point reveals that he had delivered financial help to Pasternak. The relevant passage is the following: "On March 15, 1960, I met

ning of Feltrinelli's attempt to protect his rights to *Doctor Zhivago* and to obtain from Pasternak also the extended formal rights to the *Autobiography*, to the Russian text of *Doctor Zhivago*, and to the movie rights for *Doctor Zhivago*. The story of those attempts has been recounted in detail in the third part of Mancosu 2013, where I also reconstruct the pressures leading to the need to have a clearer statement of the movie rights as a consequence of interest from the movie industry in the wake of the Nobel Prize. But in this reconstruction, the interest will be squarely on Schewe's role as a go-between for Feltrinelli and Pasternak. From this moment on, most of the correspondence between Pasternak and Feltrinelli will go through Schewe via the German embassy (Bonn and Moscow).

We hear more about financial matters in a letter from Schewe to Feltrinelli dated November 5, 1959.

> Recently in the evening Ms Olga confided the following: "The Classic [Pasternak] feels he is growing older. He is often tired. He does not want to constantly be under pressure to have to work on new translations in order to make money. He obviously has many duties. He would rather devote himself entirely to his new drama. However he can only do this if he were financially more independent than he is at the moment. He must constantly work, in order to insure the flow of rubles."
>
> Now, there is the money of "Dr. Zhivago." The Classic received in recent times offers from people who offer him large amounts in dollars from the Zhivago coffer. They promise him to deliver in some way to Peredelkino a part of his royalties in rubles. Ms. Olga commented as follows: "I would prefer if all of this were in the hands of Giangiacomo alone. We trust him. We are nervous to have to bring in additional people into this business. They are all after the money." I cannot estimate what, how much, and where, royalties for the Classic are possibly available and whether there is the possibility of transferring them here. I only convey this conversation in order to inform you. Perhaps there are possibilities to do something? (AGFE, CP, Busta 1, Fascicolo 5-Feltrinelli-Schewe; Heinz Schewe Papers, Berlin; original in German)

Boris Pasternak for the last time. A mutual friend had told me that he would have liked to see me again. . . . Two days later, the same mutual friend, whose name I must pass in silence, came to see me at the 'Central Post Office' and told me that Pasternak was *gol kak sokol* [hungry as a hawk], poor as a church mouse, and that he was getting by on loans. . . . I promised to help. We arranged a plan, which I cannot reveal in its details, and after one month I was successful in my task. Later other people generously helped Pasternak and not without taking risks" (Roberti 1968, 260–61; original in Italian).

What is interesting in this letter is not only the explicit request for financial help on the part of Olga but also her negative judgments on the help proposed thus far from d'Angelo. Olga wavered all along as to the best way of delivering money and whom to trust on the matter.

On November 7, 1959, Pasternak wrote to Feltrinelli about the financial aid in a way that reveals Pasternak's conflicted attitude:

> But even now, I refuse the idea of regular and frequent aid. But let us say quarterly allowances in the amount of the previous contributions and in such a way that in the course of further reductions, these expenditures will not deplete more than ten percent of the total income; that would be very desirable. Mr. H. Sch[ewe], through whom this should be handled, will refuse and oppose the idea, but I beg you to make the requested favor worth his while and interesting for him, at our own expense.
>
> This must in no way infringe upon my earlier instruction (on account of the list of monetary gifts) or somehow have any effect on it. And I am surprised and saddened that the matter has not yet been brought to conclusion. This is perhaps to be explained by Mme de Proyart's inexperience. With your greater experience, you should help and advise her. That you continue to quarrel and do not come to an understanding with one another is something that constantly affects me like a lack of friendly feeling towards me personally (Mancosu 2013, 335–37; original in German).

In the letter from Feltrinelli to Schewe dated November 13, 1959, we find for the first time an explicit reference to the money being sent for Pasternak:

> Enclosed please find the "loaves" [*Brötchen*]. We are baking more and will send more within a short time "as soon as possible" so that our friend can write in peace. Hopefully you will be able to deliver them to him soon. (AGFE, CP, Busta 1, Fascicolo 5-Feltrinelli-Schewe; Heinz Schewe Papers, Berlin; original in German)

Let us take stock. In 1959, Pasternak had used $112,000 of his royalties for making gifts to friends. He had instructed d'Angelo to seek permission to use $100,000 for Pasternak's own needs and was receiving money from other quarters, including Feltrinelli (through Schewe) and Proyart (through functionaries at the French embassy in Moscow and Georges Nivat). Not surprisingly, given that neither he nor Ivinskaya had yet received from Feltrinelli an exact figure for the royalties at their disposal, they felt rather confused about their financial situation. The best expression of this is in a letter from Ivinskaya to d'Angelo dated November 19, 1959:

> Unfortunately, we have now gotten completely confused regarding our financial affairs. We have received monetary transfers from different sources, and we do not know what kind of sum is now at our disposal. Primarily this mess is the result of the complicated relationship between Mister Feltrinelli and Madam de Proyart, which is still not settled. Furthermore, B.L. is very worried about the fact that his requests regarding other monetary distributions to his friends have not been fulfilled and whether he still has the possibility to set aside another one hundred thousand for his own needs. Maybe if this one hundred thousand is set aside for him, then in case of significant misunderstandings between F. and P., his royalties would be insufficient for the gifts that he had set aside for his friends so long ago. Therefore I am sending you a power of attorney for a much smaller sum for now, which will cover your expenses, and perhaps allow you to make a few more clothes shipments, which we appreciate and need very much. (SdAP, HILA; see document 14; original in Russian)

The sum in question was $10,000; I published the warrant, also dated November 19, 1959 (Mancosu 2013, 348–49; see document 16). Only three weeks later, Pasternak signed a warrant for $100,000 in favor of d'Angelo.

1.8. The Italian money carriers

We have seen in the previous section how Feltrinelli began regularly sending money through Heinz Schewe. However, d'Angelo's project had been waiting for a resolution of the conflict between Proyart and Feltrinelli. At the end of December, Olga sent Pasternak's warrant for $100,000 on behalf of Sergio d'Angelo. She gave the warrant to Mirella Garritano, who was able to bring it to d'Angelo only in mid-March 1960. At the beginning of December 1959, Olga wrote:

> I am sending you the power of attorney. Keep in mind that G.F. sometimes sends B.L. some money from the royalties. As I understand it, your transfers will be complementary, rather than against his. M-me J.P. has also sent some money (small sums). This is difficult for them to do for technical reasons, and we think that doing it from three

different sources is more reliable and convenient than from one. Anyway, everything is easier for you to see from over there. My personal idea is to sufficiently provide for B.L. for now so that he will only translate for formality's sake and work on his piece. I think that this coincides with your plan.

Big kisses,
Olga (see document 17; original in Russian)

We see Olga contradicting exactly the ideas expressed through Schewe that it would be better to have only one person in charge of payments. In any case, even before receiving the warrant (which will reach him only in March 1960), d'Angelo had already organized a substantial payment of 44,000 rubles. A receipt and a letter from February 9 confirm the payment. The courier was d'Angelo's friend Leo Paladini.

Paladini, who was a Socialist, had worked as a correspondent for the Socialist daily *Avanti* in Moscow in 1957. He and his wife, Carmela, were close friends of d'Angelo and his wife, Giulietta. But on account of an untimely scoop on the Anti-Party group and for not revealing where he got the information (see d'Angelo 2006) despite Soviet pressure, Paladini had to leave Moscow before the end of 1957. He went back on occasion (for instance, in February 1959, when he delivered a letter from d'Angelo to Pasternak) and used the opportunity to go back in February 1960 as part of a delegation of journalists for the newspaper *Il Punto*. On this latter occasion, he brought Pasternak the aforementioned 44,000 rubles. In an article in *Vita*, Leo Paladini made the following statement:

I went to see her [Olga] one evening—or better a late afternoon—in order to deliver a small packet wrapped in an issue of "Pravda." The packet contained a quantity of 100 rubles, rather greasy banknotes, and a small bottle of eye drops. I received the money from two Soviet citizens, who owned cash and were eager to convert it to a trust account in a Swiss bank. I had nothing to do with the transaction. ("Il romanzo di un romanzo," *Vita*, September 2, 1961, 12; original in Italian)

The first part of the story is correct, but the second part is not. Sergio d'Angelo, who had organized the delivery of money, explained it to me as follows:

Paladini, a very clever man and a great friend of mine, tells a lie. Perhaps he did not want to admit publicly that he had smuggled money, an activity that Moscow could still have blamed him for, declaring it not only criminal but much less noble, whatever its intent, than his notorious journalistic scoop on the "anti-Party group." . . . I confirm that I gave Paladini the rubles in Rome and his wife Carmela sewed the money inside the lining of the jacket and/or the overcoat. He traveled by joining, at my expense, a group of journalists, who included Zappulli, organized by the magazine *Il Punto*. (Personal email from Sergio d'Angelo, October 20, 2014; original in Italian)

Incidentally, d'Angelo gave a letter of introduction to Paladini, which is now somewhere in the files of the former KGB. Passages from this letter were used in the indictment against Ivinskaya:

The bearer of this letter—Leo Paladini—is a very close and reliable friend of mine, whom you can trust completely. Unfortunately, he knows few Russian words. . . . I still have a lot of your money. Therefore I will not only give the agreed-upon sum to our friend. . . . From my side, I can still—safely and quickly—perform the operation which I offered to you. (See document 50; original in Russian)

However, the indictment gives the impression that "our friend" refers to Paladini, whereas it was actually Garritano. Fortunately, a copy of this letter is found in the Feltrinelli archives (why it is found there is explained in section 2.2). It is published here as document 18.

At this point, the timeline of d'Angelo's deliveries becomes somewhat confused. In one of his 1961 articles in *Vita* ("Olga è innocente"), d'Angelo declared that before the final delivery on August 1 by the Benedettis, there had been only two deliveries, one in October 1959 and the one by Paladini just described. However, in the shortened, English version of the article, he spoke of several deliveries between February and August 1960. In his 2006 book, he stood by the account given in *Vita* in 1961 but also claimed that after receiving the $100,000 in March, he immediately sent some money to Pasternak (p. 169). What renders the situation more confused is that we have a precise dating in the indictment against Ivinskaya and Emelianova that fixes to March 1960 the meeting at the post office where Irina Emelianova and Mitia (Irina's younger half-brother) received a suitcase from Mirella Garritano containing 180,000 rubles.[26] Consulted on the

26. While the delivery of money by Mirella Garritano to Irina Emelianova is confirmed by several sources, the exact amount of 180,000 rubles rests on the indictment published as document 50. None of the other sources specifies a precise amount.

matter, Sergio d'Angelo insists that he only organized three deliveries—one in October 1959, one in February 1960, and one in August 1960—and that he did not send the 180,000 rubles. But if he did not send it, who did? While one could claim that the exact date is relatively unimportant, one ought to keep in mind that it was the evidence of her meeting with Mirella Garritano at the post office that sealed Emelianova's fate.

Furthermore, the discovery of a letter in the Feltrinelli archive seems to me to clarify the situation. D'Angelo wrote to Ivinskaya and Pasternak on March 19, 1960:

> Dear friends, greetings!
>
> In a few days, you should receive from me part of what I owe you. And relatively quickly, as I promised you, there will be other transfers. (See document 22; original in Russian).

There is no doubt in my mind, *pace* d'Angelo, that the 180,000 rubles Irina received at the post office were sent through d'Angelo. When queried by Feltrinelli at the beginning of June about the status of the deliveries, d'Angelo replied on June 9:

> Dear Giangiacomo,
>
> The matter you mentioned in your letter is proceeding in the most regular way. O. (who asked me to split the work in the span of a few months) has already received with great satisfaction two big packages. A third package is already in the making. (SdAP, HILA; original in Italian)

Of course, this letter is consistent with the possibility that the two payments d'Angelo refers to are the one he claims to have made in October and the February one. In any case, further letters quoted in chapter 2 will provide additional evidence of the delivery of money through Mirella Garritano in late March (or early April) 1960.

The Garritanos had been instrumental in delivering packages that were sometimes sent through the mail from d'Angelo or his wife and for deliveries of money throughout the period 1958–60, until their departure from Moscow in June 1960, about which more will be said in chapter 2. They did not carry money across the border but received the money already inside the Soviet Union. They also exchanged several postcards and letters with d'Angelo where monetary issues were discussed in a coded language.[27] Whereas Feltrinelli always spoke of "Brötchen" with Schewe, the Garritanos and d'Angelo spoke of deliveries of books. Here is a letter of November 28, 1959, from Mirella Garritano to Giulietta Pecori (d'Angelo's wife) with d'Angelo's explanations of the codes in brackets:

Dear Giulietta,

I received a few days ago news from Olga who always remembers you with affection. I have explained to her for a second time the reasons that speak in favor of the sending of books [transfer of money] but it seems that Giovanni [Pasternak] at this moment does not deem it necessary because he says he does not need them, they are too many and he would not know where to put them. Recently he received other books from his Paris friends [Proyart] who act very affectionately and desire not to appear inferior to anyone else. The inheritance issue [the controversy between Feltrinelli and Proyart] is still unresolved: it seems that Uncle Giancarlo [Feltrinelli] intends to travel to Belgium [Paris —PM] [to meet, I presume, the de Proyarts] toward the second half of December. This state of affairs worries Giovanni [Pasternak] a little, and it is for this reason that he does not want to make any decisions. Thus, one needs to wait a bit longer.

Meanwhile, Olga will send more books [money], which are quite cute and useful, of which a small part should remain at my disposal, as you know, and as is hinted at in one of the letters even if, it seems to me, in somewhat confused terms.[28] (SdAP, HILA; original in Italian)

Pasternak's reported resistance to further deliveries of money is consistent with what Pasternak wrote to Feltrinelli on November 19, 1959, in a letter I have already cited. Let me recall that the Garritanos were Italian Communists working for the daily newspaper *l'Unità*. Mirella's delivery in March/April 1960 of 180,000 rubles was more than four times as large as that made by Paladini in February. The delivery of the money took place at the Central Post Office in Moscow, but the money had certainly not arrived by mail. Who gave it to Mirella Garritano? Here d'Angelo, referring to how the money reached the Garritanos at some date or other, mentioned that a friend of his who had occasion to be in Moscow for business brought the money to the Garritanos, but d'Angelo said he promised he would never reveal his name. We will leave it at that except for the

27. All the letters between d'Angelo and the Garritanos are found in the SdAP, HILA, and are included in the documentary appendix.

28. For the entire letter see document 27.

remark that all the money given to Pasternak and Olga came in the form of rubles brought in from outside the Soviet Union. This was also true of the last, ill-fated delivery. This time the sum was enormous: 500,000 rubles. The delivery took place on August 1, 1960. The couriers were Giulio Benedetti and his wife, Claudia Mosettig (who was Slovenian). Both were Communists. Giulio Benedetti was the uncle of Giulietta Pecori (d'Angelo's wife). Without naming names, in his 2006 book, d'Angelo recounts how things went:

> Giulietta and I then accompany another couple from Rome to West Berlin in a Volkswagen Bug that has been acquired for the purposes of this trip. From there, the two of them proceed on their own to Moscow via Warsaw. We ourselves fly directly back to Rome. Two or three weeks later, we receive a phone call from Slovenia, which is where the wife was raised. During an otherwise casual conversation, they let us know that the set of crystal glasses, which they had made sure to handle with the greatest of care, was delivered safe and sound to the newlyweds on August 1. (d'Angelo 2006, 176)

The Benedettis hid 500,000 rubles in the upholstery of the car and managed to get through Soviet border controls. Then they arrived in Moscow and visited Olga a first time with a letter of introduction from d'Angelo (now probably preserved in some State Security archive of the Russian Federation). They arrived by taxi so as not to be conspicuous, given that their car had a foreign license plate. Then they came back the following day, August 1, still in a taxi and this time with the money (see *Vita*, December 22–28, 1966, letter from Benedetti; and the interview with Claudia Mosettig in *Vita*, February 2–8, 1967).[29] This large sum of money created logistical problems for Olga, who hid it in small suitcases and left the suitcases with neighbors. The KGB found the money, and Olga was arrested on August 16, 1960.

Much previous scholarship and many of the protagonists have long claimed that this last delivery of money was the principal reason for the arrest of Olga Ivinskaya. In the next chapter we will see that things are more complex than that. To understand that part of the story (and the last two letters from Ivinskaya to d'Angelo; see documents 41 and 46), we need

---

29. I should warn the reader that the articles in *Vita* are rather tendentious and often make ungrounded claims. But I have checked this part of the story with other sources.

to say more about the Garritanos. On April 30, 1960, Mirella Garritano wrote to Giulietta Pecori (d'Angelo's wife) that their time in the Soviet Union was coming to a close and that they were due back in Italy at the beginning of June.

Dear Giulietta,

Please excuse me for not having sent any news about us earlier, but these days we are very busy, for we are very close to our departure. We will come back at the beginning of June and thus we are already in the process of dismantling the camp. Frankly, we are very sad to leave earlier than expected (we were hoping to stay until August) but the magazine has decided so and we can do nothing about it. It is our intention to take a trip in the Soviet Union before coming back to Rome, but taking everything into consideration we will not be able to stay beyond June 15. Keep this date in mind for what concerns the sending of the books [money] I had asked you for and which the comrades [Pasternak and Olga] are waiting for. (SdAP, HILA; original in Italian)[30]

Not long before, the Garritanos had asked Pasternak to sign a receipt for the delivery of the 180,000 rubles. Pasternak decided to use the occasion to write a full power of attorney for Olga that allowed her to control all his financial assets abroad. This document, together with other important letters and documents, were given in April to the Garritanos. Here is how Olga described the events to Feltrinelli in a letter written on June 5, 1960, after Pasternak's death:

You already know about our terrible grief. My dear Boryusha is no more. Only two days have passed since his funeral, and yet I am obliged to write to you a letter not just as a friend, but as a business associate. Everyone is hurrying, and it is scary for us to wait.

In April, wishing to occupy himself solely with his play, and feeling a certain weakness, B. wrote me a power of attorney to be given to you. It states that he requests that my signature be trusted as his own—on monetary documents, as well as in any requests coming from him and about him. This power of attorney is written in both Russian and French and has been given [*handwritten*: by me] to friends of Sergio D'Angelo, before Mr. Heinz had returned to Moscow, so that they may personally hand it to you.

30. For the full letter see document 28.

If even after Borya's death his will is sacred to you and you still consider me his empowered representative, who has been charged with piously carrying out his will, I ask you to assure me of it. Meanwhile, I will acquaint you with my plans.

First of all, I ask you in turn to consider Mr. Heinz Schewe to be my empowered representative. Through him I will give you, as per Borya's wishes, those manuscripts that he will give to you in due time for publication. This concerns the manuscript of the novel, materials from the archives, which I will put into order without delay, as well as the play. Here, things are more difficult, the utmost care is needed, and in this both you and I will trust Mr. Heinz. (AGFE, Busta 6; and Heinz Schewe Papers, Berlin; for the full letter see document 32; original in Russian)

Thus the reason for giving this document to the Garritanos was that the Garritanos were returning from Moscow to Italy and that Heinz Schewe was not in Moscow during that period. The letter goes on to discuss how this document, a sort of "will," would easily solve the dispute with Proyart.

Ivinskaya then provided instructions to Feltrinelli for further payments Pasternak had earmarked for some of his friends and gave Feltrinelli a piece of information that must have pleased him very much. She was willing to send him the universal contract that he had been trying to get throughout 1959 and early 1960 with Pasternak's signature on it. Pasternak had in fact signed the contract but had not sent it for fear that it might damage Proyart's position. Here is Olga again:

Borya has wishes, which must be carried out after his death with the same precision as if he were alive.

This concerns monetary deductions, which he asks you to make to his friends, who helped him and colored his life. From the money that belongs to him, he wanted to set aside ten thousand dollars to Sergio D'Angelo to give to his friends, who are returning from Moscow. Ten thousand dollars to Mr. Heinz Schewe to his address in Hamburg. Ten thousand to Mr. Georges Nivat to an address in France, Paris (I will confirm the address). Five thousand to Mme. Renata [Schweitzer] (Berlin, Lankwitz Am Gemeindepark 16).

Dear Giangiacomo, I do not need to tell you that the strictest care must be observed: otherwise, I will perish, and so will Borya's manuscripts and archives.

Once I have received your letter, in which you will confirm receipt of the power of attorney in my name (it should be given to you in June of this year by D'Angelo's friends), I can also send you the contract that was signed by Boris Leonidovich while he was still alive, which he had withheld until the peaceful resolution of the conflict with Mme. P. It would be good if you would set aside some area for her to work on. This would coincide with Boris Leonidovich's wishes. Please tell me what you think about this, and I will write to her accordingly. Correspond only with Mr. Heinz, and remember that carelessness can destroy everything. Hurry with your response. I'm here waiting for the remaining sum that should be given to me by D'Angelo's friends in June (the power of attorney was in his name for one hundred thousand dollars, but only a portion had been transferred). After receiving it and settling with them with a receipt as per the agreement, I will ask you to have monetary relationships with me only through Mr. Heinz in the future. After finishing things here, I will do my best to leave for July and put the archive in order. Mr. Heinz, knowing the entire situation that has manifested itself here, approves of my plan.

Until next time, dear friend. (AGFE, Busta 6; and Heinz Schewe Papers, Berlin; for the full letter see document 32; original in Russian)

In chapter 2, I will recount how all these documents disappeared in mysterious circumstances. Indeed, before returning to Italy the Garritanos took a trip to the Caucasus, and the documents were lost. The circumstances of the disappearance remained unclear, and the loss of these important documents put Ivinskaya in a state of despair.

1.9. Conclusion

I began with d'Angelo's early interactions with Pasternak and Olga Ivinskaya and his role in bringing the typescript of *Doctor Zhivago* to Feltrinelli. This led to d'Angelo's friendship with Pasternak and Olga. We have also reconstructed the financial situation in which Pasternak found himself after the Nobel Prize. D'Angelo proposed helping Pasternak by means of a financial scheme that was meant to deliver to Pasternak part of his royalties from the West. We have reconstructed the network of couriers and contacts that helped Pasternak and Ivinskaya and delivered money to them. As the poet was feeling his age and felt a pressing need to focus on his work without being bogged down by translation work, it was important to provide him with an independent source of revenue. By late 1959 and early 1960, the money was flowing. Meanwhile, the poet was making progress with his new play, *The Blind Beauty*. In order not to be distracted, he preferred to put Olga Ivinskaya in charge of all his administrative chores, both literary and financial. It was in this connection that he decided to write a decisive document for Olga, making her in effect the designated heir of his royalties abroad and of all his literary work. As we have seen, in late March (or early April) 1960, the Garritanos delivered one part of the sum from the $100,000 that was entrusted to Sergio d'Angelo. They requested that Olga be given a document that would allow her to sign receipts on the spot. Pasternak decided to use the occasion to write a comprehensive power of attorney on behalf of Ivinskaya. Then, in mid-April, Pasternak became sick, got progressively worse, and died on May 30, 1960.

Since the Garritanos were supposed to leave for Italy at the end of May (or beginning of June) and Schewe was not in Moscow, they were given the power of attorney on Olga's behalf, as well as other documents, to bring back to Italy. The documents were lost in June during the Garritanos' trip to the Caucasus, and from the last two letters sent from Ivinskaya to d'Angelo (documents 41 and 46) the reader will be able to appreciate how deeply Olga was affected by the loss of these documents. In chapter 2 we unravel, among other things, this part of the story.

CHAPTER TWO

"Moscow Has Ears Everywhere!" From Pasternak's Death to the Arrests of Olga Ivinskaya and Irina Emelianova

I mentioned in the preface that some aspects of the so-called Ivinskaya case have so far resisted closer scrutiny.[1] A fuller understanding of the case has been hampered by the fact that, so far, only the evidence for one of the three aspects relevant to the story has been available, namely reports in the press about public statements surrounding the events. A partial reconstruction of these public statements, using newspapers from the period as well as some precious documents and personal reminiscences, has been attempted in the third chapter of d'Angelo's 2006 volume *Il caso Pasternak*, which complements other materials already published in the older but still useful book by Conquest (1961b).[2]

Except for a few exceptions mentioned below, we still lack the documents from the former KGB archives that would reveal the strategies of surveillance, the intercepted communications, and the *real* reasons why Soviet officials arrested Olga and Irina and sentenced them to eight and three years of labor camp, respectively. While some conjectures can be

1. Regrettably, recent books published on Olga Ivinskaya (e.g., Dalos 1999; Anna Pasternak 2016) are derivative of Ivinskaya's 1978 memoirs, which they follow uncritically without adding any substantially new information or sources. Exceptions are Mansurov 2009 and Emelianova 2005. For instance, Anna Pasternak's chronology of the relationship between Olga and d'Angelo is marred by the fact that she follows a mistaken account by Ivinskaya, which had already been corrected in d'Angelo 2006 and Mancosu 2013.

2. For earlier contributions by d'Angelo, see the articles written by d'Angelo in 1961 and d'Angelo 1968.

made on the latter point, nothing can replace documentary evidence from the former KGB archives (and other relevant archives, such as those of the Central Committee of the CPSU). These documents exist, and they include a good part of the supporting evidence that was cited in the indictment against Olga and Irina, yet they have not hitherto been made public. In the last two years, however, some documents have emerged that I will refer to at the appropriate junction.[3]

But there is an additional perspective, the "first-person view," so to speak. This is the firsthand account of how Olga, Irina, and their immediate contacts, including Heinz Schewe, Giangiacomo Feltrinelli, and Georges Nivat, lived through the events leading up to the arrests of the two women, and how they coped afterward.[4] It is here that I will be able to contribute many new facts to our reconstruction and understanding of the story. I use hitherto unpublished correspondence between Olga Ivinskaya, Heinz Schewe, and Giangiacomo Feltrinelli, among others, to shed light on many aspects of the story that were unknown or discussed in the press with only partial knowledge of the real state of things.

Single pieces of evidence—for instance, the letter from Feltrinelli to Olga dated July 8, 1960, which was used sensationally by the Soviets to indict Olga and vilify Feltrinelli, and which the Italian weekly *Vita* republished periodically—reveal a less conspiratorial and more human aspect

3. After the final draft of Mancosu 2018a was completed, I read Elena Pasternak 2017, which contains new KGB documents, found at RGANI, on the Ivinskaya case (see esp. 214–17). While it was too late to include an analysis of the new documents in that article, I cited some key passages in five footnotes (notes 19, 27, 28, 40, and 42). Some of those footnotes are now incorporated in the main text. A folder of new KGB documents on Pasternak and Ivinskaya has also recently been unearthed at GARF by Anna Koznova and is discussed in Koznova 2017, 2018. Finally, I show in section 2.2 that some key documents found in the Feltrinelli archives in Milan, which are transcribed in this book, are photocopies of documents included in the trial proceedings against Ivinskaya and Emelianova.

4. A "first-person view" is of course offered in Ivinskaya 1978 and Emelianova 1997, 2002. But I am referring to documents dating from the period of the events. *Caveat lector*: my treatment of the events is to a great extent dictated by the documents I am here publishing for the first time. This chapter is a contribution to certain aspects of the story and does not aim to present the full complexity of what happened to the protagonists during this fateful period. For instance, I will have little to say about Olga's grief at the loss of her beloved Boris, about Irina's and Nivat's illnesses and their desperate search for hospitals and doctors, about the constant harassment by the KGB, etc. While all these aspects are mentioned in my retelling of the story, my aim is only to make specific contributions to a better understanding of the Ivinskaya case and not to give an exhaustive treatment of it (which would require a *very* long book). Thus, this chapter only complements and at times corrects, through the presentation of hitherto unknown documents, the broader narratives given by Ivinskaya and Emelianova.

when the context is carefully reconstructed.[5] Indeed, I think the documents I present partially explain why the Soviet authorities always refused to publish more letters concerning the case, although they undoubtedly had additional letters and documents at their disposal.

The unfolding of the events leading from Pasternak's death to the arrests of Olga and Irina is a human and political drama that cannot fail to move us. While the two women's memoirs provide, of course, irreplaceable details about those tragic events, and I rely on them when needed, they were written many years after the events and without the appropriate documentation, which, at the time of writing, was inaccessible to them. Moreover, Olga wrote her memoir when she was still a citizen of the USSR, and as I show, she had reason to obfuscate some of the truth.

Thus, it is these documents, here published in the documentary appendix for the first time, that bear witness to the crescendo that characterized the events of those dramatic months following Pasternak's death.

But to get to the crucial events that are the focus of this chapter, we must take a step back to the events described at the end of chapter 1.

2.1. Pasternak's "will"[6]

At the end of chapter 1, I hinted at the strange events surrounding the loss of important documents that Olga had given to the Garritanos in April 1960, which were allegedly lost during a trip to the Caucasus in the first half of June 1960. Let us now look more carefully at the events, starting from Olga's account of them in her memoir *A Captive of Time* (1978).

Given the role of the Garritanos in one of the scariest episodes in Olga's life, it is surprising how little attention they are given in her memoir. That reticence calls for an explanation, which I believe can be offered using the documents at our disposal.

5. I thus strongly disagree, as will become clearer in what follows, with the following evaluation of the situation given by Christopher Barnes on the basis of insufficient evidence: "[Feltrinelli] and Ivinskaya thus conspired to deprive Pasternak's family of any share of his wealth, and the way was clear for them to exercise virtually complete control over his posthumous financial destiny. There was an element of poetic justice in the fact that they were eventually thwarted—partly by the devil-may-care incaution of Feltrinelli and his Italian associates, partly through Ivinskaya's vain stupidity, and partly by the vindictiveness of the Soviet state" (Barnes 1998, 370).

6. I am borrowing the word *will* from the protagonists of the story. As will become clear, the "will" was a power of attorney on Olga's behalf signed by Pasternak.

There are three important passages in which Ivinskaya speaks of the Garritanos in her memoir.[7] In two different passages (pp. 337–38, 343), Olga recounts how Irina and her younger brother, Mitia, went to the Central Post Office to receive a small suitcase from Mirella Garritano.[8] This took place in early April 1960, and the evidence for dating the event to that time has been discussed in chapter 1. It is partly on the basis of this "collaboration" and "contact with foreigners" that Irina received her harsh sentence (three years of labor camp). A third passage offers a succinct account of the Garritanos' loss of the important documents. Here is the latter passage, which also refers to April 1960:

> At a moment when Schewe was absent from Moscow, I had gone to see him [Garritano] on a peculiar errand from BL, namely to give him two blank pieces of paper with BL's signature on them, as well as certain important documents and instructions which he wanted passed on to Feltrinelli. Garritano then left Moscow—not, as we later discovered, for Italy, but for the Caucasus. When he returned—which was after BL's death—his wife Mirella told me that the basket in which they had put the documents had got soaking wet during one of the rainstorms for which the Caucasus is so famous, and then disappeared.
>
> I appealed to Heinz for help—he was by now back in Moscow. Whatever grievance he might have felt, he came straightaway. I also asked Garritano and his wife to come to the Potapov Street apartment, although the Italian, as a Communist, was at first reluctant to meet a West German. During the meeting I became hysterical and Heinz had to calm me down. After hearing the story about the basket and the rainstorm, he commented icily: "Even such things have been known to happen . . ." Then, rubbing his fingers together, he asked politely: "And how is the weather in Rome?" (Ivinskaya 1978, 296)

It is virtually impossible to make sense of Olga's reaction based on the sanitized version of the story she is offering. But before giving the full

---

7. There are also some other passages that are less important. For instance, Olga asserts that Giuseppe Garritano was an employee of Radio Moscow (p. 343), but this is not correct; similarly, she also incorrectly speaks of G. Garritano as being d'Angelo's successor (at Radio Moscow; p. 296). In addition, there is a brief passage concerning G. Garritano's meeting with Irina on October 24, 1958, when he gave Irina a Torpedo typewriter for Pasternak and Olga.

8. While of no great consequence, I remark that Emelianova (1997, 2002) claims that the small suitcase was handed to her by Giuseppe Garritano. However, the indictment against Olga and Irina (see document 50), as well as Ivinskaya 1978, indicates that it was Mirella who handed the suitcase to Irina.

background, let me add also some passages from Irina's memoir concerning the Garritanos. Indeed, Irina also describes in her memoir the episode in which her mother had a hysterical fit during the meeting with the Garritanos:

> Later, their touching shyness led to unforeseen consequences. They claimed that the contract signed by Pasternak, which they were supposed to bring to Feltrinelli, was spirited away from them in a seaside resort in the south of Russia. My God, what a tragicomedy! Giuseppe was trying to calm down my mother while she shouted: "You are a bunch of murderers! Bring me the poison!" and he meanwhile asked me, very timidly, "What would the lady like?" At the time we were sure that they had handed over the contract to the KGB. By contrast, I now ask myself whether they were not in cahoots with d'Angelo, who had fallen out with Feltrinelli, for he deemed that the contract was too favorable for the Italian publisher. (Emelianova 2002, 91–92; original in French)

There is much of interest here, but the passage contains much speculation. For instance, the alleged explanation of the Garritanos' behavior, and its apparent dependence on the animosity between Feltrinelli and d'Angelo, is probably colored by Irina's knowledge of later events, which saw d'Angelo sue Feltrinelli in 1965 for a part of the Pasternak royalties.[9] We will thus need to do some work to get a clearer picture of the events. Once we do so, we will also be able to analyze and correct the reconstruction of the facts provided by Ivinskaya, Emelianova, and d'Angelo.

Relying on what has already been covered in chapter 1, I can anticipate that what was entrusted to the Garritanos, in addition to letters for Feltrinelli and d'Angelo, was not the contract or the two empty sheets of paper with Pasternak's signature on it, but rather a power of attorney (which could also be considered a will and was referred to as such by Olga, Schewe, and Feltrinelli) that Pasternak had written in two (according to Olga) or three (according to Schewe) languages on behalf of Olga in April 1960. In addition, there was a receipt for the 180,000 rubles that Mirella (or Giuseppe) Garritano had given to Irina at the post office in April 1960. Let me summarize the evidence grounding this reconstruction.

---

9. Although it is true that signs of growing conflict between d'Angelo and Feltrinelli had reached Pasternak and Olga early in 1960 (see chapter 1).

We have, first of all, Olga's letter to Feltrinelli dated June 5, 1960, which I extensively quoted at the end of chapter 1. The letter was sent before Olga was informed of the loss of the documents. In it, she describes for Feltrinelli what he would receive through the Garritanos. She mentions a power of attorney signed by Pasternak on her behalf that Pasternak wanted sent to Feltrinelli. She specified:

In it, it says that he requests that my signature be trusted as his own—in financial documents, as well as in any requests coming from him and about him. This power of attorney is written in both Russian and French and has been given [*handwritten*: by me] to friends of Sergio D'Angelo [the Garritanos], before Mr. Heinz [Schewe] had returned to Moscow, so that they may personally hand it to you. (Ivinskaya to Feltrinelli, June 5, 1960)[10]

A letter dated June 6, 1960, from Heinz Schewe to Feltrinelli confirms Olga's statements:

According to the will of Boris Leonidovich, she is the sole literary heiress and the only one empowered to act on behalf of his fortune abroad. This I know and can testify to. Boris Leonidovich drew up a correspondent power of attorney for Ms. Olga already on the 15th of April 1960, one week before the beginning of his illness. This power of attorney was prepared in three languages and should be delivered to you by way of Sergio d'Angelo's friends [the Garritanos] in the course of this month. (Schewe to Feltrinelli, June 6, 1960)

More precise information about the documents given to the Garritanos can be obtained from letters Olga wrote after she was informed of the loss of the documents. The Garritanos came back to Moscow from their Caucasian trip on June 19, 1960. On June 22, Schewe wrote to Feltrinelli informing him of the loss of the documents. He gave the following list of documents:

10. All the correspondence between June and September 1960 exchanged among Olga, Schewe, and Feltrinelli is edited and translated in full in documents 30–49. The reader can find the full versions of the letters I cite using the date of the documents. All the letters written by Feltrinelli and Schewe cited in this chapter are in German. All the letters written by Olga are in Russian, as are those written by d'Angelo to Olga. Hence, in this chapter, the original language of the documents is specified only for the remaining letters or documents.

Among these papers were: a) the power of attorney (literary and financial) for Ms. Olga, b) a confirmation that the first installment of the $100,000 transfer had reached the Classic, c) the Classic's handwritten wish that you would transfer certain dollar sums to Renate Schweitzer, to the French student Georges [Nivat], and to myself, as signs of his thankfulness for the friendship we had shown him. (Schewe to Feltrinelli, June 22, 1960)

Not surprisingly, Schewe does not mention the present for Sergio d'Angelo (on behalf of the Garritanos), for he was suspicious of both the Garritanos and d'Angelo. D'Angelo's request for the present on behalf of Mirella Garritano was dated March 19, 1960.[11] It is possible that this present had not been explicitly mentioned by Pasternak but only in a letter from Olga. The donations to d'Angelo (meant for the Garritanos), Schweitzer, Nivat, and Schewe are also confirmed in a letter sent from Olga to Feltrinelli on June 5, 1960 (see document 32). Olga also mentioned explicitly having written on this matter in April, as she points out in a letter to d'Angelo dated July 28, 1960:[12]

I wanted to follow your advice and reward your friends [the Garritanos] for agreeing to be a link in our friendly chain. I wrote about this in a letter which was among those that were addressed to you and F and lost, together with the lost powers of attorney. But the loss of the documents robs me of the opportunity to do as I thought, and in general, completely unsettles me. (Ivinskaya to d'Angelo, July 28, 1960)

Olga, like Schewe, now expressed reservations about the appropriateness of the donation to the Garritanos. She also explicitly told Feltrinelli to halt the payment to Mirella Garritano (through d'Angelo), at least pending full clarification of the events surrounding the loss of the documents.[13]

---

11. This was discussed in chapter 1; see also commentary to document 23. The present to d'Angelo (meant for the Garritanos) is confirmed by a document addressed to Feltrinelli, dated May 25, 1960, a time when Pasternak was no longer in condition to sign anything (the document is published in Mancosu 2013, 375). Olga wrote that document, and signed it, on the strength of her power of attorney. However, the document in question, found in the Feltrinelli archives, did not reach Feltrinelli at the time and is part of a group of documents that were sequestered in Moscow by the KGB and included in the trial proceedings against Ivinskaya. See the conclusion to section 2.2 for further details.

12. In April, since that is when she had given the documents, including the accompanying letters for d'Angelo and Feltrinelli, to the Garritanos.

13. "There was also a directive regarding Sergio's friends—but let it remain unfulfilled for now. Let this be more clear first" (Ivinskaya to Feltrinelli, July 28, 1960).

We now have a very precise idea of what the batch of documents contained: 1) the power of attorney on behalf of Olga; 2) the receipt for 180,000 rubles signed by Pasternak; 3) several letters to Feltrinelli and d'Angelo, at least one of which involved Olga mentioning the donations to d'Angelo, Schweitzer, Nivat, and Schewe.

Notice that in all this correspondence among Olga, Schewe, and Feltrinelli, there is no mention of empty pages with Pasternak's signature on them, contrary to what is claimed in Ivinskaya 1978 and d'Angelo 2006. Moreover, contrary to what Irina Emelianova claimed in her memoir, there was nothing connected to the universal contract. That contract, signed by Pasternak in January 1960 but not sent to Feltrinelli, was still in the hands of Olga Ivinskaya, who, in her letter of June 5, 1960, offered to send it to Feltrinelli as soon as he acknowledged the validity of Pasternak's power of attorney on her behalf (which, at the time, she believed Feltrinelli would receive very soon through the Garritanos).

Olga's despair can now be fully understood. Her distress found expression in several letters, including the one written to d'Angelo on July 28:

> After this incident, I do not have a single minute of peace. Just imagine what will happen to me when the lost package with our correspondence finds its way into the hands of officials. I am surprised that I am still alive. (Ivinskaya to d'Angelo, July 28, 1960)

And to Feltrinelli:

> The Garritanos told me that all letters and powers of attorney were lost by them during their voyage through Georgia. Either lost or stolen, by whom they do not know. After this news, I at first did not have a single minute of peace. You understand—I was practically under the threat of death, the loss of B.'s archives, the demise of my children. If our government had wanted to publicize the matter, we would have been literally crushed by this misfortune—this criminal negligence, I still cannot understand what forced these people [the Garritanos] to carry out such a horrific act. (Ivinskaya to Feltrinelli, July 28, 1960)

If this batch of documents had ended up in the hands of the Soviet officials, it would have been clear that Pasternak had been receiving large sums from the West, and that he also had money at his disposal, of which he was making use. In addition, Olga was in just as much trouble as Pasternak, since her power of attorney showed that she had access to all this money.

Finally, there was also the issue, a very serious one, of Pasternak giving Olga complete freedom with his literary work. But did the documents end up in the hands of the Soviet officials?

2.2. The Garritanos' behavior and Olga's way out

So far we have only discussed which documents were lost. But how were they lost? The Garritanos gave conflicting conjectures as to what happened. The first reports by Schewe and Olga do not add up to much. Schewe's letter to Feltrinelli, dated June 22, only mentions the loss of the documents but provides no further details. Olga's letter from July 28 is also vague: "Either lost or stolen, by whom they do not know." Later reports, including letters from August 1960, speak of different accounts by the Garritanos. According to one of them, reported by Ivinskaya in her memoir, the documents were lost during a thunderstorm as the Garritanos ran for cover. A different account has the documents disappearing from the hotel room of a spa resort where they had been staying.[14] D'Angelo offers yet another variation, reporting on G. Garritano's suspicions:

> During one of their days in the Caucasus, they took part in the excursion where they were caught in a sudden downpour, and that same evening, they also went to a local party, where there was eating, drinking and dancing. When they got back to the hotel, and Mirella discovered that the package was no longer in her bag, she assumed that it had fallen out while they were running for shelter from the storm.
>
> Several days later, when they were back in Potapovski Lane, Mirella mentioned this supposition. Pino [Giuseppe] himself, however, was convinced that someone had tipped off the secret police about the delivery of the documents, and that they were stolen during the party when Mirella got up to dance and left the bag on the sofa for half a minute or little more. (d'Angelo 2006, 220–21)

This is important testimony, since d'Angelo's account relies on conversations he had with the Garritanos when they returned to Italy. D'Angelo, like Ivinskaya, includes among the missing documents two blank sheets of paper with Pasternak's signature and, while admitting that he only has a vague idea of what the batch contained, connects the blank sheets to

14. See for instance Schewe's letter to Feltrinelli dated July 28, 1960.

Feltrinelli's attempt to get the new universal contract. We have seen that the evidence points in other directions, but d'Angelo refers to an accusation by Surkov in this connection, to which I will return.

As for Giuseppe and Mirella Garritano, we have no documents by them referring to the event from that period. They kept their silence about the affair and in an interview given for a documentary by Valeria Paniccia, Giuseppe Garritano laconically repeats the explanation of how the documents were lost, giving the two versions already reported by d'Angelo and adding that, when he came back to Italy, the deputy secretary of the PCI, Luigi Longo, told him "di tacere, di non dare ulteriore pubblicità a questa cosa" (to be silent, not to give further publicity to this thing).[15]

At the time, Olga, Feltrinelli, and Schewe had no doubt that there was something quite suspicious about the Garritanos' behavior. The Garritanos had gone to see Olga as soon as they came back from the Caucasus, and the accounts given by Olga and Irina and cited earlier refer to this event. Schewe, who was present, offered a report on the meeting to Feltrinelli:

> All of this has supposedly gone missing. There were many tears shed by those who lost the documents, as well as by Ms. Olga, who is inconsolable. If the Soviet police find these . . . ? It is inconceivable!
>
> Mirella, that is the first name of the Italian journalist's wife, claims they possibly left these papers in the hotel of one of their resorts in the Caucasus. Well, strange matter. There is something I do not like about it. Ms. Olga also has strong doubts. She believes that the "Unita" people wanted to stash away the power of attorney for other parties' interest. But Mirella, apparently the one who lost them, confirms that she read the papers and knows exactly what was written in them. She says she will also gladly testify as much.
>
> However that may be—a mysterious thing! The only will that existed has, after the Classic's death, disappeared in a most mysterious manner. It was supposed to have been prepared in three languages, says Ms. Olga. (Schewe to Feltrinelli, June 22, 1960)

The reader will find in Olga's letters to Feltrinelli and d'Angelo a full statement of her suspicions concerning the Garritanos. These suspicions

15. Valeria Paniccia, dir., *Il caso Pasternak*, Rai educational (2012), http://www.lastoriasiamonoi.rai.it/puntate/il-caso-pasternak/963/default.aspx. Garritano's statements are found at 50:40–52:45. In this documentary Irina Emelianova repeats the story about the empty pages signed by Pasternak.

were vented openly in her memoir and in Emelianova's *Légendes de la rue Potapov*. I will refrain from going through the different variations of their accounts, for at the moment there is no way to clarify whether these accusations were justified or not. However, I will cite an email from Sergio d'Angelo, who was a very close friend of the Garritanos and yet wrote me the following:

> In my book I recounted in great detail all I knew about the loss of the envelope Olga entrusted to the Garritanos at the time when they were getting ready to go back to Italy. I can only add something in confidence. I have always suspected that the envelope had not been lost or stolen in the Caucasus but rather that the KGB, having been informed, asked the Garritanos to surrender the envelope when they were still in Moscow. The various versions by the Garritanos (thunderstorm or party with dancing) can be explained by the desire not to frighten Olga more than necessary. But since they repeated the explanation in Rome I must also suspect a case of misplaced discretion [*falso pudore*]. I must add that the Garritanos were not able to get over the judgment that Olga gave of them in her *Captive of Time*. (Personal email from Sergio d'Angelo, January 21, 2014; original in Italian)

The stress induced by the loss of the documents was to affect Olga for the last ten days of June and the full month of July. Nothing happened, however. In any case, there is no mention of the documents in the indictment against Olga and Irina. But this in itself does not prove that the documents were not intercepted by the KGB. Indeed, it is possible that the documents were not mentioned because they did not fit well with the case the Soviets had decided to mount against them. The indictment is a twelve-page document (see document 50), but there are three volumes of trial proceedings that have so far been inaccessible to researchers, which, in principle, could contain Pasternak's will. Irina Emelianova gave written permission to Sergio d'Angelo to consult these volumes about fifteen years ago, but d'Angelo, as he recounts in his preface (d'Angelo 2006), was refused permission to access this material by the director of the Russian Federal Security Service (FSB), Nikolai Patrushev.

However, it is unlikely that Pasternak's "will" is included in the three volumes in question. The defense lawyer for Olga Ivinskaya, Viktor Adol'fovich Kosachevskiĭ, published an article in 1988 on the Ivinskaya trial, in which he refers to an exchange between Ivinskaya and the prosecuting attorney:

Ivinskaya's response was clear: "Already from the end of April of 1960, Boris Leonidovich was severely ill and, as I found out after his death, sent instructions to the publisher Feltrinelli: 'All my next honoraria for the publication of the novel *Doctor Zhivago* and other works beyond the border I leave to O. V. Ivinskaya.' By sending the honoraria for the novel to me, the publisher fulfilled B. L. Pasternak's will."

Prosecuting attorney: "This document is not familiar to us, we cannot take it into account." (Kosachevskiĭ 1988, 147)[16]

I think this is sufficient to conclude that Pasternak's "will" is not to be found in the three volumes of legal proceedings against Olga and Irina that rest in the State Archives of the Russian Federation. Indeed, as we shall see, the case that was being mounted against Ivinskaya aimed to show that she was running shady, secret financial dealings and duping the gullible Pasternak. Thus, Pasternak's "will" was certainly not something that would have contributed to the evidence against Olga, for it spoke in her favor.

This was the state of my evaluation of the matter until the publication in 2017 of an article by Elena Vladimirovna Pasternak (2017). Indeed, a new document she published provides decisive evidence that the KGB did seize the documents and that this event sealed Ivinskaya's fate. It is a document signed by the head of the KGB, Shelepin, and by the prosecutor general, Rudenko. It is dated August 10, 1960, and reads as follows:

The facts show that Ivinskaya violated a written agreement,[17] given by her in 1959 to the Prosecutor of the USSR, to cease undesired communication with foreigners; furthermore, in June of this year she made an attempt to illegally send to Italy a power of attorney by Pasternak, according to which her signature on all sorts of documents and receipts would carry the same force as Pasternak's own. On the basis of this power of attorney, Ivinskaya ordered Feltrinelli to distribute large sums of money to some of Pasternak's acquaintances abroad, including Schewe and Nivat; for services rendered to her for illegally communicating with those abroad, they are supposed to receive 5000 dollars. Due to measures that were undertaken, these documents did not make it abroad. The KGB and the Office of the Prosecutor of the USSR consider it necessary to change the resolution adopted by the CC of the CPSU on February 25, 1960 to remove Ivinskaya from Moscow and to arrest Ivinskaya instead, so that the

16. Olga recounts the same exchange in Ivinskaya 1978, 351–52.

17. See the document reproduced in chapter 1, note 15.

case can be investigated and presented to a court. We ask that you consider this. Head of the KGB, Shelepin; Prosecutor General, Rudenko. August 10, 1960. (For the original text in Russian, see Elena Pasternak 2017, 215)

This is an extremely informative document, for it also mentions a hitherto unknown resolution by the Central Committee of the CPSU, dated February 25, 1960, to exile Ivinskaya from Moscow and the new decision to arrest her. Again, this shows that there are essential documents of the CC of the CPSU, as well as KGB documents, on the Ivinskaya case that still need to be located. However, the document just quoted does not clarify the role played by the Garritanos in the seizing of the documents. The document does confirm my original line of thought that we do not find any mention of the "will" at the Ivinskaya trial because the document did not lend itself to the thesis prosecutors had decided to prove.

Let us go back now to the repercussions of the loss of those documents, a situation that also preoccupied Feltrinelli. In his archive there are three pages of notes concerning the Garritanos. In one he writes:

Conclusion. It seems to me that the documents are in Italy. To give a reward for their recovery? Hear the Garritanos. Proceed with a lawsuit against them? Or is it more useful to have their declaration? Which instruments of pressure can be used, weaved, constructed, with respect to Garritano.

The idea could be that of blocking any possibility of paying for a lawsuit or any other means relying on the disappearance, the theft of the "will." (AGFE; original in Italian)

While the notes are somewhat nebulous in content, they do convey Feltrinelli's attempt to understand what happened and weigh possible courses of action.

That the Garritanos had not immediately gone to see Feltrinelli seemed, to Olga, proof of their wrongdoing. On July 28, 1960, she wrote to Feltrinelli:

The fact that these Garritanos have not been to see you still, and evidently Sergio does not know about the disappearance that took place, forces me to suppose that there is something very dark here—a maneuver of some sort. The G-nos gave me their word that they would immediately inform you of what happened [*handwritten*: but they didn't do it!].

Of course, none of us could have foreseen such baseness on their part. After all, these people are Sergio's friends. Though to be honest, B.L. did not feel particularly friendly toward these people on some instinctive level. Everything that they did was somehow tortured, the transfer of letters was always drawn out, etc.

What about the white sheets of paper with Pasternak's signature on them? It is quite interesting that the first claim about the pages signed by Pasternak initially reaches the West in 1961, through an accusation levied by Pasternak's archenemy, Alekseĭ Surkov, during his campaign to vilify Olga Ivinskaya following her condemnation.[18] The accusation comes in a letter to David Carver, dated April 3, 1961, where Surkov writes:

When Pasternak was still alive Ivinskaya made him sign blank sheets of paper (three such blank sheets with his signature affixed are in the files of the proceedings) which she later, at will, transformed into letters of attorney and used them avariciously to enrich herself. (See document 51)

It should be noted that, contrary to the way d'Angelo reported the accusation, Surkov does not mention any lost set of documents and does not connect the sheets to the universal contract. He only says that three such sheets are in the files of the trial proceedings (the three volumes previously mentioned). Given Surkov's malicious intent, it would be tempting to dismiss his accusation as mere fabrication. But in this case the story has an interesting twist that confirms Surkov's claim.

Faced with the loss of such a vital document (the power of attorney written by Pasternak on her behalf) and convinced that the Garritanos were working against her (either in cahoots with the Soviets or with d'Angelo against Feltrinelli), Olga decided to use a blank sheet of paper with Pasternak's signature to reproduce the power of attorney that Pasternak had given her. Contrary to what Olga alleges in her memoir, the sheets of paper were not given to, or intended for, Garritano. She simply had them at her disposal, and as we shall soon see, she made use of at least one of them as Surkov alleged.[19] This discovery was surprising. I earlier published a power of attorney signed by Pasternak on behalf of Olga dated

18. I describe the campaign at length in chapter 3.

19. Although Surkov got it right, this is not sufficient to infer that he had conclusive evidence for his accusation. I will argue at the end of this section that he did. Even so, it does not follow that he was correct in imputing to Olga the motives he alleged.

April 4, 1960 (Mancosu 2013, 365–66; original in Russian). The document was among the Pasternak documents in the Feltrinelli archive. I had suspected nothing wrong with the document and presented it as yet another document signed by Pasternak. It reads as follows:

G. FELTRINELLI, Milan
POWER OF ATTORNEY

I entrust OLGA VSEVOLODOVNA IVINSKAYA to place her signature on all instructions related to the publication of my works in those European countries where they have been printed or will be printed, as well as on all financial receipts and financial documents.

I ask that OLGA VSEVOLODOVNA IVINSKAYA'S signature be believed as if it were my own and to consider all instructions originating from Olga Vsevolodovna as my own.

The power of attorney which is granted to OLGA VSEVOLODOVNA IVINSKAYA is in effect indefinitely. I entrust her with the potential control over all publications, as well as financial operations in the case of my demise. I ask that all requests for information and receipts related to my literary work be addressed to her.

April 4, 1960,
Peredelkino,
[*signed*] BPasternak

It was during the preparation of the correspondence between Olga, Schewe, and Feltrinelli that I realized this document had been produced after Pasternak's death. What follows is the evidence.

We have three versions of the letter from Olga to Feltrinelli dated July 28. The first is the final version in Russian, the second is Schewe's faithful translation of the final Russian version into German, and the third is the draft in Russian (for the texts in the original language, the reader is referred to Mancosu 2018a).[20] It turns out that the draft in Russian diverges significantly from the final version (in Russian or German). In the final version of the letter, Olga wrote:

In the case of some hypothetical unforeseen event, which happened to actually take place, B. left me the possibility of restoring his directives, and I have documents, which I have preserved, as well as the possibility to send you the remaining power of attorney. It will not be of much use to me here. (Ivinskaya to Feltrinelli, July 28, 1960)

---

20. The document is a photocopy of the original draft. See the end of the section for its origin.

The corresponding passage in the draft is quite similar.[21] However, the draft and the final version differ on an essential point. In the draft, Olga tells Feltrinelli that she is sending the text of a power of attorney *along the lines of the lost power of attorney that she had received from Pasternak*. She is sending the new document to Feltrinelli to see whether the wording agrees with his needs, and asks Feltrinelli to send it back with suggestions for possible revisions. Upon receipt of the corrections she will send a signed copy. Here is the text in the draft:

Dear, kind Giangiacomo! We will be hoping that the most terrible thing will not happen, that I will be allowed my freedom for now, and I will be able to put in order all of Borya's affairs, and the fate of my children will not be as terrifying as it could have been if this loss was publicized. By good fortune, I have the ability to restore the power of attorney. ~~Observing the strictest secrecy, look at the text of the power of attorney that we – Mr. Schewe and I – are sending to you [*handwritten*: to replace the one that was lost by the Garritanos.] Is everything there to your complete satisfaction? For now, we can [*handwritten*: still] put in some insignificant changes. Please send this text back to us, as soon as possible, and we will send you this power of attorney signed, and send a copy to Mme Proyart~~. Furthermore, I can ~~also~~ send you other documents, such as a power of attorney in my name, notarized by Goslitizdat [*handwritten*: from 1957], for carrying out all activities related to the publication of "D. Zh." [*handwritten*: Currently,] the documents are not at my house. Getting them out of the ~~hidden place~~ secret place is not so easy, and so I will send everything to you at once when I receive from you the text of the proposed power of attorney that [*handwritten*: you] have read. I have also hidden there the contract between you and Boris, signed by B. I will also send it [*handwritten*: if it is still needed]. (Ivinskaya to Feltrinelli, July 28, 1960; draft)

From the crossed-out parts we see that Schewe was part of the machination. In the final version of the letter, Olga said nothing about a preliminary draft of the power of attorney and sent a signed document as if the document stemmed directly from Pasternak:

Dear, kind Giangiacomo! We will be hoping that the most terrible thing will not happen, that I will be allowed my freedom for now, and I will be able to put in order all of

21. "But, in case of some potential unforeseen event, B. left me the possibility of restoring his directives, and I have documents, which I have preserved, as well as the ability to restore the text of the power of attorney that was lost and send you a copy of it signed with Borya's signature."

Borya's affairs, and the fate of my children will not be as terrifying as it could have been if this loss was publicized. By good fortune, I have the ability to send you the power of attorney. I had wanted to hide this one in case it was needed, but what else is there to do, if things turned out so badly. Furthermore, I can send you a power of attorney in my name, notarized at the time by Goslitizdat, for carrying out all activities related to the publication of "D. Zh." I'm sending you now what I have on hand. I'm not keeping papers at home right now, and getting them out of the hiding place is not so easy. But, if you need the latest contract signed by B., I will send it to you. (Ivinskaya to Feltrinelli, July 28, 1960; final)

It is absolutely obvious that to prepare the new power of attorney, a sheet of paper with Pasternak's original signature was necessary. Visual inspection of the document, dated April 4, 1960, confirms the reconstruction I am offering. In fact, Pasternak's signature is in the middle of the sheet of paper and the text has been crammed into the upper half of the page (see illustration 10).

It is thus clear that in her memoir Olga is muddying the waters. In her book, she states that in the exchange with the prosecution concerning Pasternak's "will," she claimed, "The statement existed in more than one copy, and even in several different versions—all of which had reached Feltrinelli" (Ivinskaya 1978, 351–52). If this faithfully captures what she said at trial, it could have been a way to preempt possible trouble in case the original "will" had resurfaced. Indeed, the original will, as we know from a letter from Schewe to Feltrinelli, was dated April 15, 1960, whereas Olga's reconstructed document was dated April 4, 1960.

The document was ultimately of little use to Olga, who was arrested a few weeks later. It is hard to blame her for having tried to restore a document on which her livelihood depended and which truly represented Pasternak's will.[22] Given the kind of surveillance Pasternak and Olga were subjected to, it was not unrealistic on her part to think that there was something quite suspicious about the loss of the documents; with opponents such as the KGB, restoring the lost document must surely have seemed legitimate to her.

Neither Feltrinelli nor Schewe publicly mentioned this document, although they hinted at various times during the Ivinskaya campaign that

22. Without Pasternak, she was left without any protection, and because she was not married to him, she had no claims to any inheritance.

Pasternak's wish might have been to leave his royalties to Olga. Feltrinelli's unwillingness to publish this legal document surely had to do with his work behind the scenes to help Olga and Irina after they were sentenced, while not embarrassing the Soviets.[23] As for Schewe, he knew that he had helped fabricate the document, but after Olga was arrested and his role as middleman between Olga and Feltrinelli had become clear to the authorities, his situation in the USSR became very complicated (see chapter 3).[24] But this subsequent development was still to come.

But did Feltrinelli know that the document was not genuine? And what about Surkov's accusation, reported in the letter to Carver, that Ivinskaya had used empty sheets of paper with Pasternak's signature on them? Was he making a wild guess, or did he have hard evidence? Only after Mancosu 2018a was written, while checking the original documents for publication in this book, was I struck by a detail that allows me to answer these questions. The explanation requires a little background, and I hope the reader will bear with me.

When in February 1961 a Soviet delegation went to England (see section 3.9 for extensive discussion) carrying what they considered definitive evidence of Ivinskaya's guilt, they showed, among other things, a photographic reproduction of Feltrinelli's letter to Olga, dated July 8, 1960 (see document 37), and Ivinskaya's signed "confession" (see note 63 in chapter 3). These documents were photographic reproductions from the three-volume trial proceedings against Ivinskaya and Emelianova. This is revealed by the numbering of the pages in the upper right corner of the documents, which agrees with that given in the indictment against Ivinskaya and Emelianova (document 50). For instance, the first page of Feltrinelli's letter has the number 233 on the upper right corner, corresponding to the page numbers for Feltrinelli's letter given in the indictment (where the reference is to vol. 3, pp. 233–38 and 257–59). Ivinskaya's signed confession is numbered 322 (it is unclear to which of the three volumes this refers, as the confession is not mentioned in the indictment and thus cannot be inferred from the photocopy). And now for the key observation. This numbering system is found in photocopies of four letters from

23. See chapter 3 for a full description of Feltrinelli's actions.

24. A document published by Elena Pasternak (2017, 214) shows that Schewe's role as intermediary was known to the KGB as early as February 11, 1960. A memo written on that date by Shelepin, head of the KGB, says: "Pasternak receives money through illegal channels, which is sent by foreign publishers in Soviet currency through Nivat and Schewe."

d'Angelo to Ivinskaya that are preserved in the Feltrinelli archives (see documents 5, 13, 22, 23). The numbering on these letters can easily be matched to the page numbers given in the indictment. I will only give one instance. The indictment cites d'Angelo's letter to Ivinskaya dated September 26, 1959 (document 13), and refers to volume 3, pages 249–51. These are exactly the numbers found in the upper right corner of the copy in the Feltrinelli archive.

While no number is visible in the photocopy of document 19, d'Angelo's letter to Ivinskaya dated February 2, 1960, I am virtually certain that this letter was also reproduced from the trial proceedings (both on account of the quality of the photocopy and because this letter is cited in the indictment). The same numbering is found in the document signed by Ivinskaya on May 25, 1960, discussed in note 11 of this chapter. Finally, and most importantly for our case, the draft of Ivinskaya's letter in Russian, witnessing her attempt to reconstruct the original "will," carries the same numbering system as other materials from the trial proceedings (in this case the numbers are 275, 276, 277). What this shows is that these documents were found in the search of Ivinskaya's apartment and were included in the trial proceedings as evidence. Thus, Surkov was able to see Ivinskaya's draft while studying the three volumes. And the draft gave him definitive evidence that Ivinskaya had made use of the blank pages with Pasternak's signature to fabricate a new document, as he alleged in his letter to Carver.

While this establishes the source of these photocopies, how and why they reached Feltrinelli remains shrouded in mystery. These documents could not have reached him before 1961, and I conjecture that it was only around the time of his legal battle with d'Angelo in 1965 that these copies reached Milan. But that is a guess, and lacking any evidence on who might have sent these photocopies or when, I will let the matter rest there.

Having clarified the issues related to Pasternak's will, we can now discuss in chronological order the letters of June and July exchanged among Olga, Schewe, and Feltrinelli. This will allow us to gain a fuller understanding of how the events unfolded.

2.3. June and July 1960

Olga wrote to Feltrinelli on June 5, only two days after Pasternak's funeral. She was obviously very worried about the possibility that, with Pasternak no longer alive, things might take a turn for the worse. Pasternak knew all along that his presence and fame were her best protection. In the letter of June 5, Olga asked Feltrinelli, on account of Pasternak's power of attorney, to recognize her as the legitimate heir of Pasternak's literary estate and as the legal owner of Pasternak's royalties that had accumulated in the West. She explained to Feltrinelli how the power of attorney came about, something that was described carefully in previous sections. She went on to say that if Feltrinelli recognized Pasternak's wishes as expressed in the power of attorney Pasternak wrote for her, which were thus her rights, she in turn would ask Feltrinelli to acknowledge Heinz Schewe as her legitimate representative:

First of all, I ask you in turn to consider Mr. Heinz Schewe to be my empowered representative. Through him I will give you, as per Borya's wishes, those manuscripts that he will give to you in due time for publication. This concerns the manuscript of the novel, materials from the archives, which I will put into order without delay, as well as the play. Here, things are more difficult, the utmost care is needed, and in this both you and I will trust Mr. Heinz. (Ivinskaya to Feltrinelli, June 5, 1960)

Olga was thus planning to send abroad a significant part of Pasternak's literary estate. Most importantly, she also planned to send the unfinished play *The Blind Beauty*. According to Soviet laws, this transfer of literary property without permission was illegal.[25]

25. In chapter 3, I discuss the possibility that this might have infuriated the Soviets even more than the royalties issue. But see now also Elena Pasternak 2017, where we read the following document (undated but probably written in late June or July 1960) from the KGB to the CC of the CPSU: "Reporting that after the death of writer Pasternak B. L. his former cohabitant Ivinskaya O. V. recently undertook measures for leaving the Soviet Union to live abroad and because of this has categorically demanded from her daughter a formal registration of her marriage with Nivat, expecting that the presence of her daughter abroad will give her, Ivinskaya, the right to apply to Soviet agencies for receiving an exit visa. Ivinskaya expects to receive the right to manage Pasternak's multimillion fortune which is located in the banks of a number of countries. Ivinskaya intends to use Pasternak's archive and correspondence in her possession to write an anti-Soviet book and in conversation with Nivat on this matter on June 14, 1960, stated: 'I collected all the letters from the CC [of the CPSU], Borya's letters to Khrushchev, Furtseva . . . if only I could go to some free country with these documents and write a book about a Russian . . . and publish it, then it would be . . . I could rest easy after this, and my life would have some value. . . . I can write this book and bring it to you. Put together all the documents and leave them for you as an inheritance. You'll be able to see the games that the CC plays, the games of all the officials. . . . Believe me, this book would be a great success.' In this conversation, a plan to send a future book through diplomatic channels to France was discussed in detail. Ivinskaya is trying to find a way to illegally send Pasternak's play 'The Blind Beauty' to Italy to the Italian Feltrinelli, the publisher of 'Doctor Zhivago.' Ivinskaya continues to spread the anti-Soviet novel 'Doctor Zhivago' and

Olga continued by claiming that some of the documents in her possession would finally put an end to the quarrel with Proyart,[26] a thorn in Feltrinelli's side since the beginning of 1959.

Olga continued by warning Feltrinelli to be extremely careful: her life was at risk, and so was Pasternak's archive. She then offered something very important in exchange for Feltrinelli's acknowledgment of her rights:

> Once I have received your letter, in which you will confirm receipt of the power of attorney in my name (it should be given to you in June of this year by D'Angelo's friends), I can also send you the contract that was signed by Boris Leonidovich while he was still alive, which he had withheld until the peaceful resolution of the conflict with Mme. P. It would be good if you would set aside some area for her to work on. This would coincide with Boris Leonidovich's wishes. (Ivinskaya to Feltrinelli, June 5, 1960)

Olga was offering to send Feltrinelli the universal contract that Pasternak had signed in January 1960 but never sent to Feltrinelli.[27] This was a document Feltrinelli had been after for a year and a half. This contract was still in Olga's hands, and she would in fact send it to Feltrinelli in August. Therefore, all accounts in the secondary literature that connect the contract to the documents lost by the Garritanos are wide of the mark.

The last part of Olga's early June letter, peppered with constant warnings about the danger of the situation, concerns the final part of the $100,000 that remained in d'Angelo's hands. Olga was hoping to receive the outstanding portion in June and from that point on to have financial transactions only with Feltrinelli through Schewe.[28] Her plan, she

politically dubious poems by Pasternak among the unstable sections of Soviet intelligentsia and young people. She expresses libelous thoughts regarding the Communist Party and the Soviet government. Conversations of this nature took place in the presence of Moscow correspondent Schewe and Italian journalist Palladini and others" (for the original text in Russian, see Elena Pasternak 2017, 215).

26. Pasternak had named Proyart his representative in the West by means of several powers of attorney signed in 1958 and 1959. This led to a tug-of-war between Feltrinelli and Proyart. The events are described at length in chapter 2 of Mancosu 2013.

27. As explained in Mancosu 2013, the reasons had to do with Pasternak's fear that Feltrinelli could have used the contract, which was antedated to 1956, to question Proyart's activities as Pasternak's representative in the West.

28. In a letter from Mirella Garritano to Giulietta Pecori (and thus to d'Angelo, for Pecori was his wife), cited in the last section of chapter 1, Mirella tells d'Angelo to keep in mind that they will leave in June and he should try to send money by then. As it happened, this was not feasible, and the next delivery of money took place in August through the Benedettis.

informed Feltrinelli, was to leave Moscow for the month of July and spend the month putting Pasternak's archive in order.[29]

The postscript warned Feltrinelli about another potential danger, namely the possibility that Pasternak's relatives might advance claims to Pasternak's rights in the West. She wrote Feltrinelli:

> It is entirely possible that relatives of Boris Leonidovich will approach you with claims to the right to take care of his affairs in the West, in particular his sister, whom he supposedly wanted to see before his death. This is actually a lie; it was not his wish, but rather that of his relatives, who wanted to put the power in her hands.
>
> In a potential conflict with her, I will be on your side. They have no official documents to give to their publisher, as they would have liked to. The last official document was the power of attorney about which I wrote to you earlier. (Ivinskaya to Feltrinelli, June 5, 1960)

Notice that Olga, on the strength of Pasternak's "will," refers only to the inheritance related to Pasternak's affairs in the West, thus excluding the inheritance related to his affairs in the Soviet Union. The sister in question was Lydia Pasternak Slater, who had arrived in Moscow with her daughter Ann one day after the funeral, and thus had occasion to discuss with Zinaida, Pasternak's wife, the issue of the inheritance.[30] This started the thorny issue concerning the rights of Pasternak's relatives with respect to the royalties in the West, a problem that would not be resolved until 1970 (see *Le dossier* 1994).

Olga's letter was accompanied by one from Heinz Schewe to Feltrinelli dated June 6, 1960, in which he confirms Olga's account of the existence of the power of attorney. Schewe's letter begins with his disbelief concerning Pasternak's sudden passing away. He proceeds to give instructions as to the best way to handle things in line with Pasternak's wishes. First, he tells Feltrinelli that every conflict has to be resolved peacefully without publicity. Second, Olga's safety has to be a priority. He confirms that Olga had a power of attorney signed by Pasternak on April 15, 1960, according to which she was "the sole literary heiress and the only one empowered to act on behalf of his fortune abroad."

---

29. Olga spent some time in June with Ariadna Efron in Tarusa. See Emelianova 2004.

30. The correspondence between Lydia Pasternak Slater and Feltrinelli on the issue of royalties can be reconstructed in its entirety by combining the letters in the FoGF and those in the PFP at HILA.

He then touches on *The Blind Beauty*, the unfinished play by Pasternak. He reports that the original manuscript is in Olga's possession and that she has already made a few copies of it. The plan is to send a copy abroad for safekeeping, but for the moment the play should not be published there. Schewe not only warns against this but also explains that the KGB had shown interest in the matter:[31]

The Committee for State Security [KGB] is close on her tail. They recently pressured Ms. Olga even before Boris Leonidovich was under the ground. I advised her to give a copy to these people, since otherwise they will not leave her in peace. This copy will be presented to a high official of the Soviet Committee for State Security in Moscow on Tuesday, the 7th of June, 1960. It was Boris Leonidovich's wish that this new work should first be submitted in Moscow to the state publisher. And so it should happen. We hope that reason wins this time and they decide to publish the fragment. Then nothing would probably stand in the way—after a sufficient interval—of a reprint by yourself, and nobody on this side would be endangered. Be sure that no one in the West except you will receive a copy. The original should in any case remain in Ms. Olga's hands. (Schewe to Feltrinelli, June 6, 1960)

Finally, there was the larger issue of protecting Pasternak's *Nachlaß*, and Schewe reiterates the warning about the need to be more careful than ever:

I told her that everything else Boris Leonidovich ever wrote during his lifetime has now become an important piece of world literature. She collected everything, all his letters and notes. Hopefully it remains in our possession! We worry, nevertheless, that some authorities in Moscow could potentially tighten their grip. In any case we must now be more careful than ever before. I am convinced that Boris Leonidovich would never forgive us if we, by impatience, carelessness, or self-interest, were to endanger Ms. Olga. (Schewe to Feltrinelli, June 6, 1960)

Thus, Olga's safety and that of Pasternak's legacy were intertwined. Feltrinelli received this letter, together with Olga's letter, on June 15, 1960.

The next letter in the correspondence between Schewe and Feltrinelli, of June 22, 1960, announces that the batch of documents given to the

31. Both Ivinskaya (1978) and Emelianova (1997, 2002) describe at length the KGB interest in the manuscript of *The Blind Beauty*.

Garritanos has been lost. After voicing his suspicions, shared by Olga, about events concerning the Garritanos, Schewe worries about his own situation. He found himself in a difficult position, where Olga constantly needed him; he was involved up to his neck in this story but also knew he was being observed by the KGB. In addition, he was responsible to his employer, the German magazine *Die Welt*. The situation, he concluded, was very dangerous.

Schewe informs Feltrinelli that the Pasternak family had also applied to the office for authors' rights to get control of Pasternak's works and royalties. He thought that they might have a good chance of obtaining what they sought, but that this would certainly not be in line with Pasternak's explicit wishes. Finally, Schewe reports on Olga's fear of being arrested. He adds that, should this come to pass, he would have no way to help her as he was also in danger. He also points out that she has all of Pasternak's correspondence and the original manuscript of *Doctor Zhivago*. Should these materials be seized by the authorities, it would be an immense loss.

Later in the same month, on June 24, 1960, Feltrinelli responded to all of the outstanding difficulties that Olga was facing, which she had described in her letter of June 5. At this stage, Feltrinelli did not yet know about the Garritanos' loss of the documents. In his letter, Feltrinelli expresses his unqualified acknowledgment of Pasternak's will (described to him by Olga and Schewe) and his willingness to proceed according to Pasternak's wishes by giving Olga his full support. He also conveys his satisfaction at having Schewe act as liaison.

Feltrinelli confirms that transfers of money (for Schweitzer, Nivat, and Schewe), as requested by Pasternak, would be carried out and asks for advice concerning how to handle things with Proyart. He asks Olga not to write to Proyart at the moment, especially in light of the possible demands from the Moscow and London branches of the Pasternak family. Feltrinelli mentions that Lydia Pasternak had contacted him concerning her brother's inheritance but that he sent an evasive reply.[32] He advises Olga to use great caution and not to let things degenerate into a conflict with Pasternak's Moscow relatives, adding that they could be "dangerous enemies." He thus recommends that she be generous with them financially.

32. See note 30 for the correspondence between Feltrinelli and Lydia Pasternak Slater.

Finally, he inquires about the universal contract and makes suggestions for how to date and sign it in case Pasternak had not done it properly. Concerning Pasternak's legacy and the unfinished play, he writes:

> Send me a copy of Boris Pasternak's drama as soon as possible. I will not publish it as long as <u>you</u> tell me not to do so. Should it be published in Moscow, I would strongly recommend that it also be published in the West within 30 days of its appearance. Only thus can we bring it under copyright protection. Such a quick publication requires quite a preparation. (Feltrinelli to Ivinskaya, June 24, 1960)

Feltrinelli concludes the letter by stating that he eagerly awaits the promised documents, telling Olga to be careful and discreet and not to leave Moscow, for Schewe will look after her. Her main protection consisted in her being visible in Moscow, since if anything should happen to her, news would immediately reach the West, which might not happen if she were elsewhere.

Schewe's letter about the mishap with the Garritanos reached Feltrinelli in early July, and he wrote a letter to Olga on July 8 that was later used by the Soviets to vilify Feltrinelli and demonstrate Olga's involvement in the illegal deals for which she had been condemned. I discuss in chapter 3 the public use of the letter, but let us for the moment focus on its contents.

Feltrinelli asks Olga why she trusted the Garritanos when she had the possibility of sending the documents with Schewe. He asks her from now on to trust only Schewe and advises her that, should Schewe not be in Moscow at a later stage, she must trust only someone who can show her the other half of the split banknotes that he was sending her (in the postscript he adds, "If someone shows you his half [of the banknote], you will also, for your part, show yours").[33] The Soviets were later to make much of the conspiratorial nature implied by this and the following arrangement.

In reply to Olga's former requests and worries, Feltrinelli pledges, "I will try everything I can to avoid payments to third parties. Should this fail, should I be so forced, I will always do it in such a way that a substantial part of the profits remains for yourself or for Ira [Irina]" (Feltrinelli to Ivinskaya, July 8, 1960). This promise, which if considered in isolation might seem completely unfair to Pasternak's relatives, was made within

---

33. Feltrinelli had sent four split 500-lira banknotes (see chapter 3 and illustration 13).

the context of the lost "will," which had explicitly given Olga control over the finances in the West. Feltrinelli continues by listing a number of pressing issues:

Now you must, however, be careful of some things:

1) The earlier contract with Boris Pasternak concerning the publication of *Dr. Z.*, as well as the new contract (which I beg you to please send as soon as possible), can never be allowed to come into the hands of the authorities or Pasternak's family. The same goes for my letters to Boris and yourself. All these confidential documents must never be found with you.
2) Send me any other potential documents at your disposal that could be useful to me vis-à-vis Proyart. Everything I receive (I give you my word of honor) will be treated as if sent to me directly by Pasternak.
3) I will protect you in every manner with all my power. Trust me.
4) I will not be at ease until ALL of Pasternak's letters, manuscripts, etc. are in the West.

Dear Olga! Everything that has been undertaken these past years could only have been undertaken on the basis of trust. Difficulties have only arisen when other people, whom I often did not know, got involved in our affairs. Everything that can be undertaken in the future can only be undertaken if you completely trust in me.

With love and friendship I embrace you. (Feltrinelli to Ivinskaya, July 8, 1960)

This final part of the letter emphasizes the importance of not trusting anyone but Schewe, and thus indicates the need to remove d'Angelo from the financial operations. Feltrinelli asks Olga to provide him with a letter asking d'Angelo to send the remaining portion of the $100,000 back to him, cautioning in his postscript:

D'Angelo still has many things here. His route seems too dangerous to me. I would recommend you write to me that he should give everything that is left over back to me. I will communicate it to him when and how you would like. (Feltrinelli to Ivinskaya, July 8, 1960)

Olga first asked d'Angelo to send the money to Feltrinelli's lawyer, but later, having received more money from the Benedettis on behalf of d'Angelo on August 1, she changed her mind (see commentary to document 41).

On July 15, 1960, Schewe wrote to Feltrinelli from Hamburg informing him that he would soon be back in Moscow. As can be gathered from the letter, Feltrinelli and Schewe met in Vienna at some point before the letter was written, and thus it is hard to fully understand the letter, for it takes for granted those conversations. But it does seem clear that the letter concerns the transfer of the typescript of *The Blind Beauty* through some intermediaries. Schewe also announces that he would not be in Moscow between the end of August and the beginning of September, so that Feltrinelli should make sure to send "loaves" or "rolls" (i.e., money) in a timely manner. He closes the letter by announcing that his status in Moscow might change, allowing him to spend more time in Germany. This brings to a conclusion the summary of the letters exchanged in June and July. Before moving on to a chronological account of the August letters, two other key protagonists in these events need to come into clearer focus.

2.4. Georges Nivat and Irina Emelianova

The events that were to unfold bring us to a discussion of Olga's daughter, Irina, and her fiancé, Georges Nivat.

Georges Nivat was born in 1935 in Clermont-Ferrand, France, where he studied at the Lycée Blaise-Pascal. While a student at the École Normale Supérieure in Paris and the Sorbonne between 1955 and 1960, he managed to spend several periods abroad, notably at Lomonosov University in Moscow (1956–57 and 1959–60) and at St Antony's College in Oxford (1957–58 and late autumn 1960). In England, he obtained the Oxford Diploma in Slavonic Studies, and in France the *agrégation* in Russian in 1958. During his stay in Moscow in 1959–60 Nivat became close to Pasternak and Olga (see also Nivat 2007). In January 1960, he became engaged to Irina, whom he had met in 1957.

Pasternak had written to his sister Lydia about Nivat as early as May 1958:

> And now I've completely forgotten what I wanted to write about. O.V. [Ivinskaya] has a daughter who is a student, called Irochka Emelyanova. She has some friends who are students from abroad, and one of them is called Georges Nivat. He has gone to Oxford, and writes to her from there. Apparently he has made the acquaintance of one of your boys. Which is it—Michael or Nicky? A rumour has been spread that Irochka is my adopted daughter—she is a beautiful girl, very brave and very gifted.

Behind my back, she calls me "Classic." She is very well informed about everything to do with me, and sometimes supplies her friends with typed copies of my manuscripts, uncorrected and full of errors. No doubt this Nivat is a very nice fellow, and O.V. maintains that I once saw him or he saw me, but I am not sure of this. (Boris Pasternak 2010b, 395; original in Russian)

The description is similar to that given by Gerd Ruge, a German correspondent stationed in Moscow, in a letter to Kurt Wolff dated February 2, 1959. This is one of the few reports about Irina that reached the West, and Irina's fate and resilience can be better understood by comprehending her character as described by Ruge (an extended excerpt, including comments on Olga, is given in document 29).

For some reason or other, B.P. had the idea one day that I should get to know Lara [Olga]. She sent her daughter to my street corner—a girl of just about twenty whom I immediately recognized, because she looked for some reason very unusual for Moscow: blond hair bound into a "ponytail," very lively, with somewhat catlike, slanted eyes, very lively and pretty. We began at once a very natural conversation, in which she offered a stream of quite open and oppositional impressions. . . . While the boy [Mitia] is very quiet, the girl [Irina] has what one could call "a sassy mouth"—admittedly with an enormous amount of charm and wit. Her observations about art and politics in the Soviet Union were spot-on, funny, and sharp. (A few times already she has had difficulties at the university on account of such remarks.) For B.P. she came up with a fine name: she, and the others now as well, called him "Classic"—so "the Classicist," a little disrespectful but B.P. also likes it. (Ruge to Wolff, PFP, HILA; original in German)

Irina's fiancé, meanwhile, had less contact with Pasternak. In a letter dated November 5, 1959, Pasternak announces to Lydia having met Nivat at last. Writing about Nivat's trouble obtaining a visa for travel to the Soviet Union as a student in 1959–60, Pasternak describes how the couple interacted once this difficulty was overcome:

Of the refusal obtained by N[iva]t, I learned out of some Belgian clippings. Poor boy! It was even a much greater blow for Irene E[melianova], whose imagination ran high pending his arrival. Georges, having also at first been turned away, surmounted the obstacles and is visiting her every evening. I made at last his acquaintance. (Pasternak 2010b, 413; original in English)

The time Nivat spent in Moscow between October 1959 and August 1960 (with some lengthy trips back to France in between) was a nightmarish one for him. Apart from the happiness of his engagement with Irina, Nivat spent most of this time in the hospital. First, as he describes to Hélène Peltier in a letter from April 1960, he was hospitalized in Moscow between mid-January and April 15.[34] He departed almost immediately for France for further check-ups on his health, but not before having met with Pasternak, Olga, Irina, and Mitia in Potapovski Lane on April 15.[35] On that occasion, the engagement with Irina was made official, and as he wrote to Peltier at some point in late April:

> B.L. is in great form, younger, more eloquent, and more captivating than ever. He has returned to his Marburg philosophical period and only talks of neo-Kantianism. . . . He has made serious progress in the play he is writing. He read it to O.V. and intends to read it to us upon my return. You can imagine my curiosity. . . . You see now that I was certainly right to hope for the detente. Without it, I foresee catastrophe for my fiancée and me. (Hélène Peltier Archive, letter undated but datable to late April; original in French)

The facts will show that Nivat was right to worry about his and Irina's future, but to an extent that would have been unimaginable to him at that point.

Despite all these illnesses, Nivat still managed to act as a liaison between Proyart and Pasternak, and to relay important information. This is evident from the letters written by Pasternak to Proyart and published in Pasternak 1994. Some of the letters with information for Pasternak were sent from Proyart to Nivat and then shown to Pasternak (Boris Pasternak 1994, 229). In particular, Georges Nivat was instrumental in raising a powerful objection, on behalf of Proyart, against the advisability of Pasternak's signing the new universal contract for Feltrinelli (the event is described by Pasternak in a letter to Proyart dated January 17, 1960; see Boris Pasternak 1994, 217).

Pasternak had signed the contract but then he had second thoughts, for he and Feltrinelli had agreed to backdate the new contract to 1956. News

34. Hélène Peltier was a friend of Pasternak's and helped translate *Doctor Zhivago* into French. For her extensive role in the *Zhivago* saga, see Mancosu 2016. For her role supporting Nivat during the Ivinskaya case, see chapter 3.

35. This is the same day on which, according to Schewe, Pasternak signed his "will" for Olga.

of this plan created an uproar in France, with Peltier, Daniel de Proyart, Jacqueline de Proyart, and Nivat arguing that it would be a disaster and would leave Mme de Proyart hostage to possible legal consequences on account of her activity as Pasternak's representative in the West in 1958 and 1959. The reaction was successful, and although Pasternak had signed the contract, as he mentioned to Feltrinelli, the contract remained in Olga's possession (Mancosu 2013). Feltrinelli would receive it from Olga Ivinskaya in August 1960. The letter of January 17 to Proyart also brought a painful reminder that members of Pasternak and Olga's family were under constant surveillance:

> Furthermore, Georges [Nivat] could, if he liked, describe to you the concealed dependence in which our secret police (M.G.B.) perpetually maintains us (me and O.'s entire family, her son, her daughter, and herself as if hostages), always spies on us, keeps tabs on us, and admits doing so openly and impudently. And the mystery of my correspondence! Etc. etc. (Boris Pasternak 1994, 218; original in French)

These comments about what the MGB (by then called the KGB) might have known lead us back to the issue of the financial transactions originating in France. Nivat was mentioned at the trial as having been a courier for six thousand rubles that were apparently delivered to Irina in December 1959 and which, the accusation alleged, came from Mme de Proyart.[36] Previous financial transactions had gone through an employee of the French embassy, Miss Durova, but on November 14, 1959, Pasternak wrote to Proyart:

> Following several offers of aid coming from Italy (but not F-lli), and because the situation made its acceptance desirable, but in an entirely different combination, I wrote to Feltrinelli a week ago, the 5th or the 6th, in German (the letter having to pass through the hands of Mr. H. Sch.). I asked him to establish a means of assistance, which during its course would not exhaust (in its sum) more than a tenth of the total accumulated. That if this condition allows it, that he should send you each trimester, four times a year (he has already done this a number of times), sums comparable to those that

36. A document published by Elena Pasternak (2017, 214) shows that Nivat's role as intermediary was known to the KGB as early as February 11, 1960, as made clear in a memo from Shelepin, head of the KGB: "Pasternak receives money through illegal channels, which is sent by foreign publishers in Soviet currency through Nivat and Schewe."

were passed on to me by the Cavalry-Maiden D.[37] on your behalf. (Boris Pasternak 1994, 203–4; original in French)

The same letter continues:

The evening of the same day in which this letter had been given to Mr. H. Sch. in the morning, your unexpected ten thousand arrived (the first time it was twenty;—five thousand the second time—and now ten). Oh how it was, yet again, so timely! But if I knew what was waiting for us in the morning, I would not have written my letter to F. (Boris Pasternak 1994, 204; original in French)

And finally, Pasternak gives voice to his doubts about the source of the disbursement:

I am gradually coming to suspect that the money you send so regularly and abundantly has nothing to do with F. That these sums might be traced back to the money Mr. Gallimard kindly set aside for me. But no, it's enormous. The amount of your deliveries must exceed any percentage. (Boris Pasternak 1994, 206; original in French)

Moreover, on January 21, 1960, Pasternak wrote to Proyart: "Many, many thanks, indeed, for the recent money. I enclose a receipt" (Boris Pasternak 1994, 224). It is thus clear not only that Durova had given Pasternak (or Olga) money during the summer of 1959, but also that other sums sent by Proyart were received and, in particular, ten thousand rubles around the 6th or the 7th of November 1959. This coincided with Nivat's recent arrival in the USSR, and it is not unlikely that the sum was brought by him. Whether or not Nivat was involved is less significant. What is ultimately important is to show with absolute clarity that Pasternak was fully aware of the transactions. This will be central to demonstrating the bad faith of the Soviets when they later tried to make Olga a scapegoat.

Meanwhile let us go back to Nivat in the summer of 1960. He returned to Moscow from Paris, where he had been hospitalized, in early June. In July he was sick again with a skin rash and was hospitalized in Moscow

---

37. In a footnote (Boris Pasternak 1994, 204; original in French), Proyart gives further information about the identity of the person in question: "Miss Durova is the great-grandniece of a famous woman writer, Nadezhda Durova, who wrote a book on her youth adventures. In 1812 she had disguised herself as a boy, out of patriotism, in order to fight with a regiment of hussars, hence her nickname 'Kavalerist-devitsa' [the Cavalry-Maiden]."

between July 4 and July 26. A letter from Schewe to Feltrinelli dated August 1, incidentally also the date of the delivery of 500,000 rubles by the Benedettis, reports the following:

Yet another development. The French student Georges Nivat applied for marriage with Ira at the Moscow registry office. There are great difficulties. First of all, he is perpetually ill, and second, his visa expires on August 8th. The civil ceremony, however, is set for the 20th of August. Well, we will see. There will surely be a big commotion again. Honestly, an exhausting country. (Schewe to Feltrinelli, August 1, 1960)

The wedding was not to happen. The Soviets did not extend Nivat's visa, and appeals to Khrushchev and Mikoyan went unanswered. Nivat had to leave the USSR on August 10 under distressing circumstances.[38]

---

38. New KGB documents presented in Elena Pasternak 2017 allow us to see the Soviet perspective on the situation. On August 8, the French ambassador to the USSR, Dejean, appealed to the Ministry of Foreign Affairs to extend Nivat's visa. The document, signed by Shelepin (KGB) and Gromyko (Ministry of Foreign Affairs), summarizes the motivation provided by Dejean and the conclusion of the Soviet authorities: "While staying in the USSR as a graduate student, he was ill for a considerable length of time. Furthermore, and Dejean underscored this, it was particularly important that Nivat intended to marry his girlfriend I. Emelianova. The registration of marriage was scheduled by ZAGS [registry office] for August 20, but Nivat's visa for remaining in the USSR expires on August 10. The ambassador informed the ministry that earlier attempts by the embassy to contact relevant authorities did not produce the desired outcome. The ambassador requests that either the visa be extended until August 20th or that the marriage be registered on August 9. Dejean added that Nivat had already personally appealed to comrades N. S. Khrushchev and A. I. Mikoyan by telegram. According to the data available on hand, G. Nivat is a French agent who during his time in the USSR systematically maintained relationships with B. Pasternak's family (I. Emelianova is Pasternak's adopted daughter). According to the same information, Pasternak's communication with the West in recent times has occurred primarily through G. Nivat. The planned marriage between G. Nivat and I. Emelianova seemingly seeks, among other goals, to support the anti-Soviet libel campaign around Pasternak's name. Furthermore, G. Nivat clearly intends to receive Pasternak's inheritance, above all abroad. (As is well known, a large sum in foreign currency has been collected in Pasternak's name at various banks abroad after the publication, in large volumes, of the libelous anti-USSR novel 'Doctor Zhivago' in a number of countries.) All this goes to show that in this case, we are talking about a sort of arrangement in pursuit of a political goal, rather than simply a marriage. Given all of the above, the KGB and Ministry of Foreign Affairs of the USSR consider it inadvisable to allow for the registration of marriage between G. Nivat and citizen I. Emelianova, and consequently for the extension of G. Nivat's stay in the USSR. It is worth noting that the registration of marriage between Nivat and Emelianova would result in further undesired consequences (questions of Emelianova's leaving the USSR and others). As a result, the Ministry of Foreign Affairs of the USSR believes that in response to the French Ambassador's request to the Ministry, a response should be provided stating that the Ministry has nothing new to add regarding the issue at hand

At the time, Irina was also ill with a skin rash. It was the same type of illness, an atopic dermatitis, that had caused Nivat to be hospitalized. Moreover, at the airport in Moscow (where he managed to leave on the last flight of the day), he was searched and accused of trafficking in foreign currency. This is because he had been given, before leaving, some money from a Finnish embassy employee so that he could pay for his stay in Helsinki that very evening. But it is quite obvious that the search he was subjected to was not a random event. Upon his return to Paris, Nivat wrote to Peltier on August 14, 1960:

> 10 days before the wedding I had to abandon Irka [Irina], ill, bed-ridden, desperate. The USSR has thrown me out or just about. I have sent four telegrams pleading with K.[hrushchev] and Mikoyan. (Hélène Peltier Archive; original in French)

As mentioned, these pleas remained unheeded. Much worse would soon happen in the form of arrests, accusations of conspiracy, court trials, and labor camp sentences.

2.5. The arrests

On August 7, 1960, Schewe wrote three letters to Feltrinelli. The first contained two enclosures: the power of attorney dated April 4, 1960, which, as we have seen, had been fabricated by Olga with Schewe's assistance (the document is published in Mancosu 2013), and an older power of attorney dated July 10, 1958 (also in Mancosu 2013 and reproduced as illustration 10). A second letter with the same date contained more alarming news, as well as information about Irina and Georges Nivat:

> At the moment, everything is again going haywire. Monsieur Georges should leave on Wednesday, since his visa is expiring. He absolutely wants to stay in order to marry Ira on August 20th. At the same time, he seems dangerously sick (cancer of the blood???).

(earlier, the French were informed that the relevant Soviet authorities did not find it possible to fulfill Nivat's request to extend the length of his stay in the Soviet Union). A draft of the resolution is attached for your consideration. Please consider it. A. Gromyko. A. Shelepin" (for the original in Russian see Elena Pasternak 2017, 216–17).

Telegrams to Khrushchev and Mikoyan with pleas for authorization and extension of the visa. I think the thing has little chance of success.

For Ira this is not a matter of love, but simply a wish thereby to get out of this country. The idea came from the Classic. I am skeptical whether it will work. Besides, I have a feeling that this Georges has a deadly illness, ever since that smallpox vaccination here in Moscow in January 1960.

Whether Schewe was right about Irina's feelings can be doubted. He himself had been interested in Irina, and perhaps a bit of jealousy comes through in this cynical appraisal of the situation. The second part of this second letter concerned the Benedettis' delivery (on August 1) of a huge sum in rubles. Schewe first informs Feltrinelli that Olga has changed her mind about her request to d'Angelo that he give back the remaining part of the $100,000 to Feltrinelli's lawyer, Antonio Tesone. Schewe then proceeds to explain Olga's change of mind as a consequence of the visit by the Benedettis:

This new situation arose as follows: two tourists showed up from Italy, a married couple. They visited Ms. Olga. I myself did not meet them. Ira interpreted from the French as well as possible. After this conversation, Ms. Olga again decided entirely differently. Apparently the two messengers—they came at d'Angelo's instruction—reported bad things about yourself [underlined by GF], so that Ms. Olga became unsure of her earlier decision.

At this point Schewe warns Feltrinelli to cut d'Angelo off before things get out of control:

Now it looks as if we might slide into new difficulties and disarray, such as we already know from the earlier double-dealing with Madame Proyart. This time Signor d'Angelo seems to be your antagonist [underlined by GF]. To me it is a sure thing that he is intriguing heavily against you. Crush him as quickly as possible! Otherwise, we will have a new mess that is perhaps even a great deal worse than the one with your Parisian competitors. I personally, to speak frankly, would have no interest in partaking of such complicated and unpleasant matters. What does Signor d'Angelo really want anyway? Probably just to earn money. Why does he send people to Moscow to put strange doubts in poor Ms. Olga's ear about your honesty? What an abominable game! Make a stop of it! This Sergio d'Angelo, whom I have always mistrusted, wants

---

[Text continues after photo section.]

1. Boris Pasternak, Olga Ivinskaya, and Irina Emelianova, 1959

2. Sergio d'Angelo, 1957

3. Giangiacomo Feltrinelli, date unknown

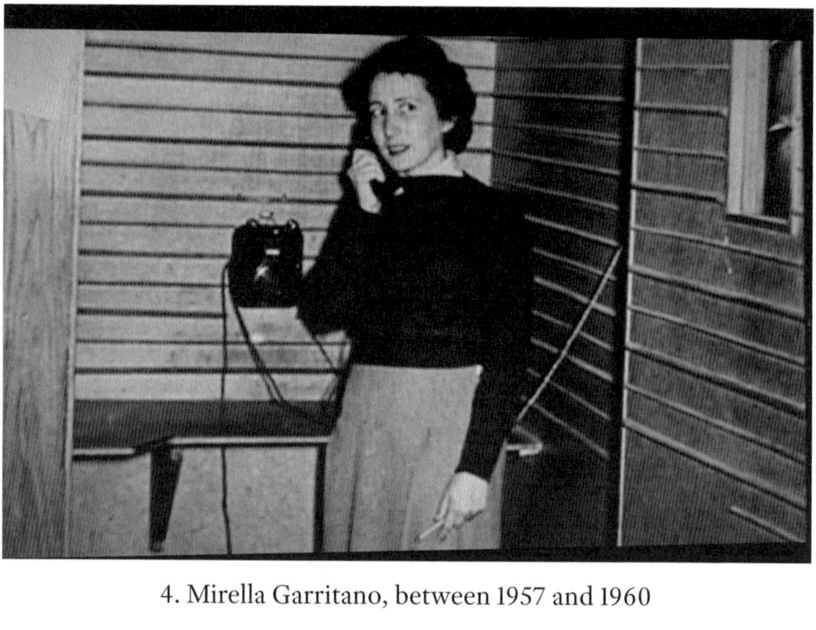

4. Mirella Garritano, between 1957 and 1960

5. Heinz Schewe, 1959

6. Olga Ivinskaya, 1959

7. Olga Ivinskaya and Boris Pasternak, 1960

8. Irina Emelianova and Boris Pasternak, 1960

9. Olga Ivinskaya, Heinz Schewe, and Boris Pasternak, 1959

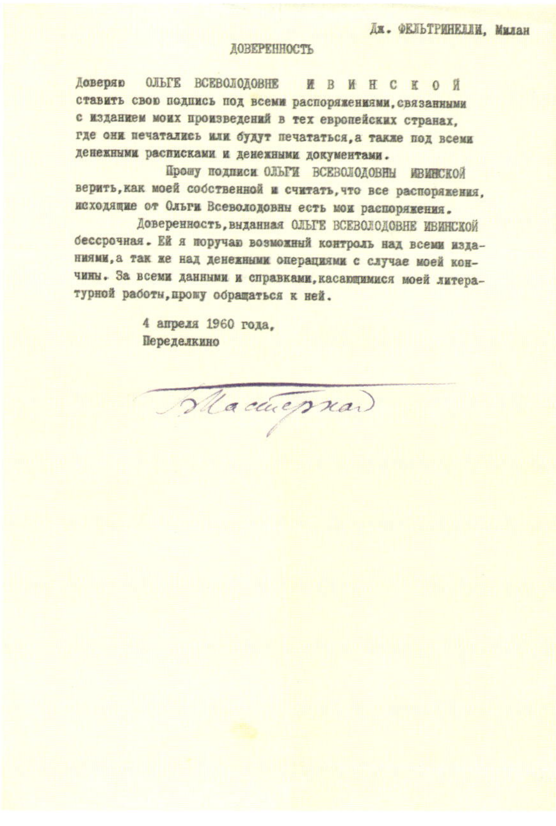

Дж. ФЕЛЬТРИНЕЛЛИ, Милан

ДОВЕРЕННОСТЬ

Доверяю ОЛЬГЕ ВСЕВОЛОДОВНЕ И В И Н С К О Й ставить свою подпись под всеми распоряжениями, связанными с изданием моих произведений в тех европейских странах, где они печатались или будут печататься, а также под всеми денежными расписками и денежными документами.

Прошу подписи ОЛЬГИ ВСЕВОЛОДОВНЫ ИВИНСКОЙ верить, как моей собственной и считать, что все распоряжения, исходящие от Ольги Всеволодовны есть мои распоряжения.

Доверенность, выданная ОЛЬГЕ ВСЕВОЛОДОВНЕ ИВИНСКОЙ бессрочная. Ей я поручаю возможный контроль над всеми изданиями, а так же над денежными операциями с случае моей кончины. За всеми данными и справками, касающимися моей литературной работы, прошу обращаться к ней.

4 апреля 1960 года,
Переделкино

10. Power of attorney dated April 4, 1960

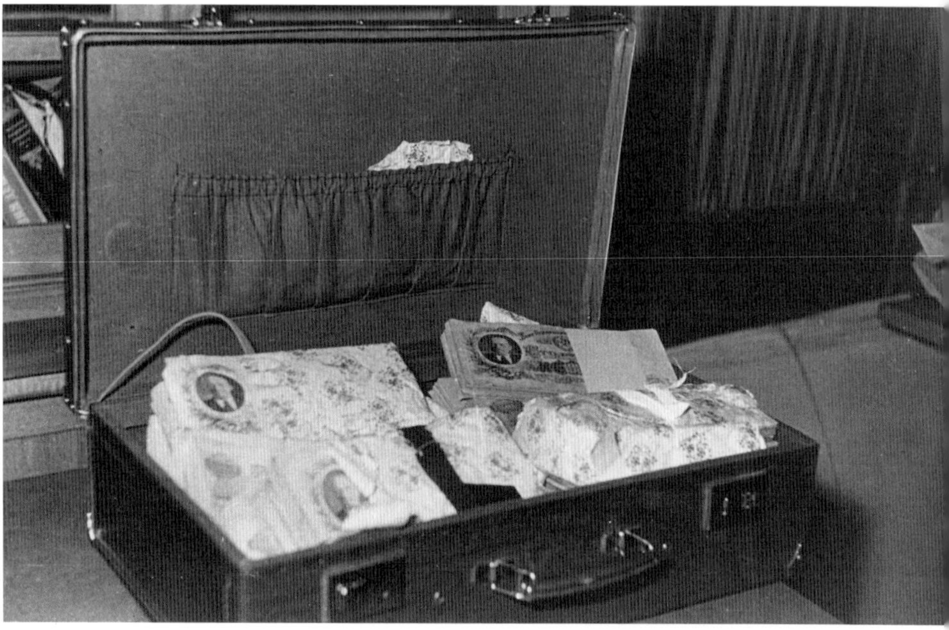

11. Rubles sequestered in Moscow by the KGB, August 1960

12. Rubles sequestered in Moscow by the KGB, August 1960

13. Split banknotes found at Ivinskaya's apartment in Moscow by the KGB, August 1960

14. George Katkov, 1962

15. Irina Emelianova in Potma (Mordovia), 1962

16. Irina Emelianova, Georges Nivat, and Vadim Kozovoï, 1972

to come to Moscow in the spring of 1961 to speak directly with Ms. Olga. More letters to follow.

Finally, in the third letter Schewe announced that he was sending as an enclosure the famous universal contract with Pasternak's original signature on it.

Schewe quickly realized that something awful was going to happen and gave expression to his feelings in the next letter, dated August 15. He tells Feltrinelli about the huge sum brought by the Benedettis, which he estimates at 200,000 rubles (in fact, it was 500,000). He warns that a sum of this kind could not escape the attention of the authorities:

I am extremely worried! Something totally unexpected has happened. Angelo sent a very large sum of money to Olga. I think it was around 200,000 rubles! The Italian tourist couple about whom I have already written to you brought the money. This will certainly not remain hidden from the security organs. (Schewe to Feltrinelli, August 15, 1960)

He heard, and apparently not through Olga, that Olga had gone on a spending spree:

As I hear it, Olga just made large purchases that will definitely attract attention. Her son Mitia bought himself a motorcycle, etc.

The danger was all too obvious, and Schewe considered this to be a huge mistake on d'Angelo's part:

My gut tells me that this will not go well. Illegal transactions of this nature get eight years in a labor camp! Remittances of smaller amounts might have perhaps been accepted. But that much goes beyond the pale. This cannot go well. It was a big mistake by d'Angelo.

Moreover, he was also worried that he might be accused of having brought the money himself:

I would not be surprised if I were dragged into this. Probably they will suspect that I brought the money. It fits almost perfectly together time-wise—my return to Moscow and the large sum. This is very unpleasant. I have good reasons to be extremely cautious. I have decided not to visit Olga for a while. D'Angelo botched the whole thing. All the consequences go on his account. I see only the black side of this!

It is too stupid. I have always recommended the greatest caution because I know the local circumstances quite precisely. I always warned: "They know everything, everything, everything!" Now everything is probably botched.

The last part of the letter reports on Olga's plans to travel south with Irina, and on Nivat's return to France after his failure to get his visa extended. Schewe also conveys Olga's request to send Nivat the sum that Pasternak had earmarked for him. Given his illness, Nivat was in need of it.

In his letter, Schewe had warned, "They know everything, everything, everything!" And they did. On August 16, Olga was arrested. Her dacha and her apartment were searched, and many confidential documents, including much of the correspondence from d'Angelo and Feltrinelli, were found by the KGB. Probably the first report to reach the West was Schewe's letter to Feltrinelli dated August 23, 1960:

Ms. Olga has been arrested. She was accused of "smuggling money." For all this we have Mr. Sergio d'Angelo to thank. He wanted to be especially smart and ruined everything. I have myself come into grave danger through this affair. As I hear it, they suspect me of smuggling this large sum of rubles (it is said to have been 200,000!!!) here and giving them to Olga. By chance the date of my return to Moscow coincided with this transaction, with which—as you know—I had absolutely nothing to do. All the documents have—so far as I hear—been confiscated by the state police. Heaven knows what sorts of unpleasant things are still to come out of this! We will surely be found out on all accounts. Ira is still at home. She is still quite sick. She advised me for the time being not to come by and to avoid any contact. Nobody can help. She says they are all in the greatest danger! I myself too! From the confiscated letters etc., my role as "family counselor and facilitator" will be discovered. Well then, thanks a million, Signor d'Angelo!

That is the state of things here. I beg you, dear Mr. Feltrinelli, for the time being do not send anything to Moscow, not even letters or mail orders. (Schewe to Feltrinelli, August 23, 1960)

In the postscript he adds a further reminder and exhortation in light of the ubiquity of Soviet surveillance: "P.S.: Please also observe the strictest discretion in Milan! Do not say anything to anyone! Moscow has ears everywhere!"

The last letter from 1960 in this correspondence is from Feltrinelli, who along with his wife read all of Schewe's letters at once upon their return from vacation on September 3, 1960:

My dear Heinz Schewe!

We read all of your letters at once, as soon as we returned from our holiday, and are absolutely horrified! The progression of events,—the crescendo in your last letter is truly terrible!

The blame unfortunately lies in carelessness and our friend's temporary mistrust in us, which the other party, whose motives are highly suspicious, exploited despite our warnings and premonitions.

With respect to d'A. I am completely in the dark,—either we are dealing with a provocateur or else with an idiot. I hardly believe that anything can be done at the moment? I am most worried about you and your safety. Hopefully the others also know, since they indeed know so much, that you had nothing to do with this matter. —En passant: d'A. applied for a visa for the Soviet Union recently and should have just departed in these past few days.

I am not at ease so long as you are not back here! Can I do anything for you, perhaps through A.[xel] S.[pringer]?

Please write without delay,—the most heartfelt wishes from Inge and me. (Feltrinelli to Schewe, September 3, 1960)

D'Angelo, as we have already mentioned, went to the Soviet Union on September 4th and tried to see Olga without success. He also failed to meet with Irina, who had been arrested the same day he arrived in Moscow, but managed to speak with Mitia and recounts his visit in d'Angelo 2006. Upon his return to Italy, Feltrinelli informed him of Olga's arrest, and this led to a breakdown of relations between Feltrinelli and d'Angelo (see commentary to document 46).

2.6. Conclusion

Previous accounts of the dramatic period between Pasternak's death and the arrests of Olga and Irina are marred by inaccuracies and a lack of documentary evidence. I hope to have improved on the prior treatment by using the essential evidence in letters exchanged between Olga, Schewe, and Feltrinelli. We have been able to clarify, among other things, what the documents lost by the Garritanos contained and how Olga and Schewe tried to replace the power of attorney that was so vital for her. In addition, only by reading the full correspondence is it possible to grasp the complexity of the events that unfolded, thereby deflating the sensationalist use to which the Soviets put fragments of the correspondence, in their attempt to cast Olga and Feltrinelli in the role of villains.

In chapter 3, I continue the story by analyzing the Ivinskaya case in the West. As mentioned in the introduction, accounts of the Ivinskaya case available so far rely on articles published in the press. But these publications are only the tip of the iceberg, since most of the campaign in favor of Olga and Irina did not play out in the public eye.

CHAPTER THREE

"We Need to Help the Russians Save Face" The Ivinskaya Case in the West

"Irke tri goda a Ol'ge Vsevolodovne vosem' let" ("Irina three years, Olga Vsevolodovna, eight years"). Speaking by phone on January 1, 1961, Georges Nivat—Irina's French fiancé—had to ask the old housekeeper at the Ivinskaya household, Polina Yegorovna Shmelëva, to repeat what she had said three times.[1] Then the enormity conveyed by the brief phrase sank in. Those were the lengths of the labor camp sentences to which Olga Vsevolodovna Ivinskaya and Irina Ivanovna Emelianova were condemned after a "closed door" trial in Moscow.

The Ivinskaya case became a cause célèbre in the West, and much has been written about it. In addition to the published articles that appeared in the international press at the time (summarized recently in d'Angelo 2006), especially valuable are Conquest (1961a, 1961b), the memoirs by Olga Ivinskaya (1978) and Irina Emelianova (1997, 2002), Emelianova 2005, and Mansurov 2009.

Of course, the Ivinskaya case does not begin or end with Ivinskaya's labor camp sentence in 1960; one can trace its roots to 1946, when Olga and Boris Pasternak started their love affair, and to Olga's first labor camp experience between 1950 and 1953. But in this chapter, I take for granted all this history, from Olga's first conviction in 1950 to the crisis surrounding the publication of *Doctor Zhivago* in 1957, to Pasternak's persecution

1. See the letter from Nivat to H. Peltier, dated January 2, 1961, Hélène Peltier Archive.

on account of the Nobel Prize in 1958 until his death.[2] Olga Ivinskaya was always at his side and at times personally shielded him. My aim is not to go over these well-known facts but rather to offer new evidence on one aspect of the Ivinskaya case that has so far not been touched upon in memoirs or by historians.

I am referring to the "hidden" campaign carried out in the West to persuade the Soviet authorities to revoke or soften the two women's sentences. Many felt that public statements would damage rather than help the cause of the two women and that a hidden campaign of persuasion would allow the Soviets to change course by saving face. That was, at least, the original plan, until the press got involved and the Soviets showed no desire to compromise. To reconstruct the events, I utilize hitherto untapped archival sources, including the Feltrinelli archives in Milan, the Max Hayward Papers at St Antony's College, Oxford, the George Katkov Papers in Oxford, the Bertrand Russell archive at McMaster University, and the Hélène Peltier Archive in Sylvanès. Given that many of these sources are not easy to access, I quote generously from the original documents.

3.1. The news of Olga's arrest reaches the West

Olga was arrested on August 16, 1960, and she recounted the circumstances of the arrest in her memoir (Ivinskaya 1978). In my reconstruction of the events between Pasternak's death and the arrest of Olga Ivinskaya (chapter 2), I used, among other sources, the correspondence between Olga Ivinskaya, Heinz Schewe, and Giangiacomo Feltrinelli to shed light on an important part of the story that could, at best, only be glimpsed through the distorted account provided by Ivinskaya and other published sources. We will now build on that revised account, focusing on the time after Olga was arrested.

Probably the first Westerner to be informed of her arrest was Heinz Schewe, the trusted middleman between Pasternak and Olga and his publisher Feltrinelli.[3] On August 23, 1960, Schewe wrote to Feltrinelli:

2. See, among others, de Mallac 1981; Barnes 1998; Fleishman 1990; Evgeniĭ Pasternak 1988, 1990, 1997; Elena and Evgeniĭ Pasternak 2004; Mancosu 2013; and Finn and Couvée 2014.

3. For biographical details of the major actors in the story presented here, I refer the reader to Mancosu 2013; Mancosu 2016; and the previous chapters. The list includes Boris Pasternak, Olga

Ms. Olga has been arrested. She was accused of "smuggling money." For all this we have Mr. Sergio d'Angelo to thank. He wanted to be especially smart and ruined everything. I have myself come into grave danger through this affair. As I hear it, they suspect me of smuggling this large sum of rubles (it is said to have been 200,000!!!) here and giving them to Olga. By chance the date of my return to Moscow coincided with this transaction, with which—as you know—I had absolutely nothing to do. (AGFE, Busta 1, fascicolo 5, "Feltrinelli-Schewe (1959 febbraio 15–1966 dicembre 07)"; original in German)

A few days after Schewe's letter of August 23 reached Feltrinelli, Irina was arrested, on September 5, 1960.

Georges Nivat, Irina's fiancé, had left the Soviet Union on August 10 because the authorities refused to extend his visa.[4] His planned wedding with Irina, scheduled for August 20, did not take place. Nothing expresses more vividly the situation and Nivat's later role in the story we are recounting than Nivat's letter to Peltier dated August 14, 1960:

I am writing to you with a heavy, desperate heart. You'll excuse me for being brief. It is so hard to speak of this. Ten days before the wedding, I had to abandon Irka [Irina], ill, bed-ridden, desperate. The USSR has thrown me out or just about. I have sent four telegrams pleading with K.[hrushchev] and Mikoyan. Our ambassador took a personal initiative on our behalf. I had to leave. Ten days before our wedding, I abandoned a young woman without whom I can no longer live. Olga V., so harshly afflicted, was marvelously tactful and kind up to the last moment. (Nivat to Peltier, August 14, 1960, Hélène Peltier Archive; original in French)

Nivat's love for Irina and his deep affection for Olga will have to be kept in mind if we want to understand his almost superhuman efforts to obtain the release of the two women—a commitment, to anticipate later events, that did not exhaust itself even when he was informed (in June 1964) that Irina had married an inmate from the camp, Vadim Kozovoĭ, in February 1964.[5] But let us now return to September 1960.

Ivinskaya, Irina Emelianova, Giangiacomo Feltrinelli, Sergio d'Angelo, Alekseĭ Surkov, Georges Nivat, George Katkov, Max Hayward, Manya Harari, Jacqueline de Proyart, Isaiah Berlin, Heinz Schewe, Gerd Ruge, Kurt Wolff, and Hélène Peltier. Likewise, no biographical information will be given for major historical figures, such as Nikita Khrushchev, Eleanor Roosevelt, etc.

4. Details on Nivat's biography, his relation to Irina, and his forced departure from the USSR are given in chapter 2. See also Nivat 2007.

5. On Kozovoĭ, a poet and literary critic, see Emelianova 2001; and Mansurov 2009, 369–77.

Nivat received confirmation of Olga's arrest from Feltrinelli. We don't have Feltrinelli's letter to Nivat, but we have Nivat's reply from around September 20, 1960:[6]

Dear Sir,

Your letter dated September 16, which I just received, has sunk me into dismay. It's more dreadful than anything I expected. I cannot sufficiently convey to you my gratitude for having notified me of this misfortune. I implore you to continue to inform me of what you learn about Olga Vsevolodovna's and my fiancée's situation. For ten days now, more, I haven't received a single letter, though Irka was writing to me every other day. I phoned their apartment on Wednesday, September 14. O.V.'s son answered in a quite perturbed tone of voice. I was still very worried. I asked to speak with Irka on the telephone, by way of advance notice, Sunday, September 18. The Post Office replied that only the maid was at the apartment. Your letter thus confirmed the misfortune I suspected. What to do? Do you have any advice? Above all, reestablish contact. Mme Hélène Peltier-Zamoyska will soon be in Moscow and will likely go to the apartment very prudently without any documents on her. (Nivat to Feltrinelli, AGFE, Busta 2, fascicolo 6, "(1960 ottobre 07–1962 aprile 17 e s.d.)"; original in French)[7]

A letter dated October 7 from Nivat to Feltrinelli clarifies that Nivat had obtained confirmation of Olga's arrest from Moscow sources.[8] At this stage he had not yet found out that Irina had also been arrested:

6. Regrettably, when asked by the author, Georges Nivat could no longer locate any letters from Feltrinelli. From Nivat's reply to Feltrinelli, one can gather that Feltrinelli had brought up the issue of Pasternak's "will" and the lost documents (see chapter 2). In addition, he told Nivat that his information was coming from Schewe.

7. In his letter, Nivat also informed Feltrinelli that he had been drafted and would have to serve in the French army in October. Actually, he began serving in March 1961. His military service complicated things, to say the least, for Nivat. He gave an overview to Isaiah Berlin at the beginning of 1962: "As you might know, I joined the army in March, specifically in Algeria. It so happened that after two months I was wounded in a small battle. The bullet hit the kidney and liver and remained in the lungs. I was in a number of hospitals, then on leave for an entire five months, recovered somehow, but thought that I would be released. That didn't happen. I'm in the army again, but in a bureau in the town of Blois. It is often boring, but it's bearable. In the evenings I work on the thesis (Belyi) or on various translations" (Nivat to Berlin, January 2, 1962; IBMC, MS. Berlin 166, fols. 10–11; original in Russian; Isaiah Berlin Literary Trust: © the Trustees of the Isaiah Berlin Literary Trust 2018). Nivat served in the army until the end of 1962.

8. The letter also thanked Feltrinelli for his intention to carry out Pasternak's wishes despite the loss of the documents (described in detail in chapter 2). This referred in particular to the sum that Pasternak had gifted to Nivat: at first $5,000, later raised to $10,000.

> Alas, the sad news concerning O.V. was confirmed. I even know some details: O.V. would be in the hands of the ordinary police; the charge would be fraudulent reception of foreign money and intent to "traffic."
>
> . . .
>
> I myself have received no word from Irka: no letters and no answer on the telephone. I am waiting to receive news indirectly. Might Herr Schewe know anything more? (Nivat to Feltrinelli, AGFE, Busta 2, fascicolo 6, "(1960 ottobre 07–1962 aprile 17 e s.d.)"; original in French)

The letter also expressed agreement with Feltrinelli that only "secret initiatives" were to be considered and that a public initiative would only result in the addition of another item to the indictment list of Olga's crimes. We will come back later to Feltrinelli's "secret initiatives."

Exploiting a trip by Peltier to the Soviet Union in late September 1960, and still unaware of Irina's situation, Nivat gave instructions to Peltier (in an undated letter from September 1960) about visiting Ivinskaya's apartment and gave her a love letter for Irina. Both Nivat's letter to Peltier and his letter to Irina are still in the Peltier archive, a sure sign that Peltier must have found out about Irina's arrest once she arrived in the Soviet Union or, in any case, found herself unable to deliver the love letter. At some point in October or November, Nivat learned that Irina had also been arrested. Hélène Peltier's archive contains many letters from Nivat written during this difficult period. Peltier was to be a constant source of support for Nivat and one of his main contacts in his attempts to mobilize a support group in France for the liberation of the two women.[9]

As it transpires from other letters, the French embassy refused to act before the end of the trial, but Nivat kept building contacts, even though, in some cases, his hopes were disappointed. For instance, writing to Peltier on December 17, he said:

9. Peltier kept a low public profile during the Ivinskaya campaign, but in Peltier-Zamoyska 1963 she brought up the Ivinskaya case (see 19–20n1 and 29n1). In 1961, she also tried to enlist the support of Professor Arne Tiselius (1902–1971), winner of the 1948 Nobel Prize in Chemistry and president of the Nobel Foundation, who declined, however, claiming that, especially after the Pasternak Nobel Prize crisis, his participation might do more damage than good. See the letter from Tiselius's secretary, M. Rudberg, to Peltier dated April 11, 1961 (Hélène Peltier Archive).

I met M. Feltrinelli in Oxford at Sir Isaiah Berlin's home, and I realized that he will do nothing for Olga Vsevolodovna.[10] She has ceased to be useful. . . . Boris Leonidovich's sister is speaking nonsense about O.[lga] V.[sevolodovna], who, according to her, is a thief. Heavens, how nauseating this is, and how the waters have muddied since the Classic disappeared (more than six months ago!)!

I saw M. François Mauriac. His reaction comforted me.[11] He fully sympathizes with my cause and proved it with his actions. I suggested to him forming a defense committee for O.V. He accepted in principle but I told him that it was not necessary right now. I suggested forming a preparatory subcommittee with Jacqueline, you, Kurt Wolff, Feltrinelli, in other words, those who know who O.V. is. In my view, I myself must attend to saving Irka. This committee would attempt to save O.V. Jacqueline rightly emphasized that she could not intervene publicly.[12] No, this subcommittee (reduced to Jacqueline and you, if the others refuse) would present the case to notable figures who would sign an appeal (Mauriac, T. S. Eliot, Hemingway maybe). Note, however, that, in my view, the time has not yet come. It's in the case of catastrophe, of heavy sentencing, if truly there is nothing to lose. The key is to win over a man like Mauriac. (Nivat to Peltier, December 17, 1960, Hélène Peltier Archive; original in French)

This plan parallels a similar initiative in Oxford that we will discuss momentarily. But first another passage from the same letter, which indicates that the accusation of smuggling levied against Olga and Irina might only have been a cover-up for something else.

A particular source informed me that the charge was "manuscript misappropriation." Have you heard about this? (Nivat to Peltier, December 17, 1960, Hélène Peltier Archive; original in French)

Nivat wrote again to Feltrinelli on December 27, 1960, mentioning the previous meeting in Oxford with Berlin. He informed Feltrinelli that he had contacted Mauriac, who had confirmed having written to the Soviet

---

10. A letter from Feltrinelli's London representative, Ruth Sanson, to Lydia Pasternak Slater (dated November 22, 1960) informs us of Feltrinelli's schedule for his visit to England: London from December 2 to December 12 with a visit to Oxford on December 10 (the letter is preserved in the PFP, HILA, Box 79, folder 6). Thus, on that day Feltrinelli met Lydia Pasternak Slater and, probably in a different meeting, Isaiah Berlin and Georges Nivat.

11. François Mauriac (1885–1970), winner of the Nobel Prize in Literature in 1952. Mauriac had already contacted Sergeĭ Vinogradov (Soviet ambassador to France) in November 1960 (see letter from Nivat to Peltier, datable to late November 1960, Hélène Peltier Archive).

12. Jacqueline de Proyart did not make any public statement during the Ivinskaya campaign.

ambassador in Paris (Sergeĭ Vinogradov). In addition, Mauriac went to speak personally with the Soviet ambassador, and from Nivat's report we learn more about the sources who had offered the "real" reason for Ivinskaya's arrest. Present during the meeting between Mauriac and the Soviet ambassador were two Soviet writers passing through Paris:

Both writers were perfectly informed of Olga Vsevolodovna's arrest, like the entire literary world in Moscow. But their accusations have nothing to do with money. They accuse her mainly of sending the manuscript abroad, namely, I think, a copy of Boris Leonidovich's last play. This is likely the core of the issue. Olga Vsevolodovna didn't want this play to be lost, and handed it over to Herr Schewe, I assume, after my departure.[13] She was then immediately arrested. Even if other accusations camouflage it, this is the crime for which she will not be forgiven. (Nivat to Feltrinelli, December 27, 1960, AGFE, Busta 2, fascicolo 6, "(1960 ottobre 07–1962 april 17 e s.d.)"; original in French)

Nivat knew or suspected that Feltrinelli had a copy of the new play and pointed out that Feltrinelli should guide his actions in light of this piece of information, meaning that one should not make Olga's situation (and thus also Irina's) worse by publishing the play abroad. And this, in particular, since the new play (*The Blind Beauty*) contained nothing that could be construed as anti-Soviet:

This is all the more true because the play written by the Classic is not dangerous for the Soviet state. Olga Vsevolodovna and the secretary of the Writers' Union were even negotiating its publication in the USSR.[14] One day he called her: "Olga Vsevolodovna, I read the copy you gave me overnight and I cried from how beautiful it is." This is part hypocrisy (what was this man doing during the Nobel Prize affair?). But this play is publishable in the USSR and it is advisable that it be published in the USSR first and then by you in the West. Otherwise, it will damn Olga Vsevolodovna (foreign submission of a Russian manuscript belonging to Russian patrimony, etc. etc.) and it will nonetheless serve the regime's Machiavellian goals, namely, gingerly pulling Pasternak back into the cradle of Soviet literature. Zhivago would only have been an accidental sin (perhaps even caused, it may be said, by Olga Vsevolodovna's influence). If

13. Actually, Olga had given the copy of *The Blind Beauty* to Schewe on July 24, before Nivat's departure on August 10.

14. The secretary of the Soviet Writers' Union between 1959 and 1977 was Konstantin Fedin.

Pasternak must be more or less completely redeemed in the USSR, this redemption should at least serve to save Olga Vsevolodovna as well. She must take advantage of this, not suffer from it. (Nivat to Feltrinelli, December 27, 1960, AGFE, Busta 2, fascicolo 6, "(1960 ottobre 07–1962 april 17 e s.d.)"; original in French)

It is striking how clearly Nivat was able to see into the motives driving the Soviets.

By the end of December 1960, several people in the West were privy to Olga and Irina's arrests. But nothing major happened until news of the stiff sentences, which Nivat learned on January 1, 1961, reached the West. It is helpful to have the following chronological table in mind. As I indicate in some of the notes, reconstructing the exact dating of some of these events is not a simple matter.

July 24, 1960. Olga hands off a copy of Pasternak's last play, *The Blind Beauty*, to Heinz Schewe to take abroad for safekeeping.

August 1, 1960. Olga receives 500,000 rubles from the Benedettis; she hides some of the money in neighbors' apartments.

August 6. Olga receives a visit from Grigoriĭ Khesin, head of the All-Union Commission for the Protection of Authors' Rights, accompanied by KGB agents, demanding the original of Pasternak's last piece, *The Blind Beauty*.[15]

August 15. Olga buys a motorcycle (model Kovrovets 175) for her son, Mitia, and a new chest. Both objects will be used as evidence at the trial.

August 16. Olga is arrested; the KGB confiscates the money that Olga had hidden in some of her neighbors' apartments. Olga is kept at the Lubianka, where she is "under investigation." The chief interrogator is Vladilen Vasilievich Aleksanochkin; her defense attorney is at first V. A. Samsonov.

August 16–September 5. Olga's manuscripts and letters (including much of the Pasternak *Nachlaß*) are confiscated. Other objects of foreign origin (clothing, Torpedo typewriter, Kovrovets 175 motorcycle, etc.) are also confiscated.

15. The All-Union Commission for the Protection of Authors' Rights was part of the Soviet Writers' Union.

September 4–10. D'Angelo returns to the Soviet Union and tries unsuccessfully to contact Olga but manages to see Mitia, Irina's half-brother.

September 5. Irina is arrested. She is also kept at the Lubianka, where she is "under investigation." Samsonov becomes her attorney. Olga's new defense lawyer is Viktor Adol'fovich Kosachevskiĭ.

November 4. Olga's "confession."[16]

November 10. Date of the indictment against Olga and Irina and "acknowledgment of guilt" by Olga and Irina.[17] The indictment refers to article 15 for Olga and articles 15 and 17 for Irina.

November 1960. At some point before the sentencing, Olga and Irina are transferred to the Lefortovo jail, where they are "under indictment."

December 1960, between 17th and 23rd. Olga and Irina are sentenced by the judge to eight years and three years of labor camp, respectively.[18]

January 1961. Olga and Irina's appeal is rejected, and the sentences are confirmed.

End of January 1961. Olga and Irina are deported to the Siberian camp of Taishet.

I refer to Ivinskaya 1978 and Emelianova 1997 and 2002 for details of the interrogations and the trial, and to Kosachevskiĭ 1988 for the retrospec-

---

16. Evidence for the dating comes from a picture of the confession, taken from the trial proceedings, which was distributed by the Soviet delegation to England (see below) in February 1961. The "confession" is translated into English in Conquest 1961b, 120; see also note 63 below.

17. The original document is found at RGANI, Moscow. A translation into English is given in document 50.

18. This date is not to be found in any of the accounts so far given in the secondary literature. Ivinskaya 1978; Kosachevskiĭ 1988; and Emelianova 1998, 2002 do not offer a precise timeline for the trial except for its beginning in November (Kosachevskiĭ 1988, 147, indicates November 10 as the beginning of the trial) and do not clearly distinguish between the date of the trial and that of the sentencing. By contrast, several secondary sources, such as de Mallac (1981, 373) and Finn and Couvée (2014, 247), make the distinction and indicate December 7 for the sentencing, but no evidence for this date is offered. The information was probably given to de Mallac by Max Hayward. It is a date found in some of the memos prepared by Georges Nivat at the beginning of January 1961. However, the date cannot be correct because we have letters (and memos) indicating that the sentencing did not occur before December 17 and perhaps as late as December 23. The date I offer is carefully reconstructed using reports by Nivat to Katkov on phone conversations Nivat had with Mitia, as well as a letter from Nivat to Peltier.

tive account of the trial given by Ivinskaya's lawyer, Viktor Kosachevskiĭ, published in *Moskva*.[19]

3.2. The savage sentences and Katkov's initiatives

Nivat's meetings in Oxford with Feltrinelli and Berlin were facilitated by the fact that, in late November and early December, Nivat was on a fellowship at St Antony's College, where he had been a visiting student in 1957. He was back in Paris by mid-December 1960. These scholarly visits to Oxford explain the close ties Nivat had with Max Hayward, one of the English translators of *Doctor Zhivago*, and with George Katkov, whose central role in the *Zhivago* saga has been extensively documented (see Mancosu 2016). These ties also help explain why the major campaign in the West on behalf of Olga and Irina was centered in Oxford: it was led by George Katkov, assisted by Max Hayward and Georges Nivat.

As we have seen, by the end of December 1960, several people in the West were privy to Olga's and Irina's arrests. Upon learning the news of the long sentences on January 1, 1961, Nivat started informing his close contacts. On January 2, he called George Katkov in Oxford.[20] Katkov reported the call to Max Hayward, who was in New York, in a letter dated January 3.[21]

Dear Maksim Maksimovich

Yesterday I sent you a telegram with the following contents: sentences of 8 and 3 years please dont publish writing George. I hope it reached you. From you [I've received] a Xmas card written on the 18th on the tenth day [the 28th] and nothing else. But from Nikol. [Nabokov?] a letter and from NY pub[lic] libr[ary] Microf [Microfilm?]. Yesterday I received word about the sentence from a sobbing Georges on the phone,

19. It will be hard to improve on these sources until the volumes containing the trial proceedings become available. The number of the volumes is given as two in Ivinskaya (1978, 344) and Kosachevskiĭ (1988, 142), and as three in Surkov's reply to Carver. The indictment against Olga and Irina (see document 50) cites from all three volumes. On April 3, 1961, Surkov wrote: "I went to the city court once more and asked them to show me the case proceedings. I studied document after document, every single sheet of the three volume file of this law suit, beginning with the warrant for the search and arrest and ending with the sentence passed by the city court" (see document 51).

20. On the same day he also wrote letters to Lydia Pasternak Slater (PFP, HILA, Box 91, folder 10) and to Peltier (see the letter cited at the beginning of this chapter).

21. The grammar in this letter is not the best; Katkov is clearly emotional and hurried.

this is a wild terror and I'm afraid that we have been too careful. Yesterday Georges called again, he received the initial notice from the housekeeper but yesterday he talked with this Mit'ka [Irina's half-brother]. He confirmed [the news], but said that the case was heard behind closed doors and that it is unknown under which article. Yesterday I darted to London. Tomorrow I am going again. I want to meet with: Freddy Ayer and Stuart Hampshire[22] (maybe) to get out of crazy old Russel what can [could have] be[en] done, that is to write Khrusch[ev] an open letter. To reach Graham Greene. Both of them cannot be suspected as F.O.'s [Foreign Office's] marionettes. But most importantly—I believe that it's time we made this matter public. I have developed a plan which I wish to carry out. I wrote about it to Georges. I am enclosing a copy of my letter to Georges, from which you will see what it entails. Read it and write [to me]. This is very important. It is very difficult for me to discuss everything and solve and ride atop the sintetyurikha[23] without you. But I end up having to do so anyway. I must finish, as I'm in a hurry as always. Harry is going to Chicago tomorrow. I firmly shake your hand, [*two illegible words*] family miss you. G.M. (MHP, Oxford; original in Russian)

It was the beginning of the British efforts on behalf of Olga and Irina. Already on January 3, 1961, Katkov wrote the following long letter to Nivat:

Mon cher Georges,

Excuse me for writing in English. I can not manage a Russian typewriter and I do not want to dictate this letter.

I have been thinking hard and have done something. Peter Norman, who had an interesting visit at the Klassiks [*sic*; Pasternak's] dacha, has gone this morning to Moscow.[24] He will try to meet Tvardovsky and explain to him, that the impression of such sentences will be disastrous for cultural relations.[25] He will speak as a private person to a private person. But he will try to find out whether T.[vardovsky] is ready

22. Both well-known philosophers. Katkov had written a dissertation in philosophy under Oskar Kraus and moved into Russian history and politics in the 1950s. This explains the presence of so many philosophers (Russell, Ayer, Kneale, etc.) in the activities on behalf of Olga and Irina. On Katkov's biography see Mancosu 2016.

23. The Cyrillic word is синтетюриха: it refers to a folklore character of a Russian woman, or the dance about her (which is a Uralic variant of the better-known Kamarinskaya).

24. Peter Norman, author and translator of Russian literature. On his meetings with Soviet writers, see Kudrova 1999. Norman was married to Natal'ia Frank, the sister of Viktor Frank, who was very close to Katkov (see note 34 below).

25. Tvardovskiĭ was the editor in chief of *Novy mir* during this time. Peter Norman had met Tvardovskiĭ in England in 1956 (see Kudrova 1999, 59–62).

to use what influence he has to help. I will have an answer from Peter before a week's time.

It is absolutely essential to mobilize public opinion here in France, in Italy, in Scandinavia and also in America. I have made preliminary steps to approach Bertrand Russell and Graham Greene and will be going to-morrow to London to meet the people who can help me to get at them. But we must be realistic. The more people will know the more probable will be a leakage to the press. I think a planned action is better than such a leakage. I had a telephone conversation with dame Rebecca [West] and she is of the same opinion, as are also the few personal friends of mine with whom I have discussed the situation.[26]

I am very much against your taking an active part in such a campaign, against your giving interviews or press conferences. But it will become known that some information comes from you, and that should not disturb you and should not damage your possible relations for the future.

I think the best way, to make the thing known, would be an article in the Sunday Press, best of all in the Sunday Times, written by Dame Rebecca, who would do it very moderately, mainly pointing out the character of the relation between the two women and the poet and expressing the hope that under the present conditions the Soviet authorities will find a way to prevent the consummation of an action reminding of the darkest days of the regime denounced at the twentieth congress. I believe this article (if Dame Rebecca agrees to produce it) should be preceded by a short item of news saying that from reliable sources the yet officially unconfirmed report has been received, that the friends of the late B.P. give full name and her daughter Irina (give age) have been after months of preliminary and strictly isolated custody sentenced after a secret trial to etc. I could make sure that that would appear in two daily papers (one conservative, one liberal) the Friday before the article in the Sunday Times.

There is one more point on which I would try to convince you, that it is necessary and beneficial. The article in the Sunday Times should be illustrated. It should have a photo of the classik [*sic*] and Irina and possibly of him and O.V. This is I believe of greater importance than any article or any words which we might use. He himself would have not spared any effort to protect them and perhaps this attitude of his is quite clearly expressed in these photographs. Your name should not be mentioned and Dame Rebecca is quite a sufficiently trusted person, that if she says that she believes the information received it can be trusted by others. She has just been awarded a prize

26. Rebecca West (1892–1983), British author, journalist, and literary critic. On her life and work see Gibb 2013.

for her reportage on South Africa, which indeed was extremely good and definitely shows that she is no reactionary. I would like your agreement in principle to this procedure and would love to hear your comment. I can not side slozha ruki [sit with my hands folded] and if I try to enlist support of public figures I am in constant fear that a stupid and inaccurate leak will do enormous damage.

As soon as I hear from you I will get in touch with Dame Rebecca. She was very sympathetic on the telephone and asked to give you her heartfelt sympathy. I am sure that she would do it very well if she agreed to do it. I would make sure that the Sunday Times is interested. They would certainly be glad to have anything she writes.

I have sent a telegram to Max [Hayward] yesterday night: Sentences of 8 and 3 years please don't publish writing George. I hope he will understand that it is from me and not from you. I did not think of it when I sent the telegram. I am writing to Max immediately.

As for France I do not know how the thing should be managed there. The best would be if Mauriac did the same as Dame R here, but he might not want to. You could write the article yourself then but on no account should it appear under your signature. Perhaps Jacqueline de P.[royart] or Hélène Z.[amoyska Peltier] could sign it. It has all to be done at a high level and in a dignified way, giving the people in Moscow every possibility for a dignified retreat. At the same time it should provide the basis in case they persevere in the line they have adopted, for official action on a diplomatic level. I do not believe that the diplomatic authorities should be approached now. They have little reason to interfere. But once public opinion is roused and has sufficiently strong support in leading literary and cultural circles, then of course the diplomats can point to it as something which must be appeased before normalization of internal relations can be achieved.

These are my reasons for advocating the course of action which I propose. I am, as I said ready to revise it, and in particular I am expecting news from you and from Peter N[orman]. But there is very little time to lose. We could not start a campaign with any hope of success in a month's time.

I feel very strained and lonely here without Max and you and I sincerely hope you will be back here soon.

God give that this year ends better than it began. With many kind regards to your much enduring parents and with all my heart, your ever,

[George Katkov] (MHP, Oxford)

Nivat consulted with Brice Parain and Pierre Pascal, who agreed with Katkov's idea of an article in the *Sunday Times* by Rebecca West, but

Nivat expressed strong reservations about going public with the information.[27]

As can be seen from Katkov's long letter, there were at least two campaigns in favor of Ivinskaya. One was centered in France, with Nivat taking the leading role, and another in Oxford led by Katkov with the assistance of Hayward and Nivat. Most of our attention will be devoted to the British campaign for the simple reason that it was the one that most successfully stung the Soviets, although from time to time I will mention events connected to the French or other campaigns.[28]

Thus the news of the long sentences began to circulate among those few people who were confidentially informed, who in turn informed other people. For instance, on the morning of January 4, 1961, Vera Traill wrote to Feltrinelli expressing anxiety about Olga's situation. A second letter, written in the evening of the same day, confirmed the correctness of her anxiety:

Dear Sir,

I hardly had the time to send you my letter this morning when a telephone call from Oxford brought the terrible confirmation of what I feared worst: during a closed-door trial this summer, Olga was sentenced to 8 years of hard labor, Irina—to 3 years. What to say, faced with such an atrocity? And what can we do? Write to me, please. Yours, Vera Traill (AGFE, Busta 3, fascicolo 2, "(1959 luglio 06–1961 gennaio 04)"; original in French)

Vera Traill (1906–1987), an émigré from Russia, lived in London, and not surprisingly, she heard the news from Oxford. The person who informed Traill was most likely George Katkov, or someone whom he had just informed. It turned out that Vera Traill was very much in favor of making the news public and had to be kept in check. By contrast, Nivat—just like Feltrinelli and contrary to Katkov's suggestion of January 3—was adamant that no news about the arrest of the two women should be released to

27. See undated letter to Katkov, obviously an answer to Katkov's letter dated January 3, found in the GKP, Oxford. Brice Parain (1897–1971) was a philosopher, writer, and *lecteur* at Gallimard. Pierre Pascal (1890–1983) was a French Slavist and specialist in Russian history; he was Nivat's doctoral adviser.

28. I should also mention that activities and petitions on behalf of Olga and Irina took place in other countries, including Italy, Germany, Austria, and the United States.

the press. In a letter to Feltrinelli, datable to the second week of January, Nivat wrote:

> As I told you in my telegram, your letter touched me deeply. I believe that by acting sensibly along the line you suggest you have the greatest chances of influencing these sad events. . . . Not only am I hostile toward any public revelation, but I believe that I am also fighting with all my might against the irresponsible persons trying to make a newspaper story out of this. I have twice pleaded for and succeeded in obtaining silence. But I do not know everything, and I fear that others might do it. (Nivat to Feltrinelli, datable to the second week of January 1961, AGFE, Busta 2, fascicolo 6, "(1960 ottobre 07–1962 aprile 17 e s.d.)"; original in French)[29]

In the same letter, Nivat reported having written to Guido Piovene and Nicolas Nabokov to enlist their help.[30]

3.3. Katkov and Greene

Katkov immediately contacted Graham Greene in London. Greene was the president of the British section of P.E.N. On January 6, he wrote to

29. One of the persons he had in mind was certainly Vera Traill. On January 10, he wrote to Katkov: "I wrote to Madame Traill and begged her to stop, begged her in the name of Irochka and O.V. I wrote that I understand her suffering, etc. but that she can well imagine that I too have my share of suffering and sorrow. In short, if she does not calm down after that, she is not worthy of attention or gentle treatment" (Nivat to Katkov, GKP, Oxford; original in Russian). Traill relented and did not inform the press. In this letter Nivat also mentions that he had been able to talk to Olga's mother, Maria Nikolaevna, by telephone.

30. Nabokov strongly supported Nivat's efforts in 1961, but letters from 1962 written by Nivat suggest that his support waned. In the Max Hayward Papers there is a seven-page report, marked AMConfidential, of a conversation on the Ivinskaya case, which reflects Nabokov's engagement. It will not be possible to provide a detailed account of all the individual contacts and solicitations for help carried out by Nivat during the period 1961–64. In addition to his extensive correspondence with Feltrinelli (Feltrinelli archives, Milan), Katkov (GKP, Oxford), Hayward (MHP, Oxford), and Peltier (Hélène Peltier Archive), the list includes Khrushchev, Sergeĭ Vinogradov (Soviet ambassador to France), Vijaya Lakshmi Pandit (sister of Jawaharlal Nehru and former Indian ambassador to the Soviet Union; at the time, Indian high commissioner to the UK), the queen of Belgium, Jean Laloy (minister of foreign affairs at the French Foreign Ministry), Emmanuel Jacquin de Margerie (France's first secretary in Moscow), the Soviet Red Cross, the International Red Cross, François Mauriac, Mme Lazareff, Bertrand Russell, Isaiah Berlin, Rebecca West, Eleanor Roosevelt, and many others.

Katkov, sending him a copy of a telegram he had written to Alekseĭ Surkov that read as follows:[31]

January 6, 1961

Mr. Alexei Surkov
Foreign Commission Union of Writers,
Vorovskaya Street 52,
Moscow.

Writers like myself who feel great friendship for Soviet Union highly disturbed by reports of condemnation and imprisonment of Pasternak's friend Ivinskaya and her young daughter Irina stop No one wants to see Zhivago agitation revived here and public protests in press etc. have so far been held back but pressure grows stop Can you help in any way.

Graham Greene.

Graham Greene was considered friendly toward the Soviets, and in fact Surkov, upon receiving the telegram, informed Khrushchev:

January 10, 1961

To the Central Committee
Attention: Comrade Khrushchev

I must convey to the Central Committee the telegram from Graham Greene, one of the most famous English writers. He has great influence on British public opinion. In the last few years he has shown himself relatively well disposed toward the Soviet Union.

It is for this reason that I ask you to reflect personally on the issue raised by the telegram.

Alekseĭ Surkov
Secretary of the Writers' Union (*Le dossier* 1994, 210–11; Afiani and Tomilina 2001, 307; original in Russian)

Surkov's message was sent by Suslov to Polikarpov.[32] Polikarpov noted on the document that the necessary measures had been taken and that a

31. During this period, Surkov was chairman of the foreign commission of the Soviet Writers' Union.

32. Mikhaĭl Andreevich Suslov (1902–1982) was one of the ideological hard-liners in the party. During the period we are discussing, he was chairman of the Foreign Affairs Commission of the USSR, full member of the Politburo, and member of the Secretariat. He was also the secretary of the Central Committee in charge of the section for ideology and propaganda. In his diaries, Khrushchev mentions Suslov's hard line on *Doctor Zhivago* as the reason for banning the book

telegram from Surkov to Greene had been sent on January 20 (see Afiani and Tomilina 2001, 308; and *Le dossier* 1994, 212).

On January 9, Katkov informed Hayward of the various contacts he had established in support of Olga and Irina:

Happy New Year 9/i/61 [January 9, 1961]

Dear M.M!

Urgently: sending simultaneously in a separate envelope two memoranda—mine (abusive language, maybe you will re-dictate) and Georges' (rewrote personally and it would be nice to retype)[33]

[the following] has been done:

1) After a visit with me and Viktor Frank[,] Graham Green[e] sent the following telegram:[34]

"To Mr Alexei Surkov Foreign Commission Union of Writers, Vorovskaya Street 52 Moscow

Writers like myself who feel great friendship for Soviet Union highly disturbed by reports of condemnation and imprisonment of Pasternak's friend Ivinskaya and her young daughter Irina /stop/ No one wants to see Zhivago agitation revived here and public protests in press etc. have so far been held back but pressure grows /stop/ Can you help any way, Graham Greene."

Besides that, he wrote to his publisher there, Izakov and asked his contact from the embassy to breakfast.[35]

2) On Wednesday at 11'30am I will be at Russel's [Bertrand Russell's] who promised to protest in the embassy, and if that doesn't help to write in the Times.

---

in the USSR (Khrushchev 2013, 551). Dmitriĭ Alekseevich Polikarpov (1905–1965) had been secretary of the Soviet Writers' Union between 1944 and 1946. He was chief of the Department of Culture of the Central Committee of the CPSU from 1955 to 1962.

33. The memoranda are found in the MHP, Oxford.

34. Viktor Semënovich Frank (1909–1972) was the son of an important Russian religious philosopher, Semën Frank (1877–1950). His father had been expelled from Soviet Russia in 1922, and thus Viktor grew up an émigré. He moved to England in 1939, where he worked for the BBC, and then to Munich, where he worked for Radio Liberty. Viktor was very active in TsOPE (Central Union of Political Immigrants), a political organization of anticommunist émigrés with offices in Munich and New York.

35. The contact was Leonid Zaitsev, who told Greene that no one at the Soviet embassy in London had heard anything about the case (see letter from Greene to Katkov dated January 16, 1961, in the MHP, Oxford). Boris Izakov was Greene's translator in the Soviet Union. In 1956 he was appointed to the foreign committee of the Soviet Writers' Union. A copy of the letter from Greene to Izakov, dated January 6, 1961, is in the MHP, Oxford.

3) David Astor promised Manya [Harari] to write to Khrusch, that he will have to give everything publicity if [Ivinskaya and Emelianova are] not released.[36]
4) Vera Traill is bitching and nearly disclosed everything to the Paris press. Crankshaw and Manya [Harari] are sitting on her and not letting her.[37]
5) I want to approach Noemi Mitchelson I have made contact with her daughter.[38]
6) Herbert Reid is doing something.[39]
7) Sartre and Simone de B.[eauvoir] intend to write to Furtseva[40]
8) Nabokov went to consult with Feltrinelli. Berlin says that he (F) has once again joined the party[41]
9) French ambassador in Moscow woke up and is demanding the public disclosure of the charges[42]
10) Nothing from P.[eter] Norman yet. He promised to wire if "No good."

Korneĭchuk is great, but Eleanor [Roosevelt] is much more important. She was supposed to immediately wire Khrusch and invite Ivinskaya to visit her and to relax with her daughter.[43] Exactly so. Slip her Georges' writing—it is capable of squeezing tears out of mountains.

Excerpts from Pasternak's correspondence with Proyart have not yet arrived.[44] They are terribly revealing. He asks for O.V.I.'s defense like for himself. Asks for the

36. David Astor (1912–2001), English newspaper publisher, editor of *The Observer*. See letter from Manya Harari to William Collins cited in section 3.4. "Khrusch" is an intentionally somewhat rude abbreviation.

37. Edward Crankshaw (1909–1984), author and journalist. See section 3.14.

38. Katkov's indecision as to the spelling might suggest that this is Naomi Mitchison (1897–1999), well-known Scottish writer and Socialist activist.

39. Herbert Edward Read (1893–1968), English art historian, poet, literary critic, and philosopher.

40. Ekaterina Furtseva (1910–1974) was minister of culture of the USSR between 1960 and 1964. It is unknown whether Sartre or Beauvoir wrote to Furtseva in this connection.

41. This is Nicolas Nabokov (1903–1978), secretary of the Congress for the Freedom of Culture.

42. Maurice Dejean was the French ambassador to Moscow from 1955 to 1964.

43. The reference to Korneĭchuk is an obvious reply to a suggestion made by Hayward, possibly on the phone. It is hard to see why Alexandr Korneĭchuk (1905–1972) would have been great. He was certainly close to Khrushchev; indeed, he is said to be Khrushchev's "dear friend and sycophant from Kiev" in Taubman 2003, 308. But he was so vociferous in his opposition to Pasternak that it is unclear why he would have been well disposed toward Olga. Max Hayward approached Eleanor Roosevelt in New York using a letter of introduction (dated January 11, 1961) from Charles E. Bohlen, United States ambassador to the USSR from 1953 to 1957. A copy of the letter from Bohlen to Roosevelt is in the MHP, Oxford. Eleanor Roosevelt did write a letter to Khrushchev on behalf of Irina on February 16, 1962 (see section 3.16). A letter from J. Chute to Max Hayward dated February 1, 1962, confirms that Roosevelt had also written to Khrushchev before the case became public, i.e., before January 17, 1961.

44. They arrived soon after through Georges Nivat, who had obtained them from Jacqueline de Proyart. Among the excerpts was the following: "If God forbid, they should arrest Olga, I will send you a telegram saying that someone has caught scarlet fever. In that event, all tocsins should

income to be split between her and Zinaida [Pasternak's second wife], wants to be buried in Milan (best to keep quiet about that) and for O.V.I. to look after his grave, complains that the authorities [the KGB] are tormenting him. Once I receive I will forward.

Photographs are being redeveloped will also send. But explain to Eleanor [regardless] that Nabokov says that she has already defended B.L. in 1958

I firmly shake your hand //signature//

Traveling to Wales is long and hard, but [the] lord [Russell] is there and I will ~~probably~~ have to spend 2 nights there. Today I am going to London to see Henry Shapiro[45] (MHP, Oxford; original in Russian)

We will have to keep track, as we proceed, of some of the developments originating from the initiatives mentioned in Katkov's letter.

On January 12, Katkov informed Greene that Bertrand Russell had written to Khrushchev a letter with approximately the same content as the telegram sent by Greene himself. Surkov's reply arrived on January 20 and was forwarded by Greene to Katkov, with a request that Katkov keep it confidential:

Immediately on returning Moscow looked into question raised your telegram stop case Ivinskaya and her daughter has neither political nor literary colouring they are condemned in open session of Moscow city court for criminal offence illegal currency machinations stop Pasternaks family has no relation whatsoever to this case respectfully Alexei Surkov

The documents published on the Ivinskaya case stemming from the Central Committee Archive (Afiani and Tomilina 2001; *Le dossier* 1994) contain no further mention of the Ivinskaya case until September 20, 1961. But this silence does not reflect inactivity, for things had been happening. Katkov wrote to Greene on January 29, thanking him for having forwarded the telegram and mentioning that the *Daily Worker* had published a note

ring, just as would have been done in my own case, for an attack on her is in fact a blow at me." The passage was from a letter to Proyart written by Pasternak in February 1959. Nivat thought these excerpts so explosive that he wrote to Katkov (in Russian): "Here are all the excerpts from the exchange that Mme de Proyart gave me. I have a photocopy of the second excerpt. This, as you will see, is dangerous material. We must be supremely careful with it, so that it doesn't end up anywhere. *Keep this text on your person*, if possible. Don't give it to anybody" (Nivat to Katkov, datable to January/February 1961, GKP, Oxford).

45. Henry Shapiro (1907–1991), a longtime Moscow correspondent fluent in Russian.

by Surkov along the lines of the telegram to Greene. In the remaining correspondence from late January and early February, Katkov brought Greene up to date with the latest news on the case, which we will discuss later. Noteworthy is Greene's letter to Katkov dated February 6, where he says: "I do feel that the man Feltrinelli has confused the issue badly. There is something very strange indeed behind his attitude. One wonders if he's already making peace with the Party." As we have seen, Katkov had also gotten this impression from Berlin, who had met Feltrinelli back in December.

At the risk of anticipating things that will become clear later, we wrap up this first part with a letter from Katkov to Greene dated February 7, 1961. It is a long letter, but it clearly reveals how hard it was to orient oneself in a story that was complex and about which very little correct information was available. Katkov's letter follows a declaration, which we will cite later, made by Feltrinelli on January 28.

Dear Mr. Greene,

Thank you very much for the further information about your exchange of letters with Boris Izakov.

You are absolutely right in your suspicions of Feltrinelli. The issue seems to me however so simple that it can not be confused too badly or for too long. Feltrinelli certainly had instructions from Pasternak to keep a sum of $100,000 at the disposal of his friend's family. There is no doubt that no immediate transfer of this sum to Russia was intended by Pasternak, but that he wanted, in case of his death, Ivinskaya's family supported when necessary out of this fund which should be separated from the rest of his royalties. Feltrinelli's agent Dangelo [*sic*], who was the man who originally brought Zhivago to Milan and used to travel with great ease between Italy and the Soviet Union, was to take care of these transfers. Instead Feltrinelli now claims that he gave the whole sum to Dangelo, who converted it into roubles and had it dumped on Ivinskaya by "a young Italian couple" who, as far as I know, were themselves correspondents of the Italian newspaper Unita.[46] The Moscow announcements do not say where and how the money was converted into roubles, in any case it is quite clear that Ivinskaya had nothing to do with the conversion nor did she "confess to it." What she admitted was a receipt of a large sum of money in hundred rouble banknotes. None of the people who had made the conversion were arrested or prosecuted, although Ivinskaya's arrest followed very closely on the dumping of the money onto her. She

46. Here Katkov confuses the Benedettis with the Garritanos.

is accused of knowing that the conversion was illegal, and for that they gave her the heavy sentence. Feltrinelli's role in transfering the money to Dangelo is not clear, he might himself have been a victim of his dishonest agents. Dangelo's role is quite obvious: there was a large amount of floating Soviet currency in the Soviet embassies abroad, and in view of the forthcoming currency reform it was strongly devalued. Dangelo and his friends must have purchased the large sum of money dumped on Ivinskaya, for a song, and pocketed the difference. However they either denounced her or more probably acted with the knowledge of the secret police so that the whole thing came out and they could claim that they had fulfilled their obligations towards Pasternak and Feltrinelli having transfered the money to Ivinskaya. The poor woman was not a match to this combination of mediterranean crookery and secret police cunning.

Izakov's suggestion that you might obtain confirmation of the official story from "the legal wife" is almost as amusing as it is beautifully worded. I wonder whether it is not time now to let the people who like Surkov, are entrusted with the task to sell an incredible story abroad, clearly understand that this will not do. They will have to invent something better or bear the consequences of being accessories to an act of police frame-up and persecution. Perhaps the sooner they understand the position now the quicker they will desist, and the earlier the higher authorities will decide to release their prey. What practical form such a step should take, I am loath to suggest in this letter; I wonder whether you would think of a possible public statement on the case by you? Perhaps would it be possible for us to meet either here or in Paris where I could come any day during the forthcoming weekends.

With many thanks for your help in this distressing matter.

Yours sincerely,
George Katkov (MHP, Oxford)

As it will turn out, Graham Greene would not actively participate in the Ivinskaya campaign. Katkov's confusion as to the roles played by d'Angelo and Feltrinelli in the Ivinskaya case is revealing of the situation at the time. D'Angelo's later articles will help rectify the situation, at least to a certain extent. For this reason, however, we will not spend too much time reproducing or analyzing the memos that were prepared at the time, lest we get involved in an endless game of pointing out the inaccurate information and misrepresentations.

3.4. Katkov and Russell

In his efforts to enlist help in putting pressure on the Soviets, Katkov contacted the philosopher A. J. Ayer, who wrote to Bertrand Russell on January 5, 1961:

Dear Russell,

I have been asked to send you this by my friend George Katkov, a Russian who has been living in Oxford since before the war. He knew Pasternak and is very deeply concerned about the fate of these women. He thinks that this is one of the periods in which the Russians are sensitive to public opinion and that if you were willing to intervene on their behalf, whether by writing privately to Khrushchev or in some more public way, there is a chance that the women would be released.

If you are interested in the case and would like more information about it, Dr Katkov will be very happy to come and see you and answer any questions that you care to put to him. I don't like to press this because I know how busy you are. But he has great faith in your influence and it would be a great kindness on your part at least to see him. (BRA, McMaster University)

The rest of the letter went on to discuss Ayer's recent Oxford lecture on the philosophy of language. The letter contained a five-page enclosure written by Katkov concerning the Ivinskaya case. During the month of January, Katkov would write many more such accounts, always including new information as it came in. The principal source of the account was Nivat. We cite from the last part:

All attempts to find out exactly the charge against the two women remained ineffectual. In December, however, Nivat managed to speak to Ivinskaya's son Dimitri by telephone, who could not give any information apart from saying that the fate of his mother and sister would be decided on the 17th of December.[47]

It was only on the 1st of January, however, that Nivat learned by telephone that Ivinskaya had been given—after what his [*sic*] son called a "secret trial"—a sentence of 8 (eight) years, and his bride-to be Irina one of three years; but the nature of the penalty (prison or labour colony) was not specified.

47. This is one of the sources for my previous claim that the sentence did not take place before December 17. A letter from Nivat to Peltier (dated December 17, 1960) indicates that the sentencing might have taken place as late as December 21.

It should be noted, that the arrest of Ivinskaya took place three months after the death of Pasternak. We do not know what formal charges the secret police brought against Ivinskaya and her daughter to obtain such savage sentences, but there is little doubt that the real crime of these women in their eyes was that they aided and abetted Pasternak whom the authorities did not dare to prosecute because of his international reputation.

All inquiries made through the French Embassy in Moscow and a second appeal by Nivat to Khrushchev asking him to spare his fiancée were unanswered.

At the express wish of Nivat, friends of Pasternak, his publishers abroad and others refrained from communicating this matter to the press for fear of making the position of Irina and her mother even more difficult, and in the hope that the new liberal trend in the Soviet internal policies would make an act of reprisal on the part of the Soviet secret police impossible. These hopes are now seen to have been unfounded. The silence of the world press over this affair might even have given the Soviet authorities the false impression, that such arbitrary treatment of defenceless women, whose only crime was their devotion to a defiant poet, would pass unnoticed.

We believe that there is a good likelihood of them revising their attitude if an independent and authoritative figure would disillusion them with regard to the probable reaction of public opinion in the west towards such actions. (Katkov, Memorandum, January 5, BRA, McMaster University)

Bertrand Russell responded positively to the request on January 7:

Dear Ayer,

Thank you for your letter. I look forward with pleasure to your inaugural lecture which you have so kindly promised to send me.

I am quite willing to see your Russian friend whose name I cannot quite make out in your handwriting. Assuming that the facts are as stated in the statement you enclose, I shall be quite willing to do something for the two ladies. I suppose that the first step would be to approach the Russian Authorities privately, probably the Soviet Ambassador.[48] Assuming, as I fear we must, that this approach would be fruitless, I should think the next step would be a letter to The Times. But, as to the proper moves, I shall suspend judgement until I have seen your Russian friend. I will be grateful if

48. The Soviet ambassador to England for the period 1960–66 was Aleksandr Alekseevich Soldatov.

you or he would telephone me to fix a time if he is willing to come here. Unfortunately, I have no spare room at present as the house is full of grandchildren.

Your sincerely,
Bertrand Russell. (BRA, McMaster University)

A similar request to Russell arrived by way of Herbert Read on January 9. Read was writing on behalf of another admirer of Pasternak, Manya Harari, one of the English translators of *Doctor Zhivago*. The request was for a direct letter to Khrushchev. Harari had also prepared a confidential statement which was more explicit than Katkov's and fully revealed the sources of information on which the statement was based. Harari indicated Georges Nivat and Giangiacomo Feltrinelli as the two major sources.[49]

Russell's reply to Read on January 12 confirmed that Katkov and Russell had met on the 11th and reported that "with his [Katkov's] concurrence, [I] composed a letter to Khrushchev which I sent via the Soviet Embassy. I enclose a copy and hope that you and Mme Harari will approve" (Russell to Read, carbon copy, BRA, McMaster University).

Here is Russell's letter to Khrushchev (which Katkov also translated into Russian):

To H.E. N. S. Khrushchev

Your excellency

I learn that two ladies Olga Vsevolodovna Ivinskaya and Irina Emelyanova who are mother and daughter, and were friends of Pasternak, have been condemned to sentences of eight years and three years respectively. Hitherto, this news has been kept from the British and French Press, but it is becoming increasingly difficult to prevent publication. I personally, and those who work with me, fear that publication, unless accompanied by a pardon, will have a very damaging effect upon our efforts to improve East-West relations. We have had reason to believe that the Soviet Government approves of these efforts. We find it hard to believe that these two ladies, if released, could do as much harm to Soviet interests as will be done by their continued detention. I hope you will not think it an impertinence on my part to address you on an internal Soviet matter but I must ask you to accept my assurance that it is my urgent and ardent desire to improve relations between our governments and those of Western countries which has led me to venture upon this letter.

49. Perhaps Harari met with either or both of them in London or Oxford in December 1960. See section 3.1.

With all respect and good wishes
I remain
yours faithfully

[Bertrand Russell] (BRA, McMaster University)

The contact between Katkov and Russell led to an extensive correspondence, in which Katkov kept Russell updated about the various pieces of news that he received about Olga and Irina, mainly through Nivat. Between January 1961 and Olga's liberation in 1964, Russell wrote at least three letters to Khrushchev (one of which received a reply).

The idea of keeping the case out of the press is well summarized by Manya Harari's letter to William Collins, head of Collins Publishers, written probably around the second week of January 1961:

Dear Billy,

I enclose a note about "Lara" [Olga Ivinskaya]. At the moment Bertrand Russell has been asked to write to Khrushchev and Graham Greene has written to Surkov. —the idea is to give the Russians the chance to say we have been misinformed and to produce the two women safe and sound, that is why we are trying to keep it out of the papers for the present, though I don't know if we'll succeed. Crankshaw is also asking David Astor [editor of *The Observer*] to write to K.[hrushchev] saying there are these rumours going round but he is not printing anything about them until he hears whether they are true. And the French government is supposed to be making representations, but I don't know if they are.

One other thing has been suggested—that C. P. Snow should be asked also to write either to K or to the Union of Soviet Writers—he is in very good standing. But I don't know him or anyone who knows him. I wondered if by any chance you did?

Yours, Manya (Collins Archives, Glasgow)

Despite the efforts to keep the issue out of the press, the news broke out on January 17, and the source of the leak was not the West but the Soviet Union.

3.5. The case comes out in the press

On January 17, the *Daily Herald* published on page 8 an article from its correspondent in Moscow, Alan Moray Williams. It was the first report in the news of anything connected to the Ivinskaya case. It was an attack on Ivinskaya, apparently stemming from an official of the State Publishing House [Goslitizdat], but with a surprising twist. First of all, it did not mention the trial or the sentences. Secondly, the article reported that Ivinskaya was accused of having plagiarized other people's work. It was the beginning of the smear campaign orchestrated by Moscow. Here is the text:

PASTERNAK'S FRIEND BANNED
Russia stops publishing all her new works
From
Alan Moray Williams
Moscow. Mon.

A Woman who was a close friend of the late Boris Pasternak, Russia's rebel writer, has been "outlawed" by the Soviet authorities.

She is Mrs Olga Ivinskaya, who was the model for Lara in Pasternak's famous novel "Dr Zhivago"—the book that was banned in Russia.

Mrs Ivinskaya is well known in Russia as a translator of poetry. She lived two miles from Pasternak's home at Peredelkino.

Moscow state-owned publishers, Goslitizdat, have refused to handle any more work from her because they say she has employed "ghost writers" to make translations published under her name.

Illegal.

Officials claim that she paid young students of Moscow University two or three roubles a line for poetry translations for which Goslitizdat paid her about 10 roubles a line.

Under Soviet law this is illegal and can be punished by prison sentence.

A Goslitizdat official told me: "We have broken all connections with Ivinskaya. Our managing director is very angry with her. In 1959 she delivered 15000 lines of rhymed verse, earning her about 150.000 roubles—then worth over $5000.

"No one person could translate so much poetry in one year. It's probable that legal action will be taken against her."

Attractive.

Mrs Ivinskaya, an attractive woman with red hair, has been married several times and has three children. She is in her forties.

Pasternak, who died last May, made no secret of the fact that he met her often in the last five years of his life and that she was the model of Lara.

Pasternak's wife tolerated the friendship, but disapproved of her.

Pasternak's widow is still living at Peredelkino on royalties received on her husband's translations.

It is more than likely that the information given to Williams was intended as part of a campaign to discredit Ivinskaya, but if this was the case the authorities soon changed plans and decided to stick to the smuggling charges. But they made sure to also smear her character with allegations of sexual promiscuity.

Williams's article was only a harbinger. The news created some confusion at the beginning, but it was no longer possible to remain silent. The first detailed Western article about the case was written by David Floyd in the *Daily Telegraph*. He concluded his article:

> Since news of Mrs. Ivinskaya's arrest and sentence reached the West several distinguished literary and public figures have tried to intervene on their [Ivinskaya and Emelianova's] behalf. Every effort has been made to spare the Russian authorities the embarrassment of publicity. But the misleading statement made this week by a Soviet official persuaded friends of the West that no further good purpose would be served by concealing the fate of Pasternak's two devoted friends. (*Daily Telegraph*, January 18, 1961, p. 19)

What followed was an avalanche of articles on the Ivinskaya case, much of it confusing. For instance, *The Times* (London) on January 19 correctly reported the prison sentences but still repeated that the charge against Olga was that of having sold the work of Moscow students as her own. On January 20, *The Times* reported that Feltrinelli had denied the rumor that Pasternak had sent a copy of *The Blind Beauty* to his Western friends.

Things picked up speed after Radio Moscow's broadcast, in English, of a program devoted to Ivinskaya on January 21. The text is well known and has been published in Conquest's book *Courage of Genius* (1961b, 182–86).[50] While presenting the accusation as one of money smuggling, it also smeared Olga's character by portraying her as an adventuress who had acted behind Pasternak's back. In addition, Feltrinelli was implicated through the mention of one letter written to Ivinskaya on July 8, 1960. Taken out of context, the letter seemed damning.[51] The smearing was also applied to Nivat: "One ill-fated Frenchman, Georges Nivat, had his eye on the royalties banked abroad and gave his heart and hand to Ivinskaya's

50. There was also a second broadcast in Italian on January 27. Since Conquest's book is easily available, I have not reproduced here the long transcripts of the two broadcasts by Radio Moscow (Conquest 1961b, 182–91).

51. For a contextual discussion of this letter, see chapter 2.

daughter. This nobleness was rewarded. Ivinskaya instructed Feltrinelli to pay the fiancé 10,000 dollars" (Conquest 1961b, 183).[52]

This broadcast by the Soviets led to more articles in the press and to feverish activity in Oxford, where the campaign for Olga and Irina turned to analyzing and rebutting the charges coming from Moscow. Edward Crankshaw wrote an article for *The Observer* on January 22. Floyd wrote another article on January 23 (*Daily Telegraph*), in which he concluded: "The story given by Moscow Radio is quite different from the one given by a Soviet official last week. But both stories appear to have the same purpose: to blacken her [Ivinskaya's] character and to depict her as Pasternak's evil genius." *The Times* published on the same day an almost complete text of the broadcast that had aired on Radio Moscow, and the *Daily Worker* published it in its entirety. The article in *The Times* subtly analyzed the broadcast's intent:

> Some of the accusations in the statement seem almost to be designed to exculpate Pasternak or at least to show that he was influenced against his better judgement by Mrs. Ivinskaya. The emphasis on her "perfidiousness" and her "deceit" in keeping money away from his legal heirs is so strongly marked that it even suggests that the authorities wish to keep a way open for his eventual rehabilitation, if that were decided on. Even so, it would be a long time before all his work, including Doctor Zhivago and some of his religious poems, was cleared. In the meantime the abuse of Mrs. Ivinskaya for her supposed influence over him might serve a narrower purpose, being designed to discredit any other manuscripts which may have survived him or found their way abroad. It is always tempting to seek tortuous explanations for Soviet acts and sometimes they turn out to be right. In this tragic case, however, the direct motive seems to be punishment and warning—punishment for being closely involved from first to last in the whole Pasternak affair: and warning to others. (*The Times*, January 23, 1961, p. 13).

On January 25, Mark Bonham-Carter, the editor who had negotiated the English rights to *Doctor Zhivago* with Feltrinelli on behalf of Collins, wrote a long article in the *Daily Telegraph*. He pointed out that the attempt had been to privately contact Soviet authorities before news got out and "spread in Moscow and from Moscow to the outside world." He continued:

52. Nivat had indeed received $10,000 as a gift from Pasternak, as had several other friends. See Mancosu 2013, 375; and chapters 1 and 2.

> The news of Ivinskaya's arrest which has been made public over last week in the British Press and by Moscow radio last Saturday, has changed the situation. The motives for silence have now disappeared and Pasternak's instruction that the tocsin be sounded must be our guide.[53]

He also emphasized that the broadcast strengthened the impression that "this bitter tragedy is part of a plan to rehabilitate Pasternak as an acceptable Soviet figure by discrediting the woman most closely associated with his later writing." Alternatively, he continued, "it may simply be an act of revenge" (*Daily Telegraph*, January 25, 1961, p. 10).

Meanwhile, Nivat in France had made his only public declaration on the case. It was reported in French newspapers as well as in the *Daily Telegraph* (January 25, 1961, p. 17). David Floyd continued the campaign in the January 26 edition of the *Daily Telegraph* (p. 18) and called on Feltrinelli to intervene and refute the charges against Olga. Sir William Hayter, former British ambassador to the USSR, stated in the January 26 edition of *The Times* that the treatment of Pasternak and his associates "suggests much more a literary vendetta armed with unusual weapons than considered decisions by political leaders as intelligent as those now in control in Moscow. The action against Madame Ivinskaya, with its varying and obviously incompatible pretexts, fits into this pattern of clumsy, low-level vindictiveness and contempt for foreign opinion." He concluded by expressing hope that Khrushchev would put a stop to this vendetta.

Katkov kept Russell abreast of the developments. Some of their correspondence concerned the fact that Russell's name had been leaked to the press on January 19. It turns out that a *New York Times* correspondent had tricked Max Hayward (then in New York but informed by Katkov as to Russell's intervention) into confirming that Russell had interceded with the Soviets. In any case, by now it was too late to worry. The whole story was out in the press. On January 23, Katkov explained to Russell how this happened. He also added that he had checked a complete and officially certified version of the Radio Moscow broadcast and stated:

> The desire to justify in one way or another an act of inhuman vengeance, has driven the Moscow propaganda machine to transcend all limits of the plausible. But what seems

53. "Pasternak's instruction" refers to his fear for Olga's safety, as expressed by Pasternak in a letter to Jacqueline de Proyart written on February 3, 1959, which was widely cited during the Ivinskaya case (see note 44 above). For the original letter, see Boris Pasternak 1994, 140–42.

most important to me is the application of the traditional treatment to Pasternak's friends, the combination of physical punishment and the destruction of their moral status. (BRA, McMaster University)

Russell replied on the 25th saying that he had not received any reply from Khrushchev or the embassy and stating his availability for further action. He added: "To everyone in the West who wishes for friendly relations between our side and the Communist bloc such incidents are very deeply distressing." And indeed, on January 27 Russell wrote a letter to *The Times* mentioning his unacknowledged letter to Khrushchev and hoping that "second, and more reasoned, thoughts may prevail and the two ladies may be liberated." The letter was published on January 30. Katkov's reply on January 29 thanked Russell for his letter to *The Times* (which Russell had shared with him before publication) and added a new memorandum on the case (dated Oxford, January 15–28, 1961) that detailed and analyzed in fifteen pages all that was known about the Ivinskaya case up to that point. The memorandum took into account the two major recent news items: an article by Heinz Schewe in *Die Welt* and some statements by Surkov that were reported in the *Daily Worker* and in *l'Humanité* of January 24, 1961.[54]

Since both aspects are important, we will devote a section to each.

3.6. Schewe's article

Heinz Schewe, the Moscow correspondent for *Die Welt*, was by far the most knowledgeable person about what had happened in Moscow. He was the trusted middleman between Feltrinelli, Pasternak, and Olga. On January 24, he published an article in *Die Welt* that left many stunned. The article, titled "Die verhängnisvollen 500000 Rubel kamen aus Rom," described with authority what had happened in Moscow and confirmed that Olga had received 500,000 rubles from two Italian tourists. There is no trace in the Feltrinelli (Milan) or Schewe (Berlin) archives that Schewe had discussed the matter with Feltrinelli prior to publishing the article. Schewe was convinced that d'Angelo, whom he here intentionally calls d'Annunzio, was responsible for Olga's arrest. He writes:

54. On Schewe's role in the Pasternak and Ivinskaya affairs, see Mancosu 2013; and chapters 1 and 2.

Thus, both of Pasternak's closest confidants are now sitting in a labor camp. To blame for this is primarily that "Signor d'Annunzio."

The article recounts the events as Schewe knew, quite accurately, them to be. However, he also added his own interpretations of d'Angelo's actions. But what is most striking in the article is the way Schewe justified the Soviet action and claimed that the protests of the West were based on weak reasons:

> Olga Ivinskaya is imprisoned . . . because she violated national laws. From the legal point of view, there are no ifs and buts about it. All protests from the West therefore stand on weak ground. Ms. Olga accepted 500,000 (old) rubles (200,000 DM). The money stemmed from honoraria for Pasternak's novel "Dr. Zhivago." At the instruction of an Italian middleman in Rome—let us call him "Signor d'Annunzio"—an Italian tourist couple smuggled it to Moscow in August 1960.
>
> The ruble is an "internal currency." It may neither be exported nor imported. Whosoever violates these conditions can be sentenced to up to 15 years' imprisonment. (*Die Welt*, January 26, 1961)

And after describing how Ivinskaya received the money, he continued, "By accepting the money, Ms. Olga had made herself guilty."

One part of the article described how the police had seized the manuscripts and letters, and finally mentioned that smaller payments from the royalties of *Zhivago* had been tolerated by the authorities during Pasternak's lifetime. He seemed almost to implicate himself by saying, "A friend of the poet gave assistance in the matter." Schewe cited Pasternak saying that he was too old to continue earning his keep with translations, and he added that the authorities had closed one eye while trying to meet his needs as much as it was possible to do. This is why, Schewe added, it was wrong to claim that the authorities were taking revenge on Pasternak. The article concluded by mentioning that after the currency reform, the authorities could perhaps revisit the sentences against Olga and Irina, and that perhaps the sentence could be commuted to one exiling them from Moscow, otherwise allowing them to live in full freedom. In the meantime, however, "protests and half-true reports" would not help set this process in motion.

Knowing how Schewe himself had broken the law, this article cannot fail to leave one puzzled about what he was up to. The Soviet authorities were fully aware of the role he had played in smuggling the money. He was even mentioned in the second Radio Moscow broadcast (January 27), and he had been explicitly mentioned in the indictment against the two women as one of the people who had illegally brought money to them (for the official indictment, see document 50). Indeed, Schewe's involvement in delivering money to Pasternak was known to the KGB as early as February 11, 1960 (see chapter 2, note 24). Was Schewe trying to appease the Soviet authorities by making amends? Surely there was some of that. But perhaps the strategy was to show through the article that the Soviets had good legal reason to think Ivinskaya was guilty, thereby paving the way, once the correctness of their point of view had been acknowledged, for an act of mercy on their part.

That Schewe was pursuing a strategy he thought would improve the chances of Olga and Irina's release emerges clearly from several exchanges he had in reply to reactions to his article. Indeed, Schewe's article left many perplexed, to say the least. In the English press, several articles suggested that the money given to Ivinskaya had been part of a frame job. Schewe claimed that this was definitely not the case, a claim that strengthened Katkov's belief that Ivinskaya had indeed been framed.[55] For some people, including d'Angelo, Schewe's behavior betrayed that he was working as a KGB agent; for others, that he was amazingly naive. Among the latter was another friend of Pasternak's and Schewe's colleague, Gerd Ruge, who had also worked in Moscow from 1955 to 1959 (see Ruge 1958). Ruge was infuriated by the article. While this conflict never made it to the press, some documents in the Schewe archive bear witness to the clash.

Upon reading Schewe's article, Ruge wrote a letter to the director of *Die Welt*, Hans Zehrer, complaining about the article. He did not question Schewe's honesty but pointed out that he was clearly too inexperienced and gullible in regards to the Soviet way.[56] In his opinion, it was clear that the whole Ivinskaya business was a setup. In addition, he sent a teletype message to Schewe questioning ten points in his article, to which Schewe replied point by point. Schewe was calm and matter-of-fact in his replies, but at one point he took umbrage at Ruge's claim that the Soviet authorities were feeding Schewe the text in which he claimed that the

---

55. David Floyd ("Plot against Pasternak," *Sunday Telegraph*, February 5, 1961, p. 5) was also convinced that Ivinskaya was framed.

56. The letter is also of interest in that Ruge, who had left East Germany for West Germany, complained that the experience of people like himself was not valued enough in the West.

punishments would be lessened if the West stopped making a fuss about it. Judging the exchange in light of chapters 1 and 2, it is clear that Ruge did not perceive the facts of the matter accurately and that Schewe was speaking truthfully, citing facts he knew firsthand. On one point Schewe agreed with Ruge: the most pressing matter was to obtain the liberation of Olga and Irina, and disagreement concerning which strategy would yield this outcome was inevitable. He stated:

I agree entirely with you that this is about the fate of two people. You can already see from the date of our publication, which was indeed relatively late, that this was not on account of any sort of journalistic ambition. One can doubtless be of different opinions about the means and methods by which to best help the two women in Moscow. This one must settle by one's own conscience. (Schewe to Ruge, January 27, 1961, Heinz Schewe Papers, Berlin; original in German)

The situation was surely difficult to adjudicate, and as we will show in the next section, there was enough evidence of persecution on the part of the Soviets that suspicion the women had been framed was very natural.

3.7. Surkov: The poet-policeman

Surkov's first official statement, reported by the *Daily Worker* and *l'Humanité*, was the following:

It is simply a question of illegal dealings in foreign exchange and this had nothing to do with Pasternak. I have seen the Public Prosecutor and the judges. They sentenced Olga Ivinskaya to eight years' imprisonment and her daughter Irina to three years: they had illegally received sums of 300,000 and 500,000 rubles. I have received letters and telegrams on this subject from Graham Greene in particular. . . . I replied giving the true facts and expressing surprise: What, you intervene and demand the liberation of rogues of whom you know nothing? Now this is really a question of an illegal currency deal and is not concerned with Pasternak who was a great poet. His family, it must be said, has nothing to do with this sordid story. All these rumors offend the writer's memory. If people abroad wish to respect his memory then they should not stir up mud around him, just because among his friends there was an adventuress. We do not want to interfere in this affair because it has nothing to do with politics or with literature.

Russians, asked why anyone would want to attack Boris Pasternak through his friends, reply: In fact the opposite happened. It was the Writers' Union which made itself responsible for Pasternak's funeral. Last year the State Publishing House published a collection of his translations from Shakespeare and Goethe. Dozens of theaters have put on his translations of *Hamlet* and *Romeo and Juliet.* A literary committee was formed a month after the poet's death to arrange for the publication of his work of which all Russians are very fond, especially that part written before October and which represents his most beautiful poems. The Chair of this committee is Konstantin Fedin who was himself a very close friend of Pasternak and with him Vsevolod Ivanov and Tamara Ivanova, as well as the poet's widow, Zinaida Pasternak. (*l'Humanité*, January 24, 1961; English translation from Conquest 1961b, 117)

Surkov could have added that he himself was in charge of editing a volume of Pasternak's poems that came out in 1961. This, should there be any doubt, was the same Surkov who had persecuted Pasternak, had tried to stop the publication of *Doctor Zhivago* abroad, and had described Pasternak as his personal enemy (see Mancosu 2013, 88–91). To fully understand his duplicitous nature, I think it is worthwhile to recall a few statements Surkov had made earlier about Pasternak.

He [Pasternak] has alienated himself from us and we have no use for him. (Interview with a Yugoslav journalist, *Mladost*, October 2, 1957; English translation from Conquest 1961b, 67)

I do not wish to offend the ears of delegates to the Congress and pronounce the name of the renegade whom our just wrath wrenched from the friendly family of Soviet writers. I mean Pasternak. I am obliged to talk about him since the song and dance raised about the treacherous act of this man of letters is still continuing up to the present moment in the capitalist press. Up to the present time the forces now waging the cold war against us with particular bitterness are grasping convulsively at this rotten rope.

Unfortunately, the market place uproar raised by bourgeois newspapers in connection with the awarding of the Nobel prize to Pasternak and with the fact that we, angered by his unworthy conduct, which was not in accordance with the main articles of the Statutes of the Union, deprived Pasternak of the title of Soviet writer, disoriented certain progressive writers, sowing doubt in their minds as to the correctness of our decision.

To these people who doubt and do not fully understand we say: we cannot tolerate in our ranks a man who, at a time when the peoples of our Motherland are increasing the speed of their movement towards Communism dared, from the rotten émigré-philistine positions of a renegade, who has shown himself to be outside the living movement of history, to cast doubt on everything for which millions of people have given their lives, to cast doubt on everything in which our young literature, linked by thousands of threads of affection with the life of the people, takes pride. (First Constituent Congress of Writers of the Russian Federation, December 7–13, 1958; original in Russian)

And in 1959 in an interview with Alan Moray Williams:

Pasternak is my ideological enemy. I regard him as a talented poet, but a man completely alien to our Soviet way of life. He should have been born 30 years earlier—then he would have been an excellent example of Russian decadence. If I had my way I should turn him out of the country. Pasternak thinks his "Dr. Zhivago" is another "War and Peace." Actually, it is the weakest book he has ever written. It is a petty travesty of history. Throughout the book there is not one sympathetic portrait of a revolutionary. I know that the Stockholm gentlemen who awarded him the Nobel Prize did it from non-literary motives. It isn't true that it was brave of him to publish such a book. Several years ago it would have been brave, but not now. If Russia is such a prison to him, let him go abroad and live on all the money his Italian millionaire-Communist publisher has accumulated for him. (Interview with Alan Moray Williams, *News Chronicle*, January 19, 1959)

Many people, including Feltrinelli, had already seen that behind the mask of ideological opposition, a long-standing personal animosity was responsible for Surkov's stand. In an article published after the Nobel Prize in *Die Zeit*, Feltrinelli wrote:

As Surkov inadvertently said to me, the core of the whole thing is a personal divergence between Surkov and Pasternak. It seems to me that Mr. Surkov abused his political leverage in a highly personal controversy with Pasternak. (G. Feltrinelli, "Wider den Mißbrauch Boris Pasternaks," *Die Zeit*, November 15, 1958)

And this was the very same person who was now rescuing Pasternak for the glory of Soviet letters by attacking Ivinskaya as Pasternak's evil genius.

Surkov's statement preceded by only three days the second broadcast of Radio Moscow on January 27, 1961, which contained an even more scathing attack on Ivinskaya. In addition, it named the majority of foreigners who had been involved in the financial transactions. Interestingly, it also showed that there were several letters from Feltrinelli in the hands of the prosecutors, including, in addition to the one dated July 8, one from June 24, 1960, which had not been mentioned before.[57] Surkov's rancor, and the style of the man, were on great display in February when he came to England with a Soviet delegation, which will be the topic of section 3.9. But first we need to discuss Feltrinelli's declaration.

3.8. Feltrinelli's declaration on behalf of Ivinskaya

International pressure was on Feltrinelli to make a declaration in favor of Ivinskaya. David Floyd wrote an article in the *Daily Telegraph* of January 26 inviting Feltrinelli to come out of his silence: "Friends of the author are hoping that Signor Feltrinelli will shortly make a statement that will help to clear Mrs. Ivinskaya of the charges made against her." Feltrinelli did make a statement on January 27, 1961, which was published in *Avanti* on the following day and extensively quoted in *The Times* on January 30 (p. 6).

A campaign has recently developed in the Western press about the sad events which have occurred to Mrs Ivinskaya, which has resulted in a tangle of conjectures, hypotheses and deductions.

As Boris Pasternak's publisher I have preferred hitherto to refrain from making any statement, because I maintain that controversy in this matter does not help the persons involved in the case—not even the late author's family.

So gross, however, are the inaccuracies reported by the most varied sources, that it is my duty to state today a fact of which I am personally aware.

I myself know that the 100,000 dollars, converted entirely or in part into roubles and transmitted to Moscow, came from funds at the disposal of Boris Pasternak in the West. The amount in question was withdrawn on a written order in the author's own hand, dated 6th December 1959. This order arrived in the West in March 1960.

57. This letter is now published as document 36.

> The bearer of this communication, which I saw with my own eyes, was the same person whom the author designated as the one to whom the sum should be entrusted. I know that the sum was duly withdrawn on 10th March 1960. These are the facts. As for the delay of some months between the date of withdrawal and consignment in Moscow, I maintain this was due as much to the understandable difficulty which Pasternak's emissary experienced in finding the rouble equivalent, as to the actual transfer of currency.
>
> In conclusion, it is my opinion that Olga Ivinskaya is not responsible either for the transfer of the sum or for its eventual destination. In the first place the transfer order was given, I repeat, by Pasternak himself; secondly, it was Pasternak himself who wished that the sum converted into roubles should be sent, without distinction, either to himself or to Mrs Ivinskaya. Nor can one rule out that the wish of the author was, in fact, to consider Olga Ivinskaya as his heiress. I trust therefore that the Soviet judicial authorities will take into account the circumstances which I have related, which are all confirmed by irrefutable documents. (Translation from Italian into English from Conquest 1961b, 110–11)

In this way Feltrinelli, while trying not to irritate the Soviets, clearly stated that Ivinskaya was not to be blamed. It should be pointed out—and I will come back to this later—that Feltrinelli refrained from using some important weapons that he possessed. For instance, he had the signed declaration by Pasternak that granted Ivinskaya power of attorney over his possessions in the West. But all Feltrinelli said was: "I cannot exclude the possibility that the will of the author if properly understood meant that he considered Olga Ivinskaya as his heir." Of course, as shown in chapter 2, we know that Ivinskaya had fabricated the power of attorney dated April 4, 1960 (published in Mancosu 2013, 365–66; reproduced here as illustration 10) to replace the original document lost by the Garritanos. But it is unlikely, although it cannot be excluded, that Feltrinelli knew this. He also did not publish any of the letters between himself and Pasternak that clearly showed Pasternak was at the source of the financial arrangements and not Olga (d'Angelo would publish documents to this effect in May 1961). This was part of Feltrinelli's strategy.

Neither Feltrinelli nor others, such as Isaiah Berlin, had great hopes of influencing the course of events by such declarations. Upon receipt of the declaration, sent to him by Feltrinelli on January 30, Berlin replied as follows.

TO SIGNOR FELTRINELLI
8 February 1961 [*carbon*]
[Headington House]

Dear Feltrinelli,

Thank you very much for your letter and text of your official statement about that very bad and tragic case. I am very glad that you have testified in her favour, though I doubt if it will make much difference to the Soviet authorities, who are not, I think, much moved by the empirical facts of the case. Poor Nivat, I am very, very sorry for him. I do not think there is much that he can do. From the point of view of public relations, what the Soviet authorities have done seems to me a blunder—it cannot be important for internal consumption and it really has [made] an appalling impression here and I think in large circles in France as well. I really think Mr K might use a better public relations adviser.

Signor Tesone is, I hope, doing his best for us. Thank you very much for putting us in touch with him.

Yours sincerely, [Isaiah Berlin] (IBMC, MS. Berlin 164; Isaiah Berlin Literary Trust: © the Trustees of the Isaiah Berlin Literary Trust 2018)

Despite his public declaration, Feltrinelli was persuaded that only "secret" initiatives could make a difference, but things were not easy on that front. After the *Zhivago* affair, Feltrinelli was not in good standing with the Soviets. As Piero Sraffa wrote in a letter to the director of the Istituto Feltrinelli, Giuseppe Del Bo (at the time a member of the Central Committee of the PCI), on September 15, 1960: "On account of Pasternak, the Soviets want nothing to do with Feltrinelli either as a publisher, or as an institute" (cited in Feltrinelli 1999 [English translation], 249). But this was to change in 1961, and we will come back later to Feltrinelli's work behind the scenes on behalf of Olga and Irina.

3.9. The conference on coexistence

On February 23, 1961, British and Russian politicians met at Wiston House, near Stying, Sussex, for a four-day conference on "the principles and practice of coexistence." The conference was organized by the Great Britain–USSR Association, presided over by Earl Attlee. The Russian delegation was headed by Alekseĭ Surkov and included Alekseĭ Adzhubei, editor of *Izvestia* and son-in-law of Khrushchev. In addition, Georgiĭ Zhukov, a minister in charge of cultural relations with foreign countries, was part of the delegation. On the British side, the delegates included, among others, William Hayter, former British ambassador in Moscow, and Isaiah Berlin.

Katkov was able to prepare the ground with the British delegates, as the following letter to Max Beloff (All Souls College, Oxford) shows.[58] Katkov had sent Beloff, one of the British delegates, some materials on the Ivinskaya case probably in late January. Beloff replied on February 9, thanking Katkov for the useful memo and informing him that the Ivinskaya issue would be raised with a Russian delegation coming to England on February 23. On February 16, Katkov informed Beloff about the Soviet composition of the delegation.

16th February 1961

Dear Professor Beloff,

Thank you very much for your letter of the 9th February. It is a wonderful thing that you might have the opportunity of raising the question with that delegation. I understand that it is highly probable that the delegation will include Alexei Surkov the poet and head of the foreign Relations Department of the Soviet Union of Writers. You will probably know that he has been for many years one of the main enemies and detractors of Pasternak; he has behaved abominably in the present affair, his inclusion into a delegation of good will appears to me to be an insult to all those who were working for it in this country. I will receive further documentary information on Surkov's baiting of Pasternak to-morrow night and could make this material available to you in one form or another, if you so desire. But you probably know enough about it as it is. On the other hand I hear that Adzhubei, Khrushchev's son-in-law, might be coming as well. He is an able journalist and has managed to transform Komsomolskaya Pravda and now the Izvestya into almost readable papers. There is a rumour (unconfirmed) that at the height of the Zhivago nobel prize scandal he intervened on behalf of Pasternak with Khrushchev. Another rumour (confirmed) credits him with holding a protecting hand over Dudintsev, the author of "Not by Bread Alone." I have personal knowledge of one case when, at a private request, he intervened and helped a young man who had been sentenced in the Soviet Union. Any approach to Adzhubei should be on a personal basis and certainly not in the presence of Surkov.

58. Max Beloff (1913–1999), British historian and public figure. Beloff's sister, Nora (1919–1997), had visited Pasternak in 1956 and written about him in *Encounter*.

I enclose a further memo on the Ivinskaya case on an analysis of the second Soviet broadcast. I possess the text of the Soviet broadcast as well as the text of Feltrinelli's declaration which I would be glad to show to you, if you think this might be useful. I will be in Oxford during this weekend, and at your disposal at any time.

Your sincerely,
George Katkov (MHP, Oxford)

With this letter in mind, we are now ready to see what happened at the conference on peaceful coexistence, which took place on February 23–26.

The *Daily Telegraph* of February 24 (p. 22) pointed out that Alekseĭ Adzhubei "devoted much of his time in Britain to foisting on the British Press documents intended to blacken the character of Mrs. Olga Ivinskaya, friend of the late Boris Pasternak. The ostensible reason, for his visit to Britain is to spend a week-end in Sussex at a 'peaceful co-existence' conference." Adzhubei presented four items as proof of Ivinskaya's guilt (see illustrations 11, 12, and 13), described as follows in the *Daily Telegraph*:[59]

1) Photographs of bundles of Russian money.[60]
2) Photographs of Italian banknotes cut in two.[61]
3) A photographic copy of a letter said to have been written by Signor Feltrinelli, Pasternak's Italian publisher, to Mrs. Ivinskaya.[62]
4) An all-embracing "confession" addressed by Mrs. Ivinskaya to the interrogation department of the Soviet secret police.[63]

---

59. Copies of the photographs circulated by the Soviets are collectively found in the MHP and the GKP in Oxford.

60. There were three such pictures. See illustrations 11 and 12 for two of them.

61. Many secondary sources are quite inventive as to the exact denomination of the banknotes. Since I have seen the picture brought by the Soviets to England in the Katkov archive in Oxford (see illustration 13), I can correct the false accounts: the banknotes were five-hundred-lira banknotes. This is also confirmed by the other halves of the banknotes (four in total with serial numbers matching the Moscow banknotes), which are still in the Feltrinelli archive in Milan.

62. This is the letter dated July 8, 1960, published in its entirety as document 37.

63. The confession reads:

In the Investigation Department, K G B
STATEMENT
of the accused
Ivinskaya, O.V.

Everything in the accusation is the essential truth. For my part I dispute none of it. (Perhaps with the exception of details about which I myself may have become confused owing to my nervous condition.) On the other hand, I wish to thank the investigator for

The *Daily Telegraph* continued by reporting that an examination of the documents did nothing to substantiate the charges against Ivinskaya, and that "they would not be accepted as evidence in support of the charges in any Western court of law." Moreover, Adzhubei charged the British press with censorship when it declined his request to publish the documents without comment:

> Mr. Adzhubei demanded more than the publication of these documents in the British Press. He wanted them published "without any comment whatsoever" and preferably after the "peaceful coexistence" conference had ended. Mr. Adzhubei has complained that the unwillingness of the British Press to publish his documents shows that there is a censorship working in Britain. He has not however, explained why his own newspaper in Russia has so far contained no reference to the Ivinskaya case about which the Russian public has not been informed. ("'Confession' of Pasternak's friend," *Daily Telegraph and Morning Post*, February 24, 1961, p. 22)

It is remarkable that Feltrinelli's letter dated June 24 was not included in the documents provided by the Soviets. I think it is clear why: the letter indicated that Feltrinelli was in possession of a power of attorney on behalf of Ivinskaya, signed by Pasternak, which gave Ivinskaya the right to sign for him. In short, using letters by Feltrinelli could soon reveal itself a double-edged sword for the Soviets, for they demonstrated just how much Pasternak was in charge of the various business transactions, completely stripping the case against Ivinskaya of substance. Indeed, when Surkov asked the Central Committee for permission to use other documents from the trial proceedings in order to reply to the attacks coming from the P.E.N. Club, his request was denied (see *Le dossier* 1994, 216, 236; Afiani and Tomilina 2001, 309–10, 326). This will be discussed further in the next section.

Let us turn to the reports on Surkov's performance in Sussex as found in letters by Isaiah Berlin and George Katkov. Here is Berlin in a letter to Rowland Burdon Muller from mid-March 1961. The report is too beautiful

---

his tact and correctness, not only in connection with me, but also with my archives, which have been carefully sorted, part of them returned to me, part delivered to the literat. archive, and nothing which I wanted to preserve destroyed.

O. IVINSKAYA

4/xi 1960 (English translation from Conquest 1961b, 120; original in Russian).

not to be quoted at length, for no official report could approximate the vividness of Berlin's description of the events:

My last powerful experience was with the Russian delegation in Sussex. The idea ws that thy shd send some people to meet corresponding British journalists, dons, M.P.'s etc. for a "free" discussion of coexistence. There arrived Mr Adjubey, son in law of Khrushchev: Mr Surkov, the ex-secretary of the Writers' Union & Pasternak's chief persecutor, demoted for the repercussions of his efforts & the fame he brought his enemy, but still a power: Mr Zhukov, Minister of Foreign Cultural Contacts: the editor of *Pravda*, a Professor & lawyer or two & a[n] obvious Secret Policeman who was obviously in charge of them all. "We" were: Fitzroy Maclean M.P.: Nigel Birch M.P. (C) Christopher Mayhew M.P. Dennis Healy M.P. (labour) John Strachey M.P., Profs Beloff & Berlin from Oxford, Alastair Buchan, the foreign editor of the *Times*, Kenneth Younger, the editor of the *Manchester Guardian*, Mr Crankshaw of the *Observer*, an economist or two, etc. You get the general "set up." The whole thing presided over by William Hayter. I didn't join them in the first two days: but I arranged for them all to the opening night of *Fidelio*—a *splendid* performance with Jurinac & Frick & Holter & Vickers conducted *incomparably* by Klemperer, which the Russians apparently *resisted*: why music? why culture? thy hd come to discuss "coexistence" & this ws an irrelevant interruption. However the vy firm Quaker who ws in charge said that all had been arranged, & firmly took them in hand. Once orders are issued thy behave like Prussians or lambs. I went with Aline & Princess Schwarzenberg the Austrian Ambassadress & joined the party at the reception in Cov. Garden. A bunch of thugs they looked & were. In the bus on the wy to the country house in which Germans used to be indoctrinated into British democracy—& which is therefore full of German notices which annoyed the Russians—as well as that *Fidelio* was sung in German—in the bus, Mr Surkov began to tell me why Pasternak's mistress had to go to jail for 8 years for receiving money from P.'s royalties abroad. She ws described as a filthy whore; a woman engaged on subverting not only the financial but the moral politics of the Soviet State; a liar, a cheat, & an evil influence. I ws told that while the English clapped their hands with joy when the bloodstained murderer Hammarskjöld—the enemy of liberty & justice—murdered Lumumba, they cried out with hypocritical horror when a squalid prostitute—who led a man of genius to write his worst book—the worthless Zhivago—ws imprisoned for receiving stolen goods—100-000 dollars sent by the pimp Feltrinelli through the spies he filtered into Russia for P.'s ill gotten royalties obtained by betraying his country—*then* the great British public threw up its hands in horror! Did I know with whom I was sympathising? this woman's husband committed suicide in 1941 why? because he found her secret diary: containing no fewer than

74—74 he repeated in a voice of thunder which reverberated down that poor bus—*lovers*! *this* is the strumpet the British public felt sorry for, Lord Russell wrote about in the *Times* etc. etc. etc. I cd only riposte by saying that I cd not check or deny their *facts*: the trial had not been attended by foreign journalists: but that (a) Pasternak ws the second most famous author in the world now, never mind whether justly or not; anything touching him automatically obtained world wide repercussions; (b) nobody wd *believe* the Russian story, however true: for the motives for persecution were too great. If, I said, the governor of Napoleon III, who had been denounced by, say, Victor Hugo, had put *his* mistress, Mme Sainte Beuve, a widow, in gaol for alleged currency offences, *who* wd have believed them? Karl Marx? One can imagine what *he* wd have written! or Herzen? or Mazzini? Thy cd imprison "evil influences" (it is now plain to me that thy mean to canonise Pasternak, who really *did* loathe them, on the principle of "if you can't beat 'em, join 'em") as much as thy wished: but the effect in the West cd be very melancholy. Thy wd alienate even the left wing intelligentsia, etc. So we went at it ding-dong till we got to Wiston House, Wilton Park, Sussex, & dropped to bed exhausted at 2 a.m.—On the next day we "debated" hammer & tongs. The Russians made nothing but loud propaganda speeches: thy said the *Times* ws a fascist sheet—the poor foreign editor, Trench Macdonald, a most mild, temperate, if anything mildly pro-Soviet man, nearly had a fit: thy said thy didn't read the *M. Guardian* because it ws a worthless liberal paper, the editor there & then left the meeting: they complained that the press hd not given their speeches enough space: thy read long intolerably dreary statements obviously made up in Moscow: "our" delegates, particularly the socialists were fearfully upset: I did not mind: this is mechanical behaviour for them, & after heaping horrible insults of a personal kind on us, thy lunched & dined amiably, as if nothing were the matter. They feel at *war*: war hs certain rules, e.g. sitting on common talks during truces: but as soon as the truce is over, one shoots to kill. It is difficult to get [across] to anyone not there, how vy unnatural & inhuman, these naturally quite human beings, artificially, under orders, become. It is not diplomatic but army training: I prefer the non-dissimulated to the white sepulchres like Surkov or Malik whom I thought of *infinite* nastiness. The new ambassador, Soldatov (appropriately so called) is *much* nicer. I enjoyed it all. I talked their language: I saw, or thought I saw, how and why thy behaved as thy did & what thy wanted & why; & ws instructed. I was amused during the visit to the Brighton Pavilion to a civic reception by the Mayor, to see that thy *could* not decide if the Pavilion ws comical or serious; to laugh or express admiration for this Bokhnan-Chinese rococo fantasy. I loved their insistence on a joint Communiqué which neither side desired to subscribe to few platitudes, because otherwise thy wd be upbraided in Moscow for incurring expenses & doing "no work" etc. I complained to Surkov that I hd just been described in a Soviet publication as "a shameful ignoramus with aspirations to knowledge of 19th Russian culture, expectorating filthy drivel & uttering unoriginal libels against Lenin"[64] he laughed amiably & said that did not matter provided I ws not called by the name of a beast e.g. a hyena, like T. S. Eliot, Hammarskjöld, Auden, Gaitskell etc. which *might* be fatal! So we parted. Much love to you, & do write again: your last letter was quite brilliant.

I.B. (IBMC, Ms. Berlin 269, fols. 178–81; Isaiah Berlin Literary Trust: © the Trustees of the Isaiah Berlin Literary Trust 2018; an excerpt of the letter was already published in Berlin 2013, 29–32)

The second report is found in a letter from Katkov to Graham Greene, written three days after the conference:

27th February 1961.

Dear Mr. Greene,

It is sometime since I received your last kind letter and things have been happening in the Ivinskaya case almost uninterrupted. I enclose a further memo, bringing the thing more or less up to date. What happened since is the arrival of the delegation which was to discuss cultural contacts with a number of public figures under the chairmanship of Sir William Hayter. The delegation included Alexei Surkov and Khrushchev's son in law, Adjubei; I am sure it is not an exaggeration to say that while the main purposes of the delegation was [*sic*] to justify the action the Soviet authorities had taken, with regard to Ivinskaya and her daughter, to blacken their characters and to find out what lies behind the revulsion these events, which are in themselves not exceptional in the Soviet Union, have produced in the public opinion abroad. The delegation tried to foist some photographic copies of documents, kept by the secret police in the Soviet Union, including a letter of confession by Mme Ivinskaya and three

64. As it transpires from a letter to S. M. Breitburg, this refers to a review of Franco Venturi's book on Russian Populism by V. Malinin, which appeared in the January 1961 issue of *Nov'iie Knigi Za Rubezhom* (*Po Obshchestvenn'iim Naukam*). Venturi's book had a preface signed by Berlin. On p. 46 of the review Malinin's references to Berlin were abusive and offensive. The exchange with Breitburg began with a letter from Berlin dated March 9, 1961, and it is found in IBMC, MS. Berlin 164, fols. 189–90; Isaiah Berlin Literary Trust: © the Trustees of the Isaiah Berlin Literary Trust 2018. In a letter to Crankshaw, dated March 16, Berlin quoted a translation of the passage in which he was described as "a vicious reactionary publicist, an ignoramus with pretentions to knowledge about Russian culture, without whose spoonful of tar the barrel of honey constituted by Venturi's Russian Populism would not have been allowed to be translated into English—a contemptible ignoramus who expectorates such pieces of contemptible nonsense as that 'the Populists were by nature religious' and 'Chernyshevsky believed in a simple materialism' etc. etc." The letter is found at IBMC, MS. Berlin 164, fols. 182; Isaiah Berlin Literary Trust: © the Trustees of the Isaiah Berlin Literary Trust 2018.

letters by Feltrinelli to her.[65] I have read these papers and they bring no clarity into the case. Surkov himself has declared both publicly and in private, that Mme. Ivinskaya was "an immoral woman." The Russian expression which he used in a conversation with a friend of mine [Isaiah Berlin] was far more precise, although not quite printable. It appears that the delegation would like public opinion in this country to understand that it is ridiculous to make all that fuss about a whore and her brat caught in dishonest currency dealings. Surkov claimed to know that the first husband of Mrs. Ivinskaya committed suicide having discovered the register she kept of her lovers, he was rather disappointed at my friend's lack of interest for further details. He had also claimed that the first arrest of Ivinskaya had nothing to do with Pasternak and volunteered the information that Mme. Ivinskaya was then in 1948 working for him on the staff of the popular illustrated journal Ogonek, where she had misappropriated some petty cash. The interrogation by Abakumov (Beriya's assistant who was later shot) exists according to Surkov, only in her imagination.

All this does not tarry [*sic*] with other information I have received. A former colleague of Ivinskaya's first husband now in Munich reports that in 1941, he was working in the publishing department of the Central Committee of the C.P. in Moscow. He was denounced by Stalin's private secretary, Poskrebyshev (never heard of since Stalin's death) of having sabotaged the work of his department by filing Central Committee publications under the wrong categories. According to my informer the accused man hanged himself in the lavatory on the premises of the Central Committee. The case aroused much excitement at the time (Spring 1941). The allegation that Ivinskaya was arrested for petty thieving, also does not hold water. She spent over a year in prison and was then sent without being sentenced to concentration camps, from which she was released and restored to all honours of Soviet citizenship immediately after Stalin's death. All this is quite compatible with a political prosecution but not with one for petty thieving.

The important thing is however that Surkov and the other members of the Soviet delegation were firmly persuaded that the fuss about the case in the West will stop in the course of the next two months. Surkov mentioned that you had wired to him for information on the case, and said that he could satisfy you in every respect. On the other hand he was worried about Lord Russell's attitude to the case and wondered who had disturbed the peace of mind of the venerable old gentleman.

From all this you will see that the various interventions, including yours, have on the one hand not led to an immediate release of the two ladies, but have stung the Soviet

65. In the documents preserved in the Max Hayward Papers and the Katkov Papers there is only the letter of July 8. This is probably a misstatement by Katkov.

authorities most painfully and forced them into a defensive attitude in which they have committed further blunders. I have no doubt that by persevering in requesting a clarification and revision of the case, we can hope to make them drop it altogether. I would very much like to discuss with you the practical steps in which this can be done. My friend in his long conversations with Surkov, left him in no doubt that this would be the best course of action for the Soviet authorities in order to avoid Ivinskaya's case in becoming cause celebre in which they would play the part of a historical villain.

I hope I don't bore you too much with this matter, but without a description of these picturesque details, I do not know how to present it adequately.

Your sincerely,
George Katkov (MHP, Oxford)

The information about Olga's first husband had been sent to Katkov by Viktor Frank, who was a colleague in Munich of Vasil'iev Antonovich Chulgoi, who had worked in the Agitprop committee of the CC of the CPSU.[66]

The third report is by Katkov in a letter to Bertrand Russell. While the source of Katkov's report is Berlin, the letter is important because it marks the birth of the Ivinskaya Committee in Oxford.

March 14, 1961
As from:
8, Chalfont Road,
Oxford

Dear Lord Russell,

Please excuse me for not having written earlier. Things in connection with the matter of Mme Ivinskaya have been happening more or less uninterruptedly since your letter appeared in The Times. You will have heard of the conference on coexistence which took place a few weeks ago. At this meeting Isaiah Berlin had a long conversation with the Soviet writer Alexei Surkov who is the head of the Foreign Department of the Union of Writers, and one of Pasternak's main detractors for many years. Surkov started the conversation and expressed amazement at the persistent interest aroused by Ivinskaya's case in this country. He was particularly incensed by the fact that you had taken it up in the press, and wanted to know who had drawn your attention to it. Surkov, who claimed to have studied the case, did not go into any details of the legal

66. The letter from Frank to Katkov is dated January 22, 1961, and is found in the MHP, Oxford.

proceedings against the two unfortunate women, but was very profuse on the theme of Mme Ivinskaya's personal immorality. He even offered to provide a list of her lovers in the thirties and was rather disappointed at Berlin's lack of interest in this story. The delegation to the conference was well supplied with photographs purporting to prove the guilt of Mme Ivisnkaya. I am in possession of copies of these photographs and can only agree with those editors of British papers who decided against publishing them because they throw no real light on the question of whether Mme Ivinskaya was guilty or not, and do not mention the case of her daughter at all. The only important point which emerged from Isaiah Berlin's conversation with Surkov was that they hope in Moscow that the case will soon be forgotten. It is this which I believe should now be prevented. Evidence that the Ivinskaya case will remain in the minds of all those people who will, it is hoped, negociate with representatives of the Soviet Union, might in the end induce the Soviet authorities to put an end to an intolerable situation, and release the two women. It is mainly in order to put this pressure on a permanent basis that the idea was put forward, of forming a committee which would, without undue publicity, serve as a permanent reminder that an error and an injustice has been committed and that an improvement of relations should be greatly helped if reparation was done. I have discussed the matter with Professor Ayer and with Sir Maurice Bowra, Warden of Wadham College, and we have approached a number of personalities in the academic and artistic world asking them to join such a committee. I need not say how important your intervention has been and how valuable your support would be if you could agree to join this committee. This would not involve any loss of time or other trouble for you. All necessary correspondence would be carried out from here and you would be kept informed of any progress.

I am enclosing a memo containing the essential aims of the committee and am sending this letter via Professor Ayer, hoping you will endorse and support my request to you.

Your sincerely,
George Katkov (BRA, McMaster University)

3.10. The Oxford Committee

Russell happily accepted membership in the committee on March 23, 1961. The document outlining its aim, written by Katkov, gave the basic facts of the Ivinskaya case. It stated that the behavior of Soviet authorities gave "rise to suspicion that her [Ivinskaya's] currency offences are in fact only an excuse for settling accounts." It then went on to say that the behavior of Soviet delegates at the conference on "peaceful coexistence" only served to "strengthen this suspicion" and that Surkov and Adzhubei's defensive attitude "suggested that they had much to hide." Katkov then described two of the documents displayed by the Soviets: Olga's "confession" and Feltrinelli's letter dated July 8, 1960. The third part of the document stated the brief of the committee:

> In view of this it is felt by friends of the late poet in the West that there should be continuing efforts to demand further explanations from the Soviet authorities. This is certainly what Pasternak himself would have wished, and it is proposed therefore to set up a committee to explore every possibility of clarifying the position, and of trying to help these two women in their distress.
>
> The aims of the committee will be:
>
> a) to test every possibility of getting the sentences revised, or preferably to obtain a pardon for Ivinskaya and her daughter;
> b) to ascertain the present whereabouts of the two women and the conditions under which they are serving their sentences;
> c) to find out in what way their fate could be alleviated either by the sending of parcels or by visiting them;
> d) to try to ensure that if on her release Ivinskaya's daughter still wanted to marry her fiancé, Georges Nivat, a French citizen, she would be permitted to do so.
>
> The committee will not pursue the task of mobilizing public opinion in the West or of using the Ivinskaya case as a stick to beat the Soviet regime; rather it would try to elicit a sympathetic hearing from Soviet representatives in this country with a view to impressing on them the consternation felt by many people here, and in the hope that such representations might lead to an improvement in the situation of the two women.
>
> It is hoped that the committee will be joined by leading personalities in the academic, literary and artistic worlds and that it will have the benefit of the advice of an eminent lawyer. Apart from a press release on its formation, it is not envisaged that its activities will be publicised in any way. (MHP, Oxford)

Although Katkov was the organizing mind, he was not officially part of the committee. Not all those approached by Bowra, Ayer, and Katkov signed. Here is the list of signatories:

> Kingsley Amis, author, lecturer in English, University College, Swansea
> Noel J. Annan, provost of King's College, Cambridge

Dame Peggy Ashcroft, D.B.E., actress
A. J. Ayer, Wykeham Professor of Logic at Oxford University, fellow of New College, fellow of the British Academy
Sir Maurice Bowra, warden of Wadham College, president of the British Academy
Herbert L. A. Hart, professor of jurisprudence, Oxford University, fellow of University College, Oxford
W. F. Kneale, White's Professor of Moral Philosophy, Oxford University, fellow of Corpus Christi College, Oxford, fellow of the British Academy
John James Osborne, dramatist and playwright
The Earl Russell (Bertrand Russell, O.M.), philosopher and writer, fellow of Trinity College, Cambridge
Dame Rebecca West, D.B.E., author and publicist

The first item on the agenda was to write to the Soviet ambassador in Britain, Soldatov, to secure his "co-operation and recognition of the Committee as body." The hope was that the Soviets "might consider that it is better to be polite with such a Committee than to have a rebuke of it splashed in the press with a renewal of the press campaign which worried them so much in the past."

With this hope in mind, the committee sent a letter on May 27, 1961, under the names of Bowra, Ayer, and Kneale, but signed also on behalf of the remaining members. It requested a meeting with Ambassador Soldatov to discuss the case of Ivinskaya and Emelianova. But the Soviets had no intention of being polite, and the ambassador sent no reply. This lack of success is also evidenced by a memo Ayer sent to the members around June 1961. He informed them that after Soldatov's long silence, he wrote again to Soldatov and again received no reply. Then he and Herbert Hart sent a letter to Madame Furtseva at the Soviet embassy during her visit to London. Once again, there was no reply.

Katkov then mentioned that "another private attempt to approach Soviet authorities, though it has not been totally ignored, has elicited a most unsatisfactory and disturbing reply." He was referring to the exchange between David Carver, the secretary of International P.E.N., and Alekseĭ Surkov. Mention was also made of d'Angelo's reply to Surkov's letter. Katkov ended the memo by wondering "whether the time has not come for us to consider, as a last resort, a public appeal to the Soviet authorities by the committee."

We now turn to the Carver-Surkov-d'Angelo exchange.

3.11. Carver and Surkov

On September 22, 1961, Helen Rogers, secretary to David Carver, sent a letter to Edward Crankshaw that contained important materials Crankshaw needed for an article he was preparing on the Ivinskaya case (which appeared in October 1961). The letter read:

Dear Mr. Crankshaw,

I enclose the promised material concerning Olga Ivinskaya, Alexei Surkov, Mr. Carver and Sergio d'Angelo. This consists of:

1. The relevant portion from Mr. Carver's letter to all Centres, which we hope to despatch to them on Monday (by air, of course). The third paragraph of this stresses the point Mr. Carver wants made clear—that he is at a loss to know how D'Angelo obtained a sight of the letter addressed to Mr. Carver by Mr. Surkov in April.

2. Memorandum for the Centres, containing the texts of the telegrams and the letters exchanged between Mr. Surkov and Mr. Carver (including paragraphs which I have crossed out, on the relations between P.E.N. and Russian writers, which is NOT for public release).

3. Sergio d'Angelo's open letter addressed to Mr. Surkov.

4. Comments made by Max Hayward—but he does NOT wish his name to appear in connection with these, preferring that they be entitled only "Comments by an English friend of the late Boris Pasternak." Naturally, he has no objection to your knowing that he is their author.

Please accept my apologies for the scruffy copy of number 4. . . .

I know Mr. Carver will be very glad to know that you have agreed to tackle this matter, and hope very much that it will be possible to include a great deal of the material. (MHP, Oxford)

Despite their importance, these documents have never been published in the original English. They appeared in Italian in September–October 1961 in *Tempo Presente*, and then as part of the Pasternak dossier from the Central Committee of the CPSU; in French in *Le dossier* 1994, 216–34; and in Russian in Afiani and Tomilina 2001, 309–25, translated from the Italian published version. Since the documents are long, I will briefly summarize their contents here and refer the reader to document 51, where I publish them in their entirety.

The exchange between David Carver and A. Surkov began in January with a telegram from Carver to Surkov expressing concern about the condemnation of Ivinskaya and Emelianova. A press release dated January 19, 1961, informed the public of the contents of Carver's telegram to Surkov, which urgently appealed to Surkov to intervene to "secure [the] release [of] Madame Olga Ivinskaya and her daughter." A telegram along similar lines was sent in January by the English Centre of International P.E.N.[67] Surkov replied on January 24, dismissing the relevance of the Ivinskaya case to a body such as P.E.N. According to Surkov, there were neither moral nor legal grounds for intervening in the case, for Ivinskaya and her daughter had been condemned in a court of law for criminal offenses related to "currency machinations." Carver replied on January 24 by pointing out that everyone in the West was well aware of who Ivinskaya was and of her relation to Pasternak. Carver asked that the trial proceedings be made public. He also wrote a longer letter on January 30 in which he reiterated his plea for clemency and pointed out how badly this case would affect the relations between P.E.N. and the Soviet Writers' Union.

No answer was sent to this request, but Carver met Surkov while the latter visited England with the Soviet delegation in February 1961. Surkov replied to Carver on April 4 with a long letter that summarizes the Soviets' point of view on the Ivinskaya case. Surkov claimed to have studied the three thick volumes making up the trial proceedings and, while he made no concessions on any point, his letter delivered some interesting infor-

67. The Austrian P.E.N. Club also sent a telegram of protest to the Soviet embassy in Vienna. It was published together with another document of protest sponsored in France by the philosopher René Tavernier (1915–1989) and addressed to Khrushchev, which was signed by prominent intellectuals such as Pierre Emmanuel, Denis de Rougemont, Stephen Spender, Reinhold Niebuhr, Ignazio Silone, and Lionello Venturi. See the published protests in *Forum* 8, no. 16 (February 1961): 48. As for the American Centre of P.E.N., its president, V. J. Chute, informed Max Hayward on February 9, 1961, that she had recorded an interview on the subject for Radio Liberty the previous week, and also provided the text of the cablegram sent to Khrushchev and the minister of justice of the USSR. The letter is found in the MHP, Oxford. Later correspondence between Chute and Hayward provides details of the activities of the American P.E.N. Club (see especially the letter from Chute to Hayward dated February 1, 1962), with an impressive list of American intellectuals mobilized to try to appeal to Soviet writers on behalf of Olga and Irina. The only reply, addressed to Edgar Johnson (P.E.N. president), came in August 1961 from Marietta Shaginyan, who emphasized the plight of Pasternak's widow, Zinaida Nikolaevna.

mation.[68] In that letter he accused d'Angelo of being an "international swindler." Surkov then expressed his point of view on the proper way to establish relations between P.E.N. and the Soviet Writers' Union.[69]

Carver closed the exchange with a letter dated April 26. Surkov, as we know, did his best to smear Ivinskaya's reputation, but he also made a terrible blunder. At a reception at the Soviet embassy in February, he promised that Ivinskaya would be released within a few months. Carver reminded him of that promise in his last letter, dated April 26, 1961. This was certainly a source of embarrassment for Surkov, who probably had to justify his statement in front of higher authorities in the USSR.

We now turn to d'Angelo's reply.

3.12. D'Angelo strikes back

On account of Olga's arrest, Sergio d'Angelo broke off relations with Feltrinelli in September 1960. D'Angelo had gone to Moscow as a tourist in September 1960 (entering the USSR on September 4 and leaving on the 10th) with his wife, Giulietta, but did not manage to meet either Olga or Irina. He met Mitia, Irina's half-brother, but the latter was too terrified to admit that his mother and his sister had been arrested. When d'Angelo returned to Italy he met with Feltrinelli, who confronted him with the news and accused him of having been the cause of Olga's arrest. At that moment neither Feltrinelli nor d'Angelo knew that Irina had also been arrested. On September 22, Feltrinelli circulated a memo informing other

68. In chapter 2, I have, for instance, made use of the reference made by Surkov to the three blank sheets of paper with only Pasternak's signature, which were included in the files for the trial.

69. A report from Moscow originating with the news agency Reuters, published in *The Times* of April 1, shows how stung Surkov was by the polemic from P.E.N. and that he was also meeting some opposition among his colleagues: "Moscow, March 31. Mr. Alexei Surkov, secretary of the board of the Soviet Union of Writers, today attacked western writers over the Ivinskaya affair, which he described as a 'shameful action perpetrated against the memory of our late highly respected colleague, Boris Pasternak.'" After giving some background, the article continued: "Mr. Surkov, speaking today at a meeting of Soviet Writers, attacked the International P.E.N. Club and suddenly raised the subject of Mrs. Ivinskaya. . . . Mr. Surkov's attack on P.E.N. as an 'aristocratic association of anti-Soviet cold war émigrés' was frequently interrupted by Marietta Shagginyan [*sic*], a seventy-three-year-old poetess, with cries of 'nonsense, nonsense.' At one point she protested, 'I met P.E.N. Club members and they were very kind to me and the Soviet Union.' Mr. Surkov replied, 'They said they did not want to meet Soviet writers, as their hands were dirty with blood. You shut up, you don't know what you are talking about'" (p. 7).

members of his publishing house that d'Angelo no longer worked for the publishing house.

In September 1960 very few people in the West knew about Olga's arrest. D'Angelo was one of them, but he did not go public with the news. He later explained his silence on account of his not being sure whether the news was correct. Be that as it may, d'Angelo's name was certainly mentioned, and often not very charitably, by those who had an interest in the Ivinskaya case. Katkov, for instance, had no doubt that the Italians had engaged in foul play (he spoke of "mediterranean crookery"). Feltrinelli was the first to state, at the end of January 1961, that it was Pasternak who had requested a sum of $100,000. But it was left to d'Angelo to provide the evidence, in a series of articles that came out in May 1961. In addition, in June 1961 his open letter rebutting Surkov's charges appeared in *Vita* and was soon circulated in Britain.

D'Angelo had a chance to tell his side of the story in two long articles in Italian for *Vita* published on May 11 and May 18, 1961, respectively. A shortened version of the two articles (with some minor discrepancies) appeared in English (*Sunday Telegraph*, May 7, 1961, pp. 7–8) and French (*Paris Jour*, May 7, 8, and 9, 1961). The English and French versions both included a photographic reproduction of Pasternak's handwritten note authorizing Sergio d'Angelo to access $100,000 of his royalties.

I think it is fair to say that these two articles constituted a major step forward in the understanding of the affair. This was not secondhand gossip, but rather the account of someone who had been in the very eye of the hurricane.

In addition to a quite reliable account of the facts, d'Angelo also published photographic reproductions of several documents: one letter from Pasternak to Proyart; one letter from Pasternak to d'Angelo; the warrant for d'Angelo to obtain $100,000 on behalf of Pasternak signed by Pasternak himself; a receipt for 44,000 rubles signed by Pasternak on February 8, 1960, namely the sum Paladini had brought to Pasternak; and a letter from Ivinskaya to d'Angelo.

D'Angelo's explanation for his long silence was also motivated, as he was to state in a later letter to Khrushchev in March 1962, by a desire not to add to the heated exchange.[70] He spoke of an "error" and did not accuse

70. The draft of the letter is preserved in the SdAP, HILA.

the Soviets of "calculation" (d'Angelo 2006, 210). In an article published on May 11, 1961, he wrote:

> There is one explanation that I would like to make at the outset. When it was learned in the West that Olga IVINSKAYA and her daughter Ira had received prison sentences I was asked by many people to make a public statement on the matter, especially those aspects with which I was directly or indirectly concerned. Since my first impulse had been to take this step I found the request quite natural. Nevertheless, after considering my position with care, I was seized by some doubts; if I made a statement to the press at the very time that Radio Moscow was giving an entirely different account of the affair it seemed to me that my move might be interpreted by Soviet authorities simply as a hostile gesture intended not so much to favour the cause of justice as to throw further oil on the flames. I might thus have aggravated the plight of IVINSKAYA and her daughter and have made it less likely that their sentence would be annulled or at least reduced by means of a new trial, or through some act of clemency.
>
> I expressed these thoughts in a talk with the legal adviser of FELTRINELLI and was advised by him to wait. He told me that FELTRINELLI would make a short statement (which in fact appeared immediately afterward in the newspapers) promising to contact qualified Soviet representatives as soon as the IVINSKAYA news dropped out of the headlines and could be discussed in private in clearer and more practical terms. He pointed out that the numerous letters which PASTERNAK had sent to FELTRINELLI had not been published and that this was the best possible proof of a reasonable and conciliatory attitude. A meeting at a later stage might therefore be expected to produce useful results.
>
> I accepted this advice, not so much out of optimism as because I felt that even the faintest hope of saving the two women should not be prejudiced by too precipitous action. I realize that my silence may have aroused doubts in many people's minds, and that it caused many erroneous ideas about the PASTERNAK case to establish themselves, but I am still not sure that my action was ill considered. Three months have now passed since the sentence was passed, and though there has been complete silence about the affair for several weeks there has been no encouraging move or indication from the other side. At least my silence up to now allows me to speak in a less heated and perhaps more attentive atmosphere, and I hope that what I have to say will be heard not only by public opinion in the West but also—and above all—by the Soviet authorities. I should like to speak with complete frankness and hope to avoid any kind of resentment and recrimination. ("Olga è innocente," *Vita*, May 11, 1961, p. 8; original in Italian.)

Unfortunately, this part of the article was not translated into English, but it was included in the French article. In any case, the Italian and French articles were known among those in England who were concerned with the Ivinskaya affair.

In his recent book, d'Angelo (2006, 194) adds that he had a chat on October 11, 1960, with one of Feltrinelli's lawyers, who told him it was quite possible that Olga and Irina might be sentenced to reside outside Moscow and that, awaiting more precise news, it would be counterproductive to raise the issue in the newspapers. Feltrinelli owed this positive, although tentative, appraisal of the situation to Schewe, who would also state this point of view in his article in *Die Welt* in February 1961. D'Angelo's conclusion of the article published in the *Sunday Telegraph* (May 7, 1961) left no doubt as to Olga's innocence:

> Though I played a direct part in the affair I was ever conscious of the secondary nature of my role. The person who took the initiative and the decisions was Pasternak himself. Not I and not Ivinskaya.

At some point in late May or early June, d'Angelo managed to see the private correspondence between Carver and Surkov.[71] Surkov's attack on him led d'Angelo to publish an open letter in *Vita*, which appeared in the June 21 issue and was soon circulated among those in Britain who were engaged in the Ivinskaya campaign.

D'Angelo dismissed Surkov's "pornographic inventions" concerning Ivinskaya's alleged immorality, and dismantled effectively what was by then the obvious strategy of the Soviets, namely to readmit Pasternak into the realm of Soviet literature by claiming that his failures (such as *Doctor Zhivago*) were the consequence of the pernicious influence of an adventuress like Ivinskaya. D'Angelo then denounced Surkov's unctuous posturing as a friend of the poet by reminding him that his personal animosity had caused this international scandal:

71. As we saw in the previous section, Carver expressed surprise that d'Angelo had access to what was considered private correspondence. When asked about it in December 2014, d'Angelo did not recall who might have given him the materials and conjectured that it was either David Floyd or a dissident friend in the Soviet Writers' Union. Floyd strikes me as the more plausible candidate.

> I am perfectly well aware, Mr. Surkov, of your state of mind. You have always hated Pasternak, and dominated by this feeling, you carried out, as first secretary of the Writers' Union, a series of ill-considered acts that did your country a very poor service. In promoting the campaign for the banning of *Dr. Zhivago* ("a novel written against me," as you once said, not without presumption) and in pursuing it with methods both mean and childish, you transformed a literary matter, about which Soviet readers could themselves have debated without passion, into an international scandal. Then, when Pasternak was awarded the Nobel Prize, you lost your head completely and, because you have the vice of using coarse language, you said and caused to be said against the author of *Dr. Zhivago* things that aroused widespread indignation in every country and caused even in Communist circles the most profound embarrassment. Still not content, you finally demanded Pasternak's expulsion from the Writers' Union, and who knows how far you would have gone, if the highest authorities in your country, intervening out of love for their country, had not stopped you and later relieved you of your duties as first secretary. (*Vita*, June 21, 1961; original in Italian; for a full translation of the letter see document 51)

D'Angelo then challenged Surkov to publish the letters that proved his accusations. As it appears now from the documents from the CC of the CPSU, Surkov did ask permission to use more materials from the trial proceedings, but that permission was not granted. I will discuss this in the section on Crankshaw.

3.13. News about Olga and Irina

Not much was known in the West about Olga and Irina's situation during these months.[72] Nivat obtained some news from the period up to the trial, which we have reported, through Olga's mother, Maria Nikolaevna Bastr'ikina. Nivat then communicated the information to Peltier or Katkov. While serving in Algeria in 1961, Nivat received occasional news

72. In 1997, the journal *Moskovsky Komsomolets* published brief excerpts of a letter from Olga Ivinskaya to Khrushchev dated March 10, 1961. While not relevant to the topic of the news that reached the West, I mention it only for completeness. The attempts to use this letter as evidence that Olga was a KGB informer strike me as ludicrous. The excerpts were published at a time when there was a struggle between Ivinskaya's heirs and the State Archive of Literature and Art concerning the Pasternak archival material that was taken from Ivinskaya in 1960. See Toomey 1996 for an overview and Mansurov 2009, chapter 2, for further details concerning the destiny of the Pasternak archive that was taken from Ivinskaya's apartment.

through Olga's mother and through a French friend studying at Moscow State University, who collected news from a friend of Irina's, the niece of Konstantin Paustovskiĭ (see letter to Katkov dated April 18, 1961; MHP).[73] Through a card from Maria Nikolaevna, for instance, Nivat was informed that on April 6, Irina and Olga had been moved from Siberia to a new location closer to Moscow, although Maria Nikolaevna did not know where.

Maria Nikolaevna was also a source, though not the only one, for Schewe. In an article in *Die Zeit* titled "Iwinskaja aus Sibierien zurück," dated May 3, 1961, Schewe informed readers that Olga and Irina had been transferred from a Siberian camp near Irkutsk to the labor camp in Potma, Mordovia, five hundred kilometers southeast of Moscow. Their status had improved:

> Olga Ivinskaya and Irina Emelianova may write and receive letters. They correspond with close friends and relatives in Moscow. A limited number of packages—four per month—and smaller monetary remittances are allowed. Also, visitations by close relatives are permitted.

According to Schewe, rumor had it that Olga and Irina had been less unhappy in the former Siberian camp, but close acquaintances of the two women thought the transfer was a positive sign. The article conveyed much optimism that the Soviet justice system might decide to revisit the case and that the revision could take into account that Olga and Irina had not actively broken the currency law—that is, they accepted but did not smuggle the rubles. Schewe mentioned that the milder punishment might simply ban them from residing in the six main city districts of the Soviet Union, including Moscow, Kiev, and Leningrad, with full restoration of freedom apart from that restriction.

Schewe's article gave hope, at least to some people, that the Soviets might reverse their stand toward the two women. However, it was not to be so, at least not immediately.

More detailed news arrived with a letter from Schewe to Feltrinelli dated June 1, 1961:

---

73. Nivat does not reveal the friend's name, but she was Galina A. Arbuzova, a fellow student of Irina's at the Litinstitut. She is mentioned several times in the correspondence between Ariadna Efron and Irina Emelianova (Emelianova 2004). One ought to keep in mind that Ariadna Efron also had an extensive correspondence with Irina and that she was exchanging information with Maria Nikolaevna and Mitia (Emelianova 2004).

Moscow/Hotel Berlin/516
June 1, 1961

Dear Giangiacomo, dear Inge,

I have heard nothing from you for a long while. It is also difficult for me to write. Much work and little joy in Moscow.

I have carefully reestablished the connection with Olga and her relatives. I occasionally meet with Mitia, the son, and with Maria Nikolaievna, Olga's mother. This way I learn a little about how it is going for Olga and Ira. They are allowed to write letters and send packages—two packages per person per month are permitted.

Olga and Ira find themselves for the moment in camp 385/14 in Potma (Mordovian ASSR) in the Pensa province, some 500 kilometers away from Moscow. Previously, they were in a Siberian camp in Irkutsk for a few months. The trip there took three weeks in January 1961. In April they were then transferred to Potma. They fancy it there less than in the Irkutsk camp. They are together with all sorts of criminal elements. "One cannot even sleep soundly," wrote Olga recently to her mother. She wants to try getting moved to another camp section in Potma. She submitted a request for transfer from Nr. 14 to Nr. 17. Nr. 17 is said to have only "political" prisoners. At the moment, Olga is in the camp hospital. Kidney issues and other such. She feels quite awful. Both have apparently lost a lot of weight, as reported by Mitia, who visited them at the beginning of May. For 24 hours he was together with them in the camp. They live in barracks that are crowded.

They are allowed to read newspapers and go to the camp library. Letters are censored. Foreign mail or even foreign words in letters are not permitted. Thus, Ira must give up furthering her foreign language studies. I have until now sent four letters with harmless contents and an undisguised sender. Don't know whether they arrived.

At the moment, Ira is doing somewhat better. At the beginning she was doing quite poorly healthwise. Now she gets glucose injections. She has become frighteningly thin, Mitia reports.

The apartment in Potapov Street was also forcibly reduced in size. A subletter moved into Ira's room, apparently an exceptionally unbearable person. The housekeeper Paulina and Mitia live in the two remaining rooms. The dacha in Peredelkino was given up. I was at the cemetery in Peredelkino on Tuesday. I often visit Boris Leonidovich's grave. On Tuesday there were many flowers there. I brought a pretty bouquet in Olga and Ira's name, and also in yours, dear Giangiacomo. I have heard nothing from the Pasternak family.

Ms. Olga sends heartfelt greetings to you through Mitia, and the wish to indeed break with d'Angelo, who is to blame for everything. I told Mitia that that had, to my knowledge, already happened. They were apparently appalled and furious at Sergio d'Angelo's reckless behavior.

Mitia was already interrogated again on account of our meeting. He makes quite a distraught impression. They want to try, with the help of a lawyer, to get the case reopened. There is probably not much hope there. The Western scandal has worsened things needlessly. Moreover, the intensified penal laws have come out here, which also complicate an early pardon. The lawyer, though, thinks these conditions cannot be retroactively applied. Perhaps there will be an amnesty this autumn at the 22nd Party Congress. Olga also pegs her hopes on the doctor. A medical commission is expected in Potma. Perhaps her poor health will help her.

I myself had a few unpleasantries on account of the ruble affair. My position in Moscow has become quite difficult and unpleasant because of it—and on account of the staunch stance that "WELT" has taken. I am at times very tired and distressed. Both sides are at my heels. All of my goodwill to build bridges has not led to any satisfying results so far. Mostly I would like to pack up my things and go home for good. But there is Elena, who at the moment is on a longer tour in the province near Moscow. And then I need to think also of Olga and Ira. Perhaps I can yet be useful to them after all. In any case my presence in Moscow gives them courage and hope, Mitia says.

My nerves, though, have all been much taken up with these recent occurrences. I plan to take a holiday in August or September. This time still without Elena. A wedding under the current circumstances is unthinkable before the end of the year. The whole undertaking "wedding in Moscow" remains as doubtful as ever.

Now and again I give Olga's mother some money from my own pocket. With it she buys groceries for the packages and keeps herself provisionally above water. All of this must nevertheless happen very discreetly. I can no longer count on being a "persona grata" in Moscow.

Hoping that times will get better. Heartfelt greetings to you,

[*handwritten*] Your Heinz Schewe (AGFE, Busta 1, fascicolo 5, "Feltrinelli-Schewe (1959 febbraio 15–1966 dicembre 07)"; original in German)

Apart from a few cards from Irina to Nivat that miraculously went through and brought some news of Irina and Olga, that was pretty much all the news that arrived in the West.

3.14. Edward Crankshaw

Crankshaw had shown an immediate interest in the Ivinskaya case. On January 22, 1961, he had published an article in *The Observer* that gave basic information about the arrests and sentencing of Ivinskaya and Emelianova and suggested what might be behind it:

Speculation about the real reason for this savage reversion to the bad old ways runs wild in many directions. But only time will tell whether it was an act of clumsy revenge or part of an elaborate plan to discredit the Pasternak who wrote "Dr. Zhivago" by preparing the way to show that it was written under the influence of a worthless woman, perhaps even tampered by her. (*The Observer*, January 22)

On February 10, 1961, Katkov wrote to Crankshaw, "I would like you to know how much I appreciate and admire the stand which you have taken in this distressing affair which has been the object of my preoccupations during the last few weeks, in your articles in the Observer" (MHP). Crankshaw replied:

How very kind of you to go to the trouble of writing about my poor efforts on behalf of Madame Ivinskaya. I know from Manya Harari that you have been very active in the background; and I do deeply appreciate your words of approval. Alas, it is all too little that one can do. I cannot go on featuring it in *The Observer* week after week. But I shall not let it drop and I shall touch on it from time to time as occasion offers in public. At the same time I shall continue to work away in private as hard as I can. It is not a thing to be given up: as you so correctly say, the Russians would like nothing better than to feel that all they have to do is to brazen it out for a few weeks until the whole affair is quietly allowed to fall to the ground. In a few days' time, for my sins, I shall be meeting Surkov himself. (MHP, Oxford)

Crankshaw did not let it drop. In addition to the early articles, he wrote a major story for *The Observer* of October 1, which brought the reader up to date with the Carver-Surkov-d'Angelo exchange (which had meanwhile been sent to the different branches of P.E.N.).[74] The article repeated

74. Another article by Crankshaw published in March was praised by Berlin in a personal letter to Crankshaw dated March 4, 1961 (see IBMC, MS. Berlin 164; Isaiah Berlin Literary Trust: © the Trustees of the Isaiah Berlin Literary Trust 2018). The major story is reprinted in Crankshaw 1984, 82–88.

Surkov's obscene characterization of Ivinskaya, which bothered Nivat. However, Hayward explained to Nivat that this had been carefully planned:

> About Crankshaw (to which there has been no reaction we have heard of so far), your mixed feelings are of course very understandable, but we did go into this point very carefully with him, very much from your point of view. He succeeded in persuading us—and I really think that he is right—that it was essential to include Surkov's obscenities. It is really a matter of knowing one's public, and I can assure you that at least here and among the sort of people who read the Observer particularly, these allegations—*quite irrespective of their truth or not*—could only evoke sympathy for their target and disgust for their author. The private reaction that I have heard fully confirmed that this is so. (Hayward to Nivat, October 19, 1961, MHP, Oxford)

As Feltrinelli put it in a letter to Secchia that contained Crankshaw's article as an enclosure, Surkov's declarations did not befit a public official of the Soviet Union.[75]

Crankshaw's article and d'Angelo's reply stung Surkov. In a letter of November 25, 1961, addressed to the Central Committee of the CPSU, Surkov requested permission to use more documents from the Ivinskaya dossier to reply to the campaign against him. The campaign, he explained, described him as a "dinosaur" of the party and a "poet-policeman." He singled out the journalist E. Crankshaw and "the renegade communist" Sergio d'Angelo as the instigators (*Le dossier* 1994, 216; Afiani and Tomilina 2001, 309–10). Judging that Western forces might interpret the release of new documents as weakness on the part of the Soviets, D. Polikarpov, in a letter dated November 30, 1961, asked permission from the CC of the CPSU to inform Surkov that his request was denied (*Le dossier* 1994, 234–35; Afiani and Tomilina 2001, 326).[76] Suslov agreed with Polikarpov, and Surkov was informed of the negative decision on December 10.

3.15. Giangiacomo Feltrinelli's work behind the scenes

We have seen that Feltrinelli had intervened publicly only by means of a statement dated January 27, 1961. From the very beginning in the summer

75. The letter is dated October 12, 1961, and is preserved in the Feltrinelli archives.
76. The letter also stated that nothing had appeared in the Soviet press on the Ivinskaya trial.

of 1960, he had agreed with Nivat and Schewe that one should keep the case out of the press but was forced by events to make a public statement. By the time Nivat met him at Berlin's house in Oxford in December 1960, Nivat had become persuaded that Feltrinelli had decided to sacrifice Olga Ivinskaya:

I met M. Feltrinelli in Oxford at Sir Isaiah Berlin's home, and I realized that he will do nothing for Olga Vsevolodovna. She has ceased to be useful. (Nivat to Peltier, December 17, 1960, Hélène Peltier Archives; original in French)

But Nivat's judgment of Feltrinelli's intentions was premature, and Feltrinelli's actions may have played some role, although we cannot say for sure, in reducing the detention sentences of Olga and Irina.

Let us reconstruct what Feltrinelli was up to. Not much seems to have happened in Milan during the first few months of 1961 except for Feltrinelli's declaration. Even the correspondence between Schewe and Feltrinelli had stopped, only to be resumed by a long letter from Schewe dated June 1, 1961, informing Feltrinelli of some recent news he had obtained about Olga and Irina (the letter was quoted in section 3.13 above). In Feltrinelli's reply, dated June 21, 1961, we find Feltrinelli asking himself what he could do to improve Olga and Irina's situation and indicating that contacts with the Soviets had resumed:

Olga and Irina's situation is nothing less than appalling. What can be undertaken on that account? Should I perhaps write to Khrushchev and ask him to exercise mercy in this case, also in order to shut up those people who only care about Irina and Olga because they want to inflate themselves with a cheap anticommunism? The attitude of the Russians vis-à-vis the Feltrinellis has changed this year. Although they entirely ignore the publishing house, they have reestablished scientific relations with the [Feltrinelli] Institute, and indeed went so far as to invite three colleagues to the Marx Engels Institute in Moscow.

It would also be interesting to know if we, in the case of a trial review, could undertake something or other. Do you think I could perhaps send a public ambassador of mine to Moscow, or rather come myself, to carry out some sort of negotiation? (AGFE, Busta 1, fascicolo 5, "Feltrinelli-Schewe (1959 febbraio 15–1966 dicembre 07)"; original in German)

The renewed contacts with the Institute Marx-Engels-Lenin (IMEL) in Moscow gave rise to what Feltrinelli, hoping to obtain concrete results for

Olga and Irina, later called "unilateral disarmament."[77] Attempts to reestablish contact with IMEL go back to early 1959, when Palmiro Togliatti, the secretary of the Italian Communist Party (PCI), offered support to the director of the Istituto Feltrinelli, Giuseppe Del Bo, in a letter dated March 2, to facilitate a possible invitation for Del Bo to go to Moscow with an invitation from IMEL.[78] Del Bo asked Togliatti again about this possibility in a letter dated December 11, 1959. The initiative was also supported by Mario Alicata, responsible for the Culture Department of the PCI, who, in a letter dated December 19, 1959, pointed out to Togliatti that one should make Del Bo (and thus Feltrinelli) understand that renewal of the contact required the help of the PCI.[79] But Alicata looked favorably upon the initiative because it would have given the PCI tighter control of the activities of the Istituto Feltrinelli. Togliatti wrote to Del Bo on February 22, 1960, expressing the view that "the contacts should and could be renewed."

The correspondence from this year is also remarkable in that it reveals a cordial relation between Togliatti and Feltrinelli (with greetings between Feltrinelli and Togliatti conveyed via Del Bo). But it was only in 1961 that things moved again. After the successful visit of A. E. Boltin, an IMEL specialist in military history, at the Istituto Feltrinelli in Milan in March 1961, the president of IMEL, Pëtr Pospelov, recommended to the Central Committee of the CPSU in May that they invite the top echelon of the Istituto Feltrinelli to Moscow, with a view toward establishing scientific contacts.[80] In a letter to Pospelov on October 9, 1961, Feltrinelli thanked

---

77. The details of how IMEL, by means of the PCI, brought about renewed relations with the Istituto Feltrinelli are recounted in Feltrinelli 1999, 231–35. The letters cited in this section are found in the Fondo Carlo Feltrinelli, serie Senior Service, GGF Miscellanea, fascicolo "Biblioteca e Istituto Feltrinelli 1951–1972."

78. Giuseppe Del Bo (1919–1981) was instrumental in founding the Istituto Giangiacomo Feltrinelli and the Annali dell'Istituto Giangiacomo Feltrinelli. The transformation from the original Biblioteca Feltrinelli to the Istituto Feltrinelli can be dated to 1956, when Del Bo became the director of the Istituto (which, replacing Biblioteca Feltrinelli, was formally recognized in 1960).

79. The reader needs to keep in mind that on account of the publication of *Doctor Zhivago* and its aftermath, Feltrinelli had not renewed his membership in the PCI as of 1958.

80. Between 1942 and 1949, Pëtr Nikolaevich Pospelov (1898–1979) was the main editor of *Pravda*. He was director of IMEL between 1949 and 1952. He was head of the commission that prepared the report on Stalin's crimes, read by Khrushchev at the 20th Party Congress in February 1956. During the Pasternak affair, he was both a member of the Central Committee of the CPSU and a member of the Presidium. From 1953 to 1960, Pospelov was secretary of the Central Committee of the CPSU. He was again director of IMEL from 1961 to 1967, and during the Ivinskaya affair he was also a member of the Central Committee and candidate member of the presidium of the Central Committee of the CPSU.

him for the invitation and the warm welcome that had been extended to the representatives of the Istituto Feltrinelli.

From what can be gathered from the letter, the director of the Istituto, Del Bo, and his collaborator Enzo Collotti had visited IMEL at some point in September or early October 1961. They also visited the Academy of Sciences. Taking advantage of the improved climate, Feltrinelli decided to send Pospelov a dossier consisting of several original letters Pasternak had sent him, expressing the hope that his action could lead to "a factual collaboration in the scientific realm and more generally to the strengthening of the respective cultural traditions and to the preservation, with every mean, of peace." Then he added:

> It is exactly in this spirit that I take the liberty to send you a small dossier. I deem it more appropriate that it be kept in Moscow. It is needless to explain the importance, from a human point of view, these documents have had for me. But I will have deprived myself of them all the more willingly if this decision of mine will be considered as a step toward bringing an episode to closure. (Feltrinelli to Pospelov, October 9, 1961; original in Italian)

The papers in question included five original letters from Pasternak to Feltrinelli and a photocopy of another letter from Pasternak to Feltrinelli.[81] There is no question that Feltrinelli was showing that he was ready to make amends with the Soviets. He concluded his letter by saying: "In my personal activity and in that of my publishing house, the friendship with your country and the Soviet people will always be foremost in my mind."

While this episode might be of even greater interest for reconstructing a key moment in Feltrinelli's biography, I will focus here on the specifics of the Ivinskaya case. There are, in fact, some other letters that clarify how much hope Feltrinelli had invested in the possible results of his action. Writing to Pietro Secchia on October 11, 1961, Del Bo forwarded the unsealed envelope with the dossier prepared by Feltrinelli, and asked Secchia to deliver the envelope to Togliatti with the request that Togliatti hand the envelope personally to Pospelov, something he said was, in his opinion, "extremely important."[82] And the day after, Feltrinelli wrote

81. These letters are published in Mancosu 2013, 3.3, 3.6, 3.12, 3.22, 3.38, 3.39.

82. Pietro Secchia (1903–1973) was vice-secretary of the Italian Communist Party (PCI) from 1948 to 1955, and was responsible for the propaganda section of the party. He was a close friend of Feltrinelli's. In 1954, as a consequence of the Seniga affair and increasing differences with the

to Secchia confirming the arrangements and expressing the core of his strategy:

I hope that this gesture of "unilateral disarmament" on my part might lead, in the appropriate places, to considering the opportunity to lighten the destiny of Ivinskaya and her daughter: an act of clemency or a reduction of the punishment leading in any case to their being freed, which, in addition to constituting a great relief for me personally, would also offer the Soviets the advantage of closing successfully [*in bellezza*] the polemic with political and intellectual circles in London and Paris, a polemic that otherwise risks dragging on for a long time. It would perhaps be possible to draw the attention of the Soviets to the opportunity that when one arrives in the imminent future at a détente of the situation in international politics, they would be able to include in the various actions and deeds that they will be achieving also something concerning the two Ivinskayas. I would be very grateful if you could intervene directly or indirectly in this sense. (Feltrinelli to Secchia, October 12, 1961; original in Italian)

Secchia confirmed in a letter to Del Bo, dated October 12, 1961, that he had handed the letter and the dossier to Togliatti, who "seems to have appreciated the gesture in its value" and confirmed that Togliatti would hand everything to Pospelov personally.

This, then, was Feltrinelli's attempt on behalf of Olga and Irina. By handing over the originals of Pasternak's letters without having published them or any other documents signed by Pasternak in Olga's favor, such as some of Pasternak's powers of attorney for Olga, he had saved the Soviets from public embarrassment, for those documents showed that Pasternak was in control of the financial arrangements all along, and thus would have exposed the lie in the Soviets' accusation that Olga was an adventuress who had acted behind Pasternak's back.

3.16. Irina's liberation

By the end of 1961, most felt that the best way to influence the case was through individual letters to Soviet writers and politicians as opposed to public statements. The American P.E.N. Club advised its members to do

first secretary of the PCI, Palmiro Togliatti, Secchia's influence weakened and he was replaced by Giorgio Amendola. During the period covered in this paper, he was responsible for the publishing activities of the PCI.

just that, asking them to write letters emphasizing how an act of clemency on the part of the Soviets would do wonders for improving East-West relations.[83]

In the second half of 1961, Nivat was first in Paris convalescing from the wound he had suffered in Algeria (see footnote 7). He pursued his tireless campaign with mixed results. As time went by, people seemed to lose interest and avoid him, even some very close to him. However, he did have the support of the French ambassador to Moscow, Maurice Dejean, who continued to put pressure on the Soviets. In September 1961, a letter written in January 1961 had been handed to Khrushchev under the most favorable circumstances. Nivat described the person who delivered it (in a letter to Katkov dated October 26) as "an old French political figure whom Khrushchev *needed* at the present time" (MHP, Oxford; original in Russian).

A few days later, Nivat reported to Katkov, "My letter to Khrushchev was given to him directly and accepted with the promise of reconsidering the matter with benevolence" (MHP, Oxford; original in Russian). This was at the time of the 22nd Party Congress, and there was hope for an act of clemency. Alas, the congress took place, but nothing happened. At the same time, Nivat was sending packages and correspondence through Maria Nikolaevna. Then things took a turn for the worse. The Soviet Red Cross did not reply to his two appeals, more restrictions on packages and correspondence were put in place starting in November 1961, and contact was just about lost until February 1962. In addition, he could not get discharged from the army and had to return to service in Blois.

Before Irina's liberation in June 1962, a few more initiatives were set in place. Katkov was upbeat at the beginning of 1962. In a letter to Max Hayward, dated January 11, 1962, he mentioned that Bowra was willing to sign anything ("if it was written for him") and explained the plan for a letter that could be signed by Russell and others. The reason for his optimism was the publication of a letter by Q. C. Eddy in *The Telegraph* (January 10, 1962) asking for the revision of the trial, an article by Crankshaw in *The Observer* (October 1, 1961), and a broadcast by Ronald Hingley on the overseas services of the BBC, which also mentioned the Ivinskaya case. He stated: "The whole affair seems to be warming up and we should lose no time in increasing pressure" (GKP, Oxford). A few days later (January 16)

83. The relevant documents are preserved in the MHP, Oxford.

he wrote to Carver, mentioning the recent events and even some developments in the Soviet Union: "The whole case of Ivinskaya seems to be coming back with a vengeance, both in public opinion here and in the Soviet Union itself" (GKP, Oxford). Concerning the Soviet Union, he referred to a sensational statement by Ehrenburg without giving further details.[84]

This optimistic attitude gave way to a more realistic assessment when, on March 11, 1962, Katkov approached Russell again. While conceding that "all our efforts have so far been fruitless," he also expressed the hope that "there may still be a chance of persuading the Soviet authorities to relent" (BRA, McMaster University). More concretely, Katkov enclosed another appeal to Khrushchev signed by Maurice Bowra, and asked whether Russell would also sign. Katkov also mentioned that Freddy Ayer was going to Moscow for academic reasons, and the plan was to hand the letter directly to Khrushchev. Russell was happy to sign and sent the signed letter to Ayer on March 17. From the extant correspondence in the Russell archive, we know that Russell received an explanation from Khrushchev by way of reply to a letter of his at some point between May and November. It is very likely that it would have been an answer to this letter cosigned with Bowra, although we cannot be certain.[85]

Feltrinelli heard nothing of his initiative for a while. As he wrote to Schewe on December 4, 1961,

> At the moment I still do not have an answer about our next steps, which in all this mess was hardly to be expected otherwise. (Feltrinelli to Schewe, AGFE, Quaderno Giallo; original in German)[86]

Feltrinelli was clearly referring to the issue of the Berlin Wall.

On December 21, 1961, Schewe expressed the hope that Feltrinelli's initiative might meet with success and asked again for news on February 15, 1962. On March 5, Feltrinelli replied optimistically:

---

84. Ehrenburg's statements, made in early January 1962, and references to the reports in the Western press are given in de Mallac (1981, 277, 397n60).

85. Unfortunately, some notes made on subsequent letters in the Russell archive indicate that Khrushchev's reply had been misplaced; it is not in the Russell archive at McMaster.

86. The Quaderno Giallo contains all the correspondence between Schewe and Feltrinelli in a copy sent by Schewe to Carlo Feltrinelli.

A messenger of mine will soon reestablish contact with the comrades in M.[oscow] and discuss the matter. Perhaps it will work. (AGFE, Busta 1, fascicolo 5, "Feltrinelli-Schewe (1959 febbraio 15–1966 dicembre 07)"; original in German)

The news Nivat received in March 1962 was not good. He had managed to reach Maria Nikolaevna by phone, who confirmed that correspondence had been blocked since December (she later claimed that the situation got worse after Semichastn'iĭ became head of the KGB in November 1961). Olga and Irina's situation was getting worse, and Olga was asking Feltrinelli and Proyart to write letters to the Ministry of Foreign Affairs declaring that she had only received money on Pasternak's behalf. Nivat conveyed the information to Feltrinelli on March 10, 1962. In April even telephonic contact was cut off.

A piece of positive news involved a letter Nivat received from Eleanor Roosevelt, who forwarded the letter she had written to Khrushchev on behalf of Irina and Nivat. Nivat reported to Katkov a long excerpt from the letter in English.[87] Nivat told Katkov he felt that "maybe now something will change in Irina's fate" (GKP, Oxford, letter datable to May 1962).

Irina was released on June 14, 1962.[88] Schewe conveyed the happy news to Feltrinelli on June 15, 1962:

Dear Giangiacomo,

Ira was released! She served half of her sentence, about one and a half years. She is here in Moscow and apparently received no residency restriction for the capital.

I still have not spoken to her. I must also be, as I have said, very careful. And indeed I cannot help any more, unfortunately . . . !

As I hear it, Irina quarreled in the camp with Olga Vsevolodovna. Things are difficult with Olga. Apparently she is occasionally mentally deranged. With all that she has had to go through, it is really little wonder. She supposedly always fantasizes about her "friends in the West," who one day will certainly come to free her from the camp.

This news makes me very sad.

---

87. Eleanor Roosevelt had been contacted by the warden of St Antony's College, Sir William Deakin, on behalf of Nivat while she was staying in Paris. The letter, preserved in the MHP, Oxford, indicates that Nivat had been in contact with Diana Michaelis, who was the television producer for an American TV program being recorded in Paris that was the reason for Roosevelt's presence there. Roosevelt's letter to Khrushchev, dated February 16, 1962, is also found in the MHP, Oxford.

88. In England the news was published in an article in *The Times* dated June 19, 1962, p. 10. But Schewe, see below, had already announced the news in *Die Welt* on June 15.

Probably Olga would, in the normal sequence of events, likewise be released after serving half of her sentence, or after four years—that would be in December 1964! Horrible thought that she is now alone in the camp.

One must do something! But what? Perhaps you have some advice, dear Giangiacomo? (AGFE, Busta 1, fascicolo 5, "Feltrinelli-Schewe (1959 febbraio 15–1966 dicembre 07)"; original in German)

Three days after Irina's liberation, Schewe ran into her in the street. She asked what Feltrinelli was planning to do, and Schewe responded by mentioning Feltrinelli's plan "to offer important documents through the Roman embassy." Schewe described the meeting to Feltrinelli on June 21, 1962:

Dear Giangiacomo,

What are the chances! Already on the third day after her return I met Ira on the street. I am enclosing a press copy of my report for WELT am SONNTAG.

Irina reports nothing of a quarrel with Olga. I also did not go out of my way to ask. She appeared worried. Olga sometimes seems not to be totally clear in the head any more. Irina wants to make a motion through her Moscow attorney that her money be transferred here by legal means. She asks, meanwhile, what has been undertaken from your side. I described to her your plan to offer the Russians valuable documents via the Roman embassy, but unfortunately did not know any specifics. Please report to me how things stand at present. Apart from that, I beg you to exercise the utmost, utmost caution! In a hurry, with heartfelt greetings,

[*handwritten*] Your HEINZ (Schewe to Feltrinelli, AGFE, Busta 1, fascicolo 5, "Feltrinelli-Schewe (1959 febbraio 15–1966 dicembre 07)"; original in German)

It seems quite likely that Feltrinelli had perhaps not told Schewe the details of his contacts with the PCI and the CPSU. In fact, in the next letter, dated July 2, 1962, he claimed that Irina should be kept in the dark concerning what he had done, because they had to help the Soviets "save face":

The little or much that I could do for I.'s and O.'s liberation seems to me as if it should not go further, especially not to Irina. Contact was established with the party in M.[oscow] through the party here. I have perhaps done the R.[ussians] a favor, insofar as I gave up the documentation of which you know. But this must not become known to I. Everything that the Russians have done with respect to the freeing of I., and perhaps shortly of O., they did of their own goodwill without any pressure or negotiation. We need to help them save face, and our dear girl must not show up with too much knowledge of the occurrences. I hope that you understand the situation. (Feltrinelli to Schewe, AGFE, Busta 1, fascicolo 5, "Feltrinelli-Schewe (1959 febbraio 15–1966 dicembre 07)"; original in German)

Did Feltrinelli's "unilateral disarmament" contribute to the earlier liberation of Irina and (later) Olga? Lacking further documentary evidence on the Soviet side, it is hard to evaluate whether Feltrinelli's action played an important role, but it might have.

As we saw, Irina was back in Moscow on June 16, 1962. Schewe wrote an article titled "Pasternaks Erbin freigelassen" for *Die Welt*, dated June 15, 1962.[89] In the article, he mentioned that Pasternak was determined to leave his foreign assets to Irina and Olga but that, Schewe also pointed out, "a written testament by Pasternak that indicates Olga Ivinskaya and her daughter as the legal heirs of his assets abroad does not exist."

Irina's liberation also brought back the issue of royalties. On November 7, 1962, Schewe wrote to Feltrinelli:

Many thanks for your greeting card of October 23rd, '62. Irina's exact address is:

Irina S. Emelianova
Moscow/USSR
Potapovski Pereulok 9/11, Apartment Nr. 18

I have the impression that the comrades would not have anything against you transferring, say, $100 per month. But I believe that they will, at the same time, ask what suggestions you have for an across-the-board resolution of the Pasternak estate. And to be sure a resolution in the sense of the Pasternak family, who according to the official Soviet position are in fact seen as the rightful heirs.

Thus, if you, dear Giangiacomo, take up the question of a monthly pension for Irina, you must in return count on the opposing question from Moscow: "And what is to become of Pasternak's millions?" You should consider this very precisely beforehand.

I myself probably cannot grasp all the aspects that you, dear Giangiacomo, must take into account in this matter. I would think it best if you personally came here to Moscow someday and courageously grabbed the bull by its horns. (Schewe to Feltrinelli, AGFE, Busta 1, fascicolo 5, "Feltrinelli-Schewe (1959 febbraio 15–1966 dicembre 07)"; original in German)

---

89. A second article, "Wiedersehen mit Irina," was published in *Die Welt* on June 21, 1962.

The problem of "the Pasternak millions" would only be resolved many years later in a complicated settlement among Pasternak's sons, Olga Ivinskaya, Feltrinelli, and the Soviet authorities.

3.17. From late 1962 to Olga's liberation in 1964

Despite Irina's liberation, Olga's case was still pressing. Freddy Ayer solicited Russell on November 21, 1962, to write again to Khrushchev on behalf of Olga Ivinskaya. Ayer thought the moment might be propitious, for "it is possible that Khrushchev might feel some gratitude to you for the part that you played in the Cuban affair, and, therefore, be more disposed to listen to you" (BRA, McMaster University). He added his personal congratulations on the success of Russell's intervention in the Cuban crisis.[90] The letter also contained as enclosure a letter from Georges Nivat dated November 8, 1962. Russell actually drafted an appeal to Khrushchev (dated November 26, 1962) but then decided against sending it. His change of mind can be explained by what he wrote to Ayer on November 27: "Thanks for your letter and the enclosures. I have only recently written to Khrushchev on the subject. I think it unwise to do so again so shortly upon receiving a rather long reply from him setting out his reasons for the imprisonment. I am hopeful that the release of the daughter may presage the release of Madame Ivinskaia herself."[91] It is truly unfortunate that the "rather long reply" (already mentioned in the previous section) has gone missing from Russell's archive and has not resurfaced in the archives of the Russian Federation.

Meanwhile, Sergio d'Angelo was trying to find a way to help Olga and Irina. In early 1962, he had written a letter to Khrushchev (a draft dated March 12, 1962, is in the SdAP, HILA). D'Angelo had, of course, become well known among those interested in the Ivinskaya case on account of his articles in the international press. He still had to dispose of the remaining part of the $100,000 that had not been sent to Pasternak or Olga. Realizing that he could make no legal transfers under his own name, he decided to

90. The documents relative to Russell's involvement in the Cuban crisis (including telegrams to Castro, Kennedy, and Khrushchev) are found in the Russell archive at McMaster.

91. The original of this letter is in the MHP, Oxford. A carbon copy is in the BRA, McMaster University.

approach British journalist David Floyd of the *Daily Telegraph* at some point in mid-May.[92] He wrote:

> Mr. David Floyd
> c/o The Daily Telegraph
> London
>
> Dear Mr. Floyd,
>
> I take the liberty to ask you for an advise [*sic*] and, if possible, an assistance which I was not able to find in Italy.
>
> As you know, I have in my hands a remarkable amount of money which, according to Pasternak's will, belongs to O. V. Ivinskaya.
>
> Under the present circumstances it seems to me an absurdity to wait till Ivinskaya and her daughter are released and enabled to receive their money. Having given up all hope that an act of justice or clemency will be accomplished in a short while (uselessly, some months ago, I wrote a letter to Khrushchev too), I came to the conclusion that the best to be done now is to try to help economically the two women in their present condition.
>
> Obviously, I could not apply to Soviet authority for an initiative like this. But I think that in name of another person (or, better, of a committee) it would be perhaps possible to obtain the permission of making some remittances: as a help, of course, and without revealing the real source of the money.
>
> I realize that the possession of some money would be a great relief for Ivinskaya and her daughter; and no one will be surprised if the attempt to help the two women in this way is made in Great Britain, where the consequences of Pasternak's case caused a particular emotion.
>
> Would you agree to my idea and devote yourself to carry it out. I would provide you immediately with all means that are necessary to organize the assistance.
>
> Anyway please consider my letter as confidential and forgive me for this trouble. (SdAP, HILA and MHP, Oxford)

The letter must have been written after preliminary conversations with Floyd, with whom d'Angelo had been acquainted since at least 1961 (personal email from d'Angelo, April 27, 2014). In the spring of 1961, Floyd and d'Angelo had met in Rome to discuss d'Angelo's article in the *Sunday Telegraph* (May 7, 1961; see d'Angelo 2006, 230). D'Angelo had prob-

92. The full exchange can be reconstructed by combining the SdAP, HILA and the MHP, Oxford.

ably gotten wind of the existence of the committee on behalf of Ivinskaya and Emelianova, and Floyd immediately sent d'Angelo's letter to Max Hayward. Hayward wrote to d'Angelo on May 26, 1962, informing him of the existence of the committee:

> You may like to know that there is already in existence in this country a small unofficial committee, consisting of leading figures in the academic and literary world, who have made it their business to do what they can, without any publicity, to give assistance to Ivinskaya and her daughter. On receipt of your letter I contacted the head of this committee and took the liberty of telling him in general terms about the problem raised in your letter. (Hayward to d'Angelo, SdAP, HILA)

Hayward conveyed, on behalf of the committee, the suggestion that the committee could take responsibility for the sum: "They would undertake to dispose of the money in the interest of Ivinskaya and her daughter at a time, and in such a way, as might seem most appropriate in the light of changing circumstance."

The arrangement did not go through. As is clear from the correspondence, d'Angelo wanted the small remittances to start immediately, and he offered to send part of the sum to London immediately (letter dated May 30, 1962). In a reply dated July 18, 1962, Hayward stated that the committee was in no position to start the remittances as envisaged by d'Angelo,[93] and d'Angelo replied (letter of July 24; MHP, Oxford) that lacking this condition—an immediate start of small deliveries on behalf of Ivinskaya—he was not willing to go ahead. But he reiterated his readiness to send the money if the committee found a way to carry out other concrete forms of assistance to Ivinskaya. And that was the end of it.

After the "merveilleuse nouvelle" of Irina's liberation, Nivat received a card from Irina in the summer but no letter for quite a while. In a letter to Katkov, dated October 11, 1962, Nivat reported that Irina had written, asking him to abandon any marriage plans. A friend of his reported from Moscow on threats against Irina by the KGB:

> I found out from this friend that the KGB has scared them to death. Irina was shaking. They threatened her that if she continued meeting with foreigners, she would

93. "The committee did not consider it advisable, in present circumstances, to transfer the money to either of the two women" (letter of July 18, 1962; SdAP, HILA).

receive a terribly long prison sentence. Grandmother [Maria Nikolaevna] was brought in recently because of me. In a word, I don't need to pass along all the details to you. You understand for yourself. No hope remains. Irina, the poor thing, lives a hard life. She is a typist at her former university. She agrees with me that we should regularly correspond by mail, just as friends. But nothing more. (Nivat to Katkov, GKP, Oxford; original in Russian)

In a letter to Russell dated November 8, 1962, Nivat admitted that he had no hope of seeing Irina again. In December, Galina Alekseevna Arbuzova, Konstantin Paustovskiĭ's niece, told him in Paris that there was no hope for him and Irina (see letter to Katkov, December 31, 1962, GKP, Oxford). But that did not stop Nivat's efforts on Irina and Olga's behalf.

Not much happened between Irina's liberation and Katkov's renewed attempt in June 1963 to get the ball rolling again. On June 27, he wrote to Russell, pointing out that while Irina had been freed and was living in relative freedom, her mother Olga was still serving her sentence. There was some urgency, as her health was said to be deteriorating quite seriously. He added, "I am surprised and baffled as to the reasons for the implacable cruelty shown by the Soviet authorities towards this weak and defenceless woman whose case has aroused so much sympathy in the world. Indeed, I sometimes wonder whether there is some element in the case of which I am unaware" (BRA, McMaster University). Katkov thought that perhaps Khrushchev's reply to Russell, which Russell had mentioned to Ayer the previous year, might shed some light on the motivations and asked for a copy of the letter. Russell was willing to send him the letter, which in the end could not be located. Nothing new emerged, and even the Feltrinelli-Schewe correspondence contains nothing of interest for 1963. There are also fewer letters between Nivat and Katkov.[94] In a letter dated April 26, 1963, Nivat, who had not received any letters since the previous summer, reported that a friend of his had visited Irina, and she had asked the friend to tell Nivat that she could not write on account of Olga.

It was during mid-June 1964 that rumors of Olga's impending liberation started arriving in the West. As usual, the harbinger was a letter by Schewe, who wrote to Feltrinelli on June 11:

94. In July 1962, Nivat had been offered a position at the University of Toulouse, which he accepted. In the fall of 1962 he was discharged from the army. During the academic year 1962–63, he also taught at the Lycée Fermat in Toulouse. Starting in 1963–64, he only taught at the university, where he was Peltier's assistant.

Dear Giangiacomo, dear Inge!

As I hear from a reliable source, Olga Vsevolodovna should be released already sometime this summer. She will probably be allowed to return to Moscow.

I do not want to neglect telling you this. We have not heard anything from one another for a long time.

I was recently with Ira at a Marlene Dietrich concert here. Meanwhile she has married—a young man her age by the name of Vadim,[95] whom she met in the Potma camp. He is still studying. Ira is working in an office.

Olga's son Mitia (Dmitri) has likewise married and expects an addition to the family in the next weeks. He is working in construction as a crane operator now.

Olga Vsevolodovna is apparently not doing well healthwise. She is no longer in the library, but rather occupied in the sewing room. Her eyes have apparently suffered for it. (Schewe to Feltrinelli, AGFE, Busta 1, fascicolo 5, "Feltrinelli-Schewe (1959 febbraio 15–1966 dicembre 07)"; original in German)

On October 1, 1964, Katkov forwarded to Russell another letter from Georges Nivat. Nivat pointed out that, according to Soviet law, it was possible for Olga to be freed after serving half her sentence, which she had done by then. Russell wrote his last letter to Khrushchev on the matter of Ivinskaya on October 2, 1964, mentioning the legal aspect of the matter, as suggested by Nivat.[96] Whether this letter carried more weight than the previous ones is hard to say, but Olga was finally freed on October 14, 1964, under the new leader, Leonid Brezhnev.

3.18. Conclusion

The Ivinskaya case is surely one of the most important events in the relationship between the USSR and the West during the "cultural" Cold War. It was preceded by the Pasternak case and was soon to be followed by the Siniavskiĭ and Daniel case (see Hayward 1966). The Ivinskaya case, which took place during the tensest period of the Cold War, has some peculiar characteristics.[97]

---

95. Irina married Vadim Kozovoĭ in February 1964.

96. All these letters are found in the Russell archive.

97. The downing of a U-2 plane and its pilot, Francis Gary Powers, in 1960, the construction of the Berlin Wall in 1961, and the Cuban crisis in 1962 are among the key international events of those years.

A remarkable feature of it was the attempt on the part of the Soviets to "rehabilitate" a writer, Boris Pasternak, whom they had vilified and banned from their midst. That such rehabilitation could only be envisaged by finding a scapegoat, namely the "adventuress" Ivinskaya, to account for those aspects of Pasternak's work that the Soviets did not like, is what makes the case so peculiar. It is still unclear in my mind what bothered the Soviets most. Was it the fact that they had been unable to completely silence Pasternak and were still livid about his international success and the Nobel Prize? Or were they more incensed by the fact that Ivinskaya was planning to send his literary *Nachlaß*, or parts thereof, abroad? Or that she was still gaining financially from his royalties and engaging in contact with foreigners? Or a combination of all these factors?

Be that as it may, the Soviets showed remarkable cruelty in the case, and both Irina and Olga were freed only after serving half their sentences, which made them anyway legally eligible for release. Lacking further documentation from former Soviet archives, it is at the moment hard to evaluate how effective the various types of pressure exercised by the West were, whether secret or public. These pressures did, however, force the Soviets into an unpleasant situation, especially during a period in which their rhetoric of peace seemed to clash drastically with their actions. I think one can safely say that, cumulatively, the pressure had the effect of shortening the detentions of Olga and Irina, who might otherwise have served their full sentences.

Olga's liberation did not bring to a close the Ivinskaya case. Ivinskaya renewed contact with Schewe and Feltrinelli. The latter helped financially, allowing Ivinskaya to buy an apartment in Moscow.[98] Feltrinelli also helped Pasternak's wife, Zinaida, with smaller sums. In 1966, Ivinskaya joined Pasternak's wife and sons in seeking, through the help of the Juridical College of the USSR, a share of the royalties that remained under Feltrinelli's control.[99] An agreement was reached in 1970 (see *Le dossier* 1994, 237–45; Afiani and Tomilina 2001, 298–303). At the same time, Olga led a largely unsuccessful campaign to recover the Pasternak manuscripts that had been taken from her when she was arrested (Mansurov 2009; Toomey 1996).

---

98. The extensive correspondence between Olga, Schewe, and Feltrinelli after 1965 is found in the Feltrinelli archives.

99. Zinaida Pasternak died on June 21, 1966.

In 1984, Irina moved to Paris to join her husband, Vadim, who had emigrated in 1981. She still lives in Paris. In 1988, the Supreme Court of the USSR annulled the sentences against Olga and Irina. Olga died in Moscow in 1995.

Documentary Appendix

Editorial note: In the commentaries for the three letters from Pasternak to d'Angelo (documents 1, 2, and 8) and a document signed by Ivinskaya (document 3), I include a brief commentary; for more details, refer to Mancosu 2013. The following abbreviations appear in the letters:

B.L.	Boris Leonidovich
F.	Feltrinelli
G.F.	Giangiacomo Feltrinelli
G.	Garritano
P.	Proyart

Document 1. Boris Pasternak to Sergio d'Angelo, April 16, 1957

Location: AGFE, CP, Busta 1, Fascicolo 7, "Olga Ivinskaya–Sergio d'Angelo (1959–1960)"

Format: Handwritten, signed. Original.

Original language: Russian

Previous publication: Full text reproduced in Boris Pasternak 2005, 222–23 (earlier in Elena and Evgeniĭ Pasternak 2001a, 293–94); and Mancosu 2013, 226. Fully translated into Italian in d'Angelo 2006, 81–83. Translated into English in Mancosu 2013, 227.

Additional information: There are minor variations between the original and the published Russian versions. We follow the original. Original text and English translation also published in Mancosu and Borokhov 2017.

DOCUMENT

April 16, 1957

Dear D'Angelo!

What a pity we did not see each other while I was still well! Now, I have been bedridden for a long time in the Kremlin hospital with terrifying pain in my right leg, and I cannot imagine now when and how I will recover.

The telegram concerning the postponement of the publication of the Italian edition of the novel until September 1, 1957, was sent to Feltrinelli from Goslitizdat with my consent. The September 1, 1957, deadline [for publication of the Russian text] was actually promised to me as the telegram was sent off.

Concerning the request regarding the deviation of the Italian translation from the original Russian text of the manuscript, from which the translation is being done, I had never asked Feltrinelli for anything of the sort, and the thought of a divergence of the Italian translation, done from the exact original, from the form that the text of the edited Russian edition will take had never given me pause or frightened me.

These prospective alterations will be carried out and introduced into the Russian text not by me but rather by a special editor who has been charged by the publisher with the task of smoothing out rough edges of the novel that are unacceptable in a Soviet edition. I have not yet seen the results of his work, and now, lying in the hospital with an illness that is currently unbearably excruciating and to which I see no end, I probably will not see them soon.

Given the state in which I find myself at the moment—both physically and my thoughts and the state of things with the publication of the novel here—it seems to me that the publisher Feltrinelli should not go so far in his kindnesses as he is apparently ready to go and should simply limit himself to the postponement of the printing of the novel in Italian until September 1 of this year.

I cannot at the moment imagine the shape into which the novel will be transformed to become acceptable for printing, and it is impossible to guess it. Apart from the intrinsic uncertainty involved in such conjectures, the matter has become awfully complicated for an indefinitely long time on account of my illness. Would Feltrinelli really place himself in a position that would be dependent on such as of yet undeterminable conditions?

Writing is difficult (physically painful) for me, forgive me. I hope that you will derive at least something useful from my words for making your decision. Be well; I thank you for your attention.

Your B. Pasternak.

Commentary. In the spring of 1957, Pasternak was suffering from a knee problem and was hospitalized at the Kremlin hospital. The telegram mentioned by Pasternak was one of the defining moments of the cat-and-mouse game between the Soviets and Pasternak. The Soviets were pressuring Pasternak (directly) and Feltrinelli (through the Italian Communist Party) to retrieve the typescript of *Doctor Zhivago*. On January 7, 1957, Pasternak signed a contract for the publication of *Doctor Zhivago* in the Soviet Union, and two editors, Puzikov and Starostin, were put in charge of the alterations. Pasternak was pressured to send a telegram asking Feltrinelli not to publish in any other language before the publication in Russian. But sensing that this was only a delaying tactic on the part of the Soviets, Pasternak added a firm deadline to the request, asking Feltrinelli to wait only until September 1, 1957. He also informed Feltrinelli in a separate letter that, should the novel not appear in Russia by September 1, he should go ahead and publish. For the whole episode and the relevant documents, see Mancosu 2013, section 1.8.

Document 2. Boris Pasternak to Sergio d'Angelo, October 22, 1957

Original language: Russian
Previous publication: First published in Boris Pasternak 2005, 267; translated into English in Mancosu 2013, 245–46
Additional information: Original text and English translation also published in Mancosu and Borokhov 2017

DOCUMENT

Oct. 22, 1957

My dear Sergio! I am forever grateful for your concern. It is terribly painful and embarrassing to me that you are expending so much time and effort for us. One Yugoslavian writer from Zagreb, who was in Paris in the fall, sent me a French postcard from there saying: J'ai lu dans "Esprit" un récit de vous. . . . [I read a story of yours in "Esprit."] Therefore, he's talking about prose of some sort and, apparently, in some issue from late summer or fall. It's doubtful that this writer could have gotten his facts confused to the point that he would have said récits about poems that were published in March and that he read them recently. I cannot take care of this myself via correspondence, my letter will disappear, and the response to it wouldn't make it either. If you could inquire, and if it is true that, apart from the March material, there was in fact something else printed, if you could obtain that issue! In that case, either sorrow or joy awaits me. Sorrow—if something of my old prose was translated, with little content and full of mannerisms, the texts of which are easier to obtain abroad; and joy, if suddenly, to my great fortune, these are excerpts from the autobiography that you know of and have translated yourself.

Regarding F[eltrinelli], I have two favors to ask of you! 1) That F. absolutely not respond with even one word and completely ignore this correspondence, this outrageous correspondence based on unheard-of torture (they are coercing me with threats of death and arrest and forcing me to portray my "dissatisfaction" with F. as a personal matter of a free person, in which the regime is supposedly not intervening and about which they supposedly do not know). How can one take part in such a base duplicity and mockery of one's soul, conscience, life, everything, everything that is sacred! I am undertaking all possible efforts to end this cheap and repulsive sport whenever I can.

2) That F. take care that this fictitious game of my supposed "own will" does not confuse anyone, that no one pay attention to it anywhere and that the books come out as soon as possible everywhere.

Commentary. This letter was never sent, but it bears witness to the violence exercised by Soviet authorities ("threats of death and arrest"). We are at the last stage before the publication of the Italian translation of the novel (printed on November 15, 1957), and the Soviets were becoming frantic to find a way to halt the publication. See Mancosu 2013, 245–46.

Document 3. Receipt signed by Olga Ivinskaya, December 24, 1957

Location: AGFE, CP, Busta 1, Fascicolo 2-Feltrinelli-Pasternak
Format: Handwritten, signed. Original.
Original language: Russian
Previous publication: Published in the original Russian and English translation in Mancosu 2013, 259
Additional information: Original text and English translation also published in Mancosu and Borokhov 2017

DOCUMENT

Receipt

I have received for B. L. Pasternak, from Sergio D'Angello [*sic*] a total of twelve thousand 800 (eight hundred) rubles.

24 Dec 57 O. Ivinskaya

Commentary. Just before leaving the Soviet Union, d'Angelo visited Pasternak and/or Olga at Olga Ivinskaya's place (see d'Angelo 2006, 129) and gave 12,800 rubles to Olga Ivinskaya, who signed on behalf of Pasternak. See Mancosu 2013, 259.

Document 4. Olga Ivinskaya to Sergio d'Angelo, datable to summer 1958

Location: AGFE, CP, Busta 1, Fascicolo 7, "Olga Ivinskaya–Sergio d'Angelo (1959–1960)"
Format: Handwritten, signed. Original.
Original language: Russian
Previous publication: Original text and English translation first published in Mancosu and Borokhov 2017

DOCUMENT

Dear Sergio, Serezhen'ka,

Greetings! First of all we ask you to kiss Giulietta for all of us. B[oris] and little Irina and I, we think of you more often, probably, than you of us.

Sweet Sergio dear, our main request to you is *clippings*, responses to the novel. For example, a certain *Moravio* [*sic*] (an Italian) has written a review of "D. Zh." Don't forget that we have literally nothing, and this is the most important thing for Boris Leonidovich. Not just Italian ones—all of them—after all you have the ability! And let our *friend*, who is with you now, do *everything* exactly as he deems necessary. He is tactful and smart, he holds all the cards. B.L. is *not against it*. Now regarding the settlements—after you, there have been 4! But I see that settling there, in Moscow, is hard for your friend (G[arritano]). Please think about how to make this simpler and increase the amount of a single dose. That would be better for B.L., and you will likely be able to come up with a way to get it done and then actually deliver on it. As for me personally, I have the following requests. First off, photos of our family.

Second if there will be an opportunity to get it through—pumps with stiletto heels. Giulietta knows—size 36 and 37—for me and Irishka. Third if it's possible and convenient to arrange for a typewriter—this is our dream with B. How to do this I leave to you.

Now about B.

Things are not going well. Sweet Sergio, that book "Selected works" still has not come out to this day and will not be released and they don't want to pay, even though they are supposed to. It is likely that there will be court proceedings, but for now we've gotten the runaround. Surkov continues his earlier persecution, B.L. is not being printed anywhere and no one is giving him translation work. Only theater and—for now his plays are still being performed in provincial theaters.

B.L.'s health is not good. In his right knee, the meniscus—it's a bone that needs to be removed, and it hurts. He is waiting all the time that something will bring him out of a state of stagnation and oblivion—somewhere people will say things, responses, reviews—but almost nothing reaches us. I was waiting for so long to get some reviews with your letter—and am waiting for them with the first opportunity. Though, to be fair, a letter from France did arrive.

How sorry I am that I will never see you again! It is hard to even believe it. Send us a photo of your family and F[eltrinelli], if you can.

I could not obtain "Moscow Literator" [the newspaper of the Moscow Writers' Union]—I no longer have the connection I had at that place. But I am sending all of Tsvetaeva, and B's new poems, all the ones that we have. Just be careful, remember how frightening everything is for us. B.L. sends you kisses and greetings from all of us. Irochka is currently in the field in Samarkand, Mitia is on an expedition, and I am going between the city and the country—between Goslit and Peredelkino. I can always be found.

Your O.

Address in Moscow, or even better through others . . .

Commentary. Moravia's review of *Doctor Zhivago* ("Visita a Pasternak") appeared in *Corriere della Sera* on January 11, 1958; it was published in translation in the June issue of *Preuves*.

The "friend" was certainly Giuseppe Garritano, who must have brought this letter to Rome ("who is with you now"), and from the context it appears that Garritano was instrumental in facilitating the delivery of payments to Pasternak and Ivinskaya. Among Olga's requests was one for a typewriter, which was in fact delivered by Pino Garritano to Irina Emelianova on October 24, 1958.

The letter bears witness to the ostracism suffered by Pasternak. Pasternak was not being given any more translation work, and publication projects had been stalled. For instance, the publication of his collected poems (prefaced by the autobiographical essay), which had been ready in proof for Goslitizdat since January 1956, was halted and did not appear in the USSR. Only theater work in the provinces was still available to Pasternak. This information matches other reports from the period, such as a letter from Gerd Ruge to Kurt Wolff dated August 15, 1958, cited in section 3 of chapter 1.

Document 5. Sergio d'Angelo to Boris Pasternak, February 23, 1959

Location: AGFE, CP, "Olga Ivinskaya–Sergio D'Angelo (1959–1960)," Busta 1, Fascicolo 7

Format: Handwritten, signed. Photocopy (originating from Ivinskaya and Emelianova's trial proceedings; see section 2.2).

Original language: Russian

Previous publication: Partial English translation in Mancosu 2013, 311. Original text and English translation first published in Mancosu and Borokhov 2017.

Additional information: A draft of the letter is also found in the SdAP, HILA

DOCUMENT

Rome, February 23, 1959

Dear Boris Leonidovich, greetings!

I have not written to you for a long time, but I can say that I have been constantly thinking about you, particularly after these recent developments. I have been afraid many times that you do not consider me an "angel" but rather a "devil," because I, though unwillingly, caused the most terrifying troubles to befall you.

Yes, I have left the Communist Party, became the subject of intense slander coming from many people who had been amicable toward me in earlier times: but all this, obviously, is a mere trifle compared to the things you have had to experience.

Currently, all around the world, your name is respected, people are being inspired by your novel and your poetry: but all this is not enough to put my conscience at ease. If, by fate's will, I assisted in the recognition of your mastery and talent, I consider it my responsibility to do everything possible to make your personal life easier.

I read what you told the "Daily Mail" correspondent about the difficult financial situation in which you might find yourself in a few months. But if you choose to follow my advice, it will not happen. It is well known that Feltrinelli is in possession of a sum of money that belongs to you from royalties (from Italy and other countries). I do not know exactly how large a sum, but it is big. I think it would be impossible to send you the money through official channels. But I assure you that it can be sent unofficially (and it will be completely safe).

Why have you only received small change to this day? Unfortunately, I must say that Feltrinelli has not devoted any effort to this problem. One needs to take the initiative to take advantage of unofficial channels. And not only is he not the kind of person to take the initiative, but he doesn't allow me to take the appropriate actions. I can't say what his reasons for this are. In fact, I did not want to write about this delicate topic. Recently, I attempted to explain it indirectly through our friend, but I'm afraid that the only result was an unpleasant misunderstanding.

After reading the declarations of the correspondent of the "Daily Mail," I tasked my English friend to talk with your sisters and ask them to write you a letter about this question. I do not yet know whether he has met with them and whether they will carry out my request.

But now, because an Italian journalist, my friend, is leaving for Moscow tomorrow, I decided to send you a personal letter.

And here is my recommendation to you: write to Feltrinelli in French or English (and to me, for my information), that you have decided to grant into my hands the sum that belongs to you, adding only that you wish to charge me with looking out for your interests.

In this case, I can pledge to send you the money in parts and in significant transfers (and, I repeat, completely safely).

Of course, I would take on legal responsibility for the deposit, which would always remain under your control or the control of your authorized agents.

It is a pity to talk about these things, but I hope you will understand that I am doing this with kind intentions. In any case, I entreat you to answer through our friend as quickly as possible.

My bad Russian does not allow me to express how much I wish you health, calm, and more wonderful work, how I wish for myself to see you in a better future. Until next time, Boris Leonidovich!

With the most heartfelt and warmest greetings

Your
Sergio d'Angelo.

Commentary. This is the first letter d'Angelo sent to Pasternak after the Nobel Prize award on October 23, 1958. D'Angelo informs Pasternak (who had perhaps raised the question in a previous letter now lost or directly through Garritano) that he had left the Communist Party. In the SdAP, HILA, there is a copy of the letter, dated October 8, 1958, that d'Angelo sent to the "Federazione del PCI" in Rome, explaining his decision not to renew his membership in the PCI, of which he had been a member since 1944.

The context and the details of d'Angelo's proposal to Pasternak concerning a transfer of his royalties have been clarified in chapter 1.

Document 6. Olga Ivinskaya to Sergio d'Angelo, datable to February 1959

Location: SdAP, HILA
Format: Handwritten, signed. Original.
Original language: Russian
Previous publication: Original text and English translation first published in Mancosu and Borokhov 2017

DOCUMENT

Dear Sergio

A personal request to you: please hold the list in which B.L. specifies the people to whom he wants to make small gifts. This needs to be done to make sure we don't let friends down. A new list will be sent at the first opportunity.

Your Olga.

Commentary. Pasternak had decided to make donations from his royalties to several persons in the West (see chapter 1, section 1.5). The letter from Pasternak to Feltrinelli, containing the names of the beneficiaries, was dated February 2, 1959. The same list of beneficiaries had been included in a letter to Proyart dated January 30–February 3, but it was immediately followed by a postcard from Ivinskaya to Proyart asking her to wait for a new list. The reason was that Pasternak had included in the original list a donation of $2,000 to Giuseppe Garritano, who, however, did not want his name included in the list (though he accepted the donation). Garritano's reaction led to a modification of the official list of beneficiaries. It turns out that d'Angelo, contrary to what Ivinskaya implies here, had not been sent a list of beneficiaries (see one of the crossed-out passages in the letter to Ivinskaya dated April 1959). All of this allows us to date the brief letter we are commenting upon to February 1959, though it might have reached d'Angelo as late as April 1959.

Document 7. Olga Ivinskaya to Sergio d'Angelo, datable to late March / early April 1959

Location: SdAP, HILA
Format: Handwritten, signed. Original.
Original language: Russian
Previous publication: Original text and English translation first published in Mancosu and Borokhov 2017

DOCUMENT

My dear friends!

The circumstances here were so frightening that they interrupted our correspondence and communication. I wasn't even able to thank you. Thank you very, very much.

I don't know, Sergio dear, in what form I should write the receipts—for now I'm sending them this way. If it's not any good, tell me, and I will rewrite them.

Briefly about our affairs. Personally, I don't like that Proyart is entangled in our affairs, but obviously we will have to carry them out through her *for now*. B.L. thought that she will soon return to Russia, and this is the reason for all this talk about French editions. Feltrinelli needlessly wrote about his priority for all editions, and B.L. also perfectly understands and will take his side. B.L. has no real notion of the sum for which he could write a power of attorney. Please write to us an approximate amount and the appropriate form.

Here, there is a complete boycott, civil death, orders have been given to put us outside the law. It has never been this terrifying before. At Goslitizdat, an unspoken order has been given to all workers not to print. Such a name—"P[asterna]k"—does not exist, and there are no financial relationships. No one is paying for the J. Słowacki translations, though the contract has not been legally violated or rescinded. Even for the anthologies, money has been pulled—even if they contain only ten lines. Furthermore, they have threatened us with proceedings (took signatures about nondisclosure) due to the "hostile interview" given to Brown.

Be extremely cautious, but think about what can be undertaken. There is a possibility that at the upcoming congress, the persecution will begin again. Surkov is again preparing a report! Everything that I am writing, you can understand yourself, is extremely secret—all this, if it is carelessly discovered, would cost me my freedom and my life. But I fully believe in you, you have been true friends and I cannot reproach you for anything. Write. It would be good if you would send 3–4 [copies] of the Russian editions of the novel through G-o [Garritano]—yours [the Mouton edition] and the American one and your autobiography of him!

For Irochka, in terms of clothes, I would like summer pumps and some outerwear—for example, we dream here of nylon winter outerwear, only the shoe size is 36, and not smaller, and 37–38 for me. Everything else—at your discretion. Only attach copies of receipts, which we will copy here with B.L. and send back to you for accounting for F. while you need them. Dear Serezha, please quickly obtain possession of this sum—one hundred thousand dollars from Proyart. We will do everything that we can to make this easier for you, please write precisely what is needed.

Furthermore, try to meet and correspond with her (Proyart) while G[iuseppe] G[arritano] is in I[taly] and tell us where things stand. We are waiting for frank and detailed letters from you; after all, there are so few opportunities to get them.

Y[our] O.

Warmest greetings to Giangiacomo Feltrinelli. Thanks for his tactfulness, nobility, and his wonderful energy. Kissing you and Giulietta.

Commentary. This letter was the first Ivinskaya wrote to d'Angelo after the storm of the Nobel Prize. It was written, I argue, in late March or early April 1959, not long after Pasternak was summoned by the general prosecutor Rudenko on March 14. The reference to the "hostile interview" Pasternak gave Brown indicates that the letter must have been written after February 11, 1959, the date of publication of Brown's first article. (On Brown's articles and the Soviet reaction, see Koznova 2017, 2018.) Indeed, as it appears from d'Angelo's letter to Ivinskaya sent in April 1959 (see document 9), Ivinskaya is alluding in the letter to a document dated February 17, 1959. I am referring to a receipt signed by Pasternak, written on that date, that reads:

In 1958, received items valued at approximately five thousand rub. (5,000 r) in total from S. D'Angelo (typewriter, dress shoes, books)

17 Feb 59 BPasternak

The original Russian text and the translation were published in Mancosu 2013, 300. It is not surprising that this receipt is found in the Archivio Giangiacomo Feltrinelli Editore (the location of the original document is AGFE, CP, Busta 1, Fascicolo 1-Feltrinelli-Pasternak), given that it was intended for Feltrinelli, who was in charge of Pasternak's royalties.

The reference to the power of attorney for a certain sum seems to indicate that this letter was written after d'Angelo's letter dated February 23, 1959, had reached Pasternak and Ivinskaya and thus not before the end of February. And on account of the precise figure of $100,000 and the way Proyart is mentioned without explanation, I think this letter is contemporaneous with the one written by Pasternak on April 6. In addition, Ivinskaya also mentions, just as Pasternak does in his letter of April 6, the Russian editions of *Doctor Zhivago* that were published in the West.

Ivinskaya is more forthcoming than Pasternak concerning the financial hardships Pasternak was facing because his royalties were not being paid (see section 1.4 in chapter 1).

Document 8. Boris Pasternak to Sergio d'Angelo, April 6, 1959

Location: Location of the original unknown
Original language: Russian
Previous publication: Photographically reproduced in d'Angelo 1961a, 14–15. Text reproduced in Elena and Evgeniĭ Pasternak 2001b, 245–47; Boris Pasternak 2005, 457–60; Mancosu 2013, 308–9. Fully translated into Italian in d'Angelo 1961a, 13–14; and d'Angelo 2006, 153–56. English translation: Mancosu 2013, 308–11. Original text and English translation also published in Mancosu and Borokhov 2017.

DOCUMENT

April 6, 1959, Peredelkino

Dear Sergio, I thank you for the letter. We always think of you in the most friendly and grateful terms. Since the last time we saw each other, so many unexpected and important things have come to pass. Many conjectures that I had made at the time, whether verbally or in the form of precarious and hypothetical, non–legally formalized wishes, concerning literary translations, editions, etc., have been overtaken by reality, which outpaced our boldest assumptions. Everything has developed and become more complicated, not only in a bad sense but even more so in a good sense. Although the danger with which they threatened me most recently is without exaggeration fatal, it is dwarfed by the things of immortal order that have been achieved alongside it.

I thank you for the help that you are offering me. My current situation is uncertain. They have offered an official transfer of funds to me, but I do not know whether this is a concealed trap to destroy me all the more certainly, for so great is the constant desire to ruin me that I do not see anything except this desire in their attitude toward me. All the while with complaint, as if they were preparing something good for me but ran out of time, while I again spoiled everything, and so reconciliation is impossible yet again—just think, what cheap despicable behavior! And so I have not yet decided anything on how to respond to their offer for transferring the funds officially. So, perhaps, I will resort to your willingness to help as a last resort. I'll say this, try this possibility *even now, without waiting for dire straits.*

But I cannot give you a general power of attorney for all of my funds, because I have already given it much earlier to Mme de Proyart. Plus, you do not need such a power of attorney. Appeal to her for advice on your own. If she approves your measure (and she is a friend of mine just like you are and similarly cares about me), she will set aside for you for your kind objective a sufficiently large sum (let us say, if with my previous requests and allocations I have not drained the reserve below the means for covering this amount), let us say up to one hundred thousand dollars ($100,000). Draw from it, then, *without giving an account* (I am not allowed to correspond about this matter) and with some benefit to yourself, for I would not want your efforts and your time to go for naught.

Above, I had mentioned the monetary requests that I have already addressed to Mme de Proyart, in this way reducing the initial amount of the fund. Among these requests, I sent her a list of people to whom I wished to extend monetary gifts. In this list, I assigned ten thousand dollars to you, just as for my sisters; forgive me that it is so little. This has nothing to do with your current suggestion. For the financial support that you want to provide for me, there will be a different source, which I have described above. Thus, this money ($10,000) is yours no matter what, even if you were to have a falling out with me and forget to think about me. I also asked that two thousand dollars be assigned to Garritano.

The power of attorney to Mme de Proyart arose on its own in that natural course of events in which they developed and about which I spoke in the beginning of my letter. In the same nonbinding way as with you, I spoke to her about the autobiography and about much more. She translated it, and her translation ended up coming out before the Italian edition. Furthermore, she is a kindred spirit, and I was able to entrust her with the supervision of the literary and philosophical aspects of many matters and questions (by the way, the Milanese edition of the Russian text of the novel is teeming with misprints; I am horrified by their quantity). However, do send us two or three copies with someone when you get a chance, as well as two or three copies of the American Russian edition which I have not seen at all. (Never mind the other foreign editions, not of the novel but of other works. They could perhaps be sent to me by registered mail, as books sent in this fashion generally do make it here.) And so, the power of attorney to Mme de Proyart (21, rue Fresnel, Paris XVI) arose not as a way to spite Sig. Feltrinelli, not from lack of trust in him or you, nor in preference to my sisters or to the detriment or offense of my other friends, but in parallel with and alongside these relations and as an awful burden on Mme de Proyart, writer, instructor, public figure, and mother, who does not even have a free minute for her own affairs.

Feltrinelli's letter will pass through your hands. Acquaint yourself with it. I am also enclosing a note for Mme de Proyart with which I ask you to approach her concerning your plan, either in writing or in person. You speak and write Russian wonderfully. Mme de Proyart teaches Russian. I'm telling you this just in case conversing with her would be harder for you in French or English.

Tell Garritano about his two thousand dollars.

I heartily shake your hand. Do not be angry with me if I seem to you insufficiently sympathetic and grateful.

Your B. Pasternak

Commentary. It seems obvious from Ivinskaya's letter (see document 7) and this one from Pasternak that Giuseppe Garritano returned to Italy with, in addition to this letter, Ivinskaya's letter (document 7), the receipt signed by Pasternak dated February 17 (cited in the previous commentary), Pasternak's letter to Feltrinelli dated April 4 (see Mancosu 2013, 301–8), Pasternak's letter to Proyart introducing d'Angelo and endorsing the plan for the transfer of $100,000 from his royalties through d'Angelo (the letter is published in *Le dossier* 1994), and (included in the letter for Feltrinelli) a power of attorney dated April 4, 1959, on behalf of Proyart, which gave her "the unlimited and complete management of my [Pasternak's] royalties as well as the supervision over the remittance of the sum of money that I request from you [Feltrinelli]" (see Mancosu 2013, 306, for the full text). One of the main goals of Pasternak's letters to Feltrinelli and d'Angelo was to explain Proyart's role as Pasternak's representative in the West. Pasternak's election of Proyart as his representative led to a major conflict between Feltrinelli and Proyart. That conflict is analyzed in Mancosu 2013.

The reference to the misprints in the "Milanese" Russian edition of *Doctor Zhivago* has to be interpreted—as I have argued in Mancosu 2013, 165–66—as a reference to the Mouton edition.

Document 9. Draft of a letter from Sergio d'Angelo to Olga Ivinskaya, April 1959

Location: SdAP, HILA
Format: Handwritten, signed. Original.
Original language: Russian
Previous publication: Original text and English translation first published in Mancosu and Borokhov 2017

DOCUMENT

Rome IV.1959

Olga Vsevolodovna, hello!

There's no need for you to apologize for why you didn't write to me earlier. I know ~~and very well understand the circumstances~~ how things are and completely support your caution.

~~I have not personally received the list of people to whom B.L. wants to make gifts~~

Just one comment—you wrote your letter in such a rush that it was very difficult for me to make sense of your handwriting, and perhaps, I did not understand it correctly completely.

~~I have not personally received the list of people to whom B.L. wants to make gifts~~

You ask me to hold a list containing the names of people to whom B.L. would like to make gifts. But I have not received it. Therefore, I will simply tell Mme de Proyart that the old list is no longer valid and a new one will be provided as soon as it becomes available.

~~As I wrote to B.L., it is not a good idea to meet with Mme de Proyart right now~~

I have not met Mme de Proyart yet and cannot personally say anything about her, but in general, I do think it's important that B.L. has designated a trusted person. ~~As I wrote to B.L.~~ I would like to meet with Mme de Proyart in Paris when she receives the money from Feltrinelli (who is currently in the US) and we will be able to talk concretely about its transfer to B.L. I hope that such an opportunity will arise in May.

I do not know the sum that belongs to B.L. (Feltrinelli has been rather reserved with me about such issues, and others), but I do believe that it exceeds B.L.'s expectations ~~it is bigger than what B.L. believes~~.

As far as your receipts are concerned, everything is in order. But 5,000 rubles for a typewriter and a pair of shoes is too much. Therefore, and without needing any new receipts, I am sending right now a pair of summer shoes for you and Irochka, a shawl for you, and a summer dress for Irochka; and then I will send you some nylon winter clothes in a few months (which ones I ask you to specify in more detail if possible).

You can be certain of my caution. I insist that if Mme de Proyart is not against it, I can, starting in the summer, transfer money to B.L. without any danger.

Although much time has passed since our return to our homeland, believe me, my wife and I think of you very often in the most tender and affectionate terms.

From the bottom of our hearts we send greetings to you and your family: your mother, beautiful Irochka, and your sailor son.

Yours,
S. d'A.

Commentary. This draft is clearly the reply to Ivinskaya's letter published as document 7. Using document 50, this letter can be dated to April 2, 1959. D'Angelo informs Ivinskaya that he had not received the list of beneficiaries for Pasternak's gifts but he would inform Proyart that a new list would be forthcoming. As reported in d'Angelo 2006, 160, d'Angelo went to meet Proyart and her husband at the end of May 1959. However, on account of the conflict between Proyart and Feltrinelli, the transfer of funds took much longer than expected, for d'Angelo was able to obtain the money only in March 1960.

Document 10. Draft of a letter from Sergio d'Angelo to Boris Pasternak, dated April 1959

Location: SdAP, HILA
Format: Handwritten, signed. Original.
Original language: Russian
Previous publication: Original text and English translation first published in Mancosu and Borokhov 2017

DOCUMENT

Rome, IV.1959

Dear B.L.,

I received your heartfelt letter with great joy, confirming that you never considered my ~~continued~~ long silence in bad faith.

How can I thank you for the generous gift that you are offering me? It is so large, undeserved, unexpected, that I cannot find the right words. Thank you very, very much also from my wife and from my entire family.

I am very pleased that you have given a power of attorney for all your royalties to Mme de Proyart. I have already written to her, and if she generally agrees with my proposal, I will go to Paris to convey to her my plan for transferring money in more detail. Of course, such a trip would be of use only after Mme de Proyart receives your money from Feltrinelli, who is currently in the US and will return to Italy early next month. Regarding the transfer of money (which could begin in the summer), I have no desire to undertake it without accountability. On the contrary, I consider it necessary to say that, if my plan is approved, I will be reporting to Mme de Proyart on the basis of your receipt and absolutely do not require any sort of compensation for myself.

There are two "Milanese" Russian editions of your novel. The first, full of errors, which you have already received, was released unsanctioned in The Hague with Feltrinelli's name but without his permission. A lawsuit has come from this. ~~The second has just been released, what you could call a legal one, and I hope better prepared (by whom, I do not know). I still have not seen either of them to this day (and I do not know who prepared it).~~ The second, a sanctioned edition (I do not know who edited it), came out recently. I still have not seen either one, and, unfortunately, will not be able to obtain them for you before our friend leaves. (I called Milan, but they told me that they do not have any copies in their possession these days.) Therefore, I will fulfill your request (as well as the one concerning the American Russian edition, which I still do not have) at the earliest possible opportunity. For now, I can send you your autobiography in Italian, which, to be honest, I am not very happy with, because the Milanese colleagues at the publisher took it upon themselves to insert incorrect "stylistic" corrections to my translations.

If you need anything else, write to me. With the greatest pleasure I will do everything possible to show you my eternal loyalty and gratitude.

Please accept my most passionate greetings

Your
S. d'A

I have already delivered all your letters.

Commentary. Using document 50, this letter can be dated to April 2, 1959. D'Angelo conveys his thanks for Pasternak's generous donation (he would receive his present from Feltrinelli in July, together with the gift for Garritano).

Concerning the Russian edition of *Doctor Zhivago*, d'Angelo clarifies that there were three editions. The first, the so-called Mouton edition, was a pirate edition that came out in September 1958 and carried the Feltrinelli imprint without Feltrinelli's permission. The other Feltrinelli edition (the first legitimate Feltrinelli edition) had just come out (in fact the first copies reached the Feltrinelli publishing house on April 30). Finally, the American edition was the Michigan edition that had come out in February 1959. For a detailed description of all these editions, see Mancosu 2013, chapter 2. D'Angelo informed Pasternak that he would be unable to send copies through Garritano, who was leaving soon, but that he would try to send copies at the next opportunity. He did, however, send with Garritano a copy of "Autobiografia e nuovi versi" (Boris Pasternak 1958b), which contained Pasternak's autobiography translated by d'Angelo himself.

Document 11. Sergio d'Angelo to Olga Ivinskaya, July 4, 1959

Location: SdAP, HILA
Format: Handwritten, signed. Original or draft of the original.
Original language: Russian
Previous publication: Original text and English translation first published in Mancosu and Borokhov 2017

DOCUMENT

July 4, 1959

Olga Vsevolodovna, greetings!

A few days ago, Mme de P. wrote to me that she has "theoretically" agreed with F. Currently, her husband is supposed to arrive in Milan to practically formalize the affairs.

When exactly he will arrive I do not know yet. But I am hoping that I will soon have the opportunity to carry out my promise.

Heartfelt greetings,
S.

Commentary. In this brief letter, d'Angelo informs Ivinskaya about the most recent developments concerning the transfer of funds for Pasternak. Indeed, the Proyarts went to Milan on July 21 (see document 13) to meet

Feltrinelli, who made an excuse and did not show up. Thus, although d'Angelo met with the Proyarts, no progress was made on this occasion concerning the disbursement of funds for Pasternak.

Document 12. Olga Ivinskaya to Sergio d'Angelo, after July 21, 1959

Location: AGFE, CP, "Olga Ivinskaya–Sergio D'Angelo (1959–1960)," Busta 1, Fascicolo 7
Format: Partly typed, partly handwritten, signed. Original.
Original language: Russian
Previous publication: Original text and English translation first published in Mancosu and Borokhov 2017

DOCUMENT

Sergio, my dear friend

Regarding the list—it is still current, only it should not include the last name of our friend who gave me the package from you. We would like his name to not be in the list, but we are asking for a big favor from you to do this some other way, so that it is still done.

Now: news of a disagreement between F[eltrinelli] and P[royart] has reached us. I am completely on his side. He has the first priority, while Mme P. incorrectly understood the powers granted to her. She should not argue with him and instead should agree and help him. Borya wrote to her: "If her relationship with F. is a war, then she should surrender."

I think that now everything will be resolved. B. has written letters to her, her friend Peltier, and to F. himself. Either she should understand everything correctly, or everything will need to be changed. For example, her power of attorney can be redirected to you. What do you think?

Dear Sergio, it seems to me that this time, B's letters are the right ones, she will understand, will not interfere in anything, and of course, there will be no publicity about this. In any case, it is very important to us that you will finally be able to do things the way you wanted and started. Our affairs here are still the same as they were. For now there is only talk and almost no contracts, only excuses and promises. Concrete help from you and F. is more important than anything. A big thanks to you for understanding and for your friendship and support. Do not doubt my friendship either. Please tell me whether Borya's requests regarding you have been carried out and whether the cold war between F. and P. is over. It cannot be allowed to go on, and I have done everything I can to end it. Please read all the letters and let me know if what has been done is correct. I await the news from you. Thank you very much for the packages, everything is very good, everything fits well. Don't forget that I am very fat and for winter clothes my size is 52 or 54, while Irochka's is 48. It seems that you have a different sizing system, for example judging by the pumps, your size 37 is equivalent to our 36. Irochka is currently in Estonia, on vacation; I could not give her your wonderful present, but it is waiting for her. Meanwhile I send you big kisses for mine. Borya and I both like it very much.

Thank you once again, please understand, we are tied down here in such a way that maybe in your eyes our friendship is not very active, but I hope that this is only temporary!

All news from you brings such joy to me, as if we were relatives, that is how close you are to us, and Sergio, it is so good to have friends who are so far away and yet so close!

Please send our greetings and kisses to Giulietta and to all our friends. Please inform me that you know this whole story about F. and P. and let me know your opinion. I can do a lot to make sure that Borya behaves correctly and need your advice, professional and personal.

Your O.

It is best to come to my apartment, every Tuesday night. It is safe, I am alone. This is better than writing and sending by mail [*handwritten*: ~~through other people~~]. Be careful—everything can only be this way. You can call on the phone and say that it is Yura calling [*remainder handwritten*:], this is to check that I am home. B. sends his most tender and friendly greetings. For now, not all is well with him. His relationship with those at the top is most strained, everything is still difficult. They have promised to publish Faust, but for now nothing has happened.

Commentary. By the time this letter was written, a set of letters written by Feltrinelli in February 1959 addressing his strained relationship with Proyart had finally reached Pasternak (see Mancosu 2013, 286–300). The conflict between Feltrinelli and Proyart pained Pasternak, but during this period he had come to the conclusion, expressed in a letter to Peltier that passed through d'Angelo's hands (see d'Angelo 2006, 162–63), that if the acrimonious relationship between Feltrinelli and Proyart were to turn to war, Proyart would have to concede. D'Angelo probably also saw the letters that at the same time Pasternak sent to Proyart and Feltrinelli.

Document 13. Sergio d'Angelo to Olga Ivinskaya, September 26, 1959

Location: AGFE, CP, "Olga Ivinskaya–Sergio D'Angelo (1959–1960)," b. 1, fasc. 7

Format: Handwritten, signed. Photocopy (originating from Ivinskaya and Emelianova's trial proceedings; see section 2.2).

Original language: Russian

Previous publication: English translation published in Mancosu 2013, 312–13. Original text (with English translation) first published in Mancosu and Borokhov 2017.

Additional information: Draft of the letter also found in the SdAP, HILA

DOCUMENT

September 26, 1959

Dear Olga Vsevolodovna, hello!

I received your letter. You wrote: "Do not doubt my friendship." But how could I!? You have always shown me such friendship, tenderness, generosity, that I myself fear appearing to be forgetful and ungrateful. Therefore, I in turn say: Do not doubt my friendship. Until now, unfortunately, I have not been able to provide you with the assistance that you require, but I remain at your command and will do everything possible for B.L. and you that depends on me.

News about the letter that F. wrote addressed to B.L. exceeded all my expectations. But I knew even before that F. is not on good terms with Mme. de P. and her husband (and I informed you of this through our friend). What is the reason? Many months ago now, F. told me that he was hurt by the fact that Mme. de P. and her husband do not recognize his priority as a publisher regarding B.L.'s Autobiography and threatened him with a lawsuit. Though to be honest, when I met de P. (in the second half of May, in Paris), they were clearly predisposed against F. I recommended to them that they show more moderation and tact, and they agreed that the most important, pressing matter was the resolution of the financial question of how to transfer money to B.L.

Then, for a month and a half, I could not find out anything about further developments in the situation. In the first week of July, F. arrived in Rome, met with me at the publishing office, and declared that he himself would give me a gift from B.L. (and I did in fact receive it about 10 days later). As far as the de P.'s were concerned, F. told me that he had recently met them, that they (particularly the husband) made a very bad impression on him and that he would address B.L. directly about all questions of copyright and [their respective] roles.

On July 21, the de P.'s were in Milan. From there, they called and scheduled a meeting for the following day. I went there. They had already met with F's lawyer (F. found an excuse to not receive them). From the lawyer, they found out that F. intended to immediately set aside a sum corresponding to B.L.'s royalties for 1957–1958, excluding the money received from foreign publishers in the first half of 1959—in a word, the de P's told me, approximately 115 thousand dollars. Regarding the remaining sum, no promises and no agreement were made.

It should be noted that F. received most of the sum belonging to B.L. from foreign publishers specifically in 1959. In sum, it seems that B.L.'s earnings now already comprise approximately 500 thousand dollars.

Regardless, the de P.'s expressed significant optimism. Even though I told them about F's initiative and expressed my concern, they declared that everything would work out in time.

Having received approximately 115 thousand dollars, the de P's told me that 110 was destined for gifts, while the remainder was for B.L. And they asked me to write to them as soon as an opportunity to send money to B.L. appeared. On the 16th of the current month, I wrote to Mme de P., that such an opportunity had appeared, but she responded that she had fallen ill, and that unfortunately she could not deal with it at the moment.

This, in brief, is all I can tell you. I do not know in detail the relationship between F. and P. (having no right to meddle in it), and I cannot make judgments about the behavior of the two sides. But, since you had asked me for my "professional, personal opinion," I will tell you very honestly my opinion about the whole affair, that is, about the question of transferring money to B.L.

Only I can present the opportunity to give money to B.L. completely safely and *not in a trickle.* In what way, our friend will explain to you. Yet I do not consider it appropriate to redirect to me the power of attorney, as you suggested. It is likely that F. would not accept such a decision with pleasure, and new difficulties would arise.

In my opinion, B.L. needs to be a realist, that is, write to F. that he is ready to satisfy his demands when it is possible to do so, that he will limit the powers of de P., that he will not sharply raise the question of finances (undoubtedly, F. would very much like to administer part of B.L.'s funds for some time), that he will also give him priority regarding the new book. . . . But, *in return* (of course, that should be the meaning, but not these exact words), B.L. should demand that F. transfer to me, *immediately and in one transaction*, 100 thousand dollars. For what purpose, it is not necessary to describe in writing. It is sufficient to write that I will describe it myself.

100 thousand dollars is a sum that B.L. has wanted to receive for a long time; this is a sum that could forever secure him against all sorts of financial worries and difficulties.

If B.L. will listen to my advice and trust me, F. will probably be happy, and I would be able to transfer the entire sum in the shortest amount of time. But the letter to F. should be written very soon (and to me, for my information), because I do not know whether I will have the opportunity that I have now in a couple of months.

Given the current situation, in my opinion, there is absolutely no other way. Therefore please excuse me for my absolutism.

I bought for you and Irochka some winter clothes with your money. If you like the fur coat, I will buy another, when our friend goes on another trip (one cannot send two fur coats together).

Giulietta and I kiss you and ask you to send the most heartfelt greetings to B.L., your mother, Irochka, and your son.

Your
Serezha.

Commentary. Here d'Angelo rejects as unfeasible the proposal Ivinskaya made to transfer the power of attorney from de Proyart to him. D'Angelo also gives advice on how to advance the plan for sending Pasternak $100,000.

Document 14. Olga Ivinskaya to Sergio d'Angelo, November 19, 1959

Location: SdAP, HILA
Format: Partly typed, partly handwritten, signed. Original.
Original language: Russian
Previous publication: Original text and English translation first published in Mancosu and Borokhov 2017

DOCUMENT

Dear Serezhen'ka,

We still have not had an opportunity to thank you for the package. Thank you very much. The fur coat fit me very well and I liked it a lot, while Irochka got everything else. The clothes are all very nice.

I am sending you a letter B.L. started writing at the dacha, but then changed his mind, asking me to write about everything in detail. But it seems to me that even his draft will be interesting to you. There was no paper there at all and so he had to write on some scraps, and this embarrasses B.L.

Unfortunately, we have now gotten completely confused regarding our financial affairs. We have received monetary transfers from different sources, and we do not know what kind of sum is now at our disposal. Primarily this mess is the result of the complicated relationship between Mister Feltrinelli and Madam de Proyart, which is still not settled. Furthermore, B.L. is very worried about the fact that his requests regarding other monetary distributions to his friends have not been fulfilled and whether he still has the possibility to set aside another one hundred thousand for his own needs. Maybe if this one hundred thousand is set aside for him, then in case of significant misunderstandings between F. and P., his royalties would be insufficient for the gifts that he had set aside for his friends so long ago.

Therefore I am sending you a power of attorney for a much smaller sum for now, which will cover your expenses, and perhaps allow you to make a few more clothes shipments, which we appreciate and need very much.

If there is an opportunity to send with someone, please also send Irochka a fur coat, only in a significantly smaller size and in a more junior style. And if you will be sending me a dress, then the opposite, of a much larger size than you have ever sent me. I would also like a knit cap or beret, something stylish for my head. Irochka is again asking for pumps, but this time with a low heel, or no heel at all. We are sending you the sizes. Yes, I would also like a large bag.

Somehow we have made too many requests, but send whatever is more easily available and less burdensome to you. Please let me know the form of the receipts that are easier for you to make use of without any detriment to you.

Dearest Sergio, forgive me for such an incomprehensible and boring letter. My hand hurts, and Irochka is typing on the typewriter.

The health of the classic is not very good. His heart aches. If possible, please send some heart drops,[1] but ones that do not act too quickly. Things are not very good with his eyes. There are drops called "Intermidinii," it is impossible to obtain them here, perhaps you have them? Or some others.

Hugs and kisses. Your friends.

---

1. *Heart drops* is a term widely used in the USSR and still used to this day in the countries that belonged to the former Soviet Union. It refers to over-the-counter concentrates that are mixed with water and consumed to relieve stress, anxiety, and "heartache." Typically, they consist of concentrates of valerian root (*Valeriana officinalis*), hawthorn berries (*Crataegus* spp.), and motherwort leaves (*Leonurus cardiaca*).

Dear Giulietta, I have a special, feminine request for you. Perhaps there is some good antiwrinkle cream? Because I don't want to age, I want to be beautiful: kissing you once more

Olga.
November 19, 1959

Measurements for pumps
Ira — length 24 cm
width 8 cm
Olga Vsev[olodovna] length 24½,
and width 11–12 cm

Commentary. Pasternak had received news that the gifts he had asked Feltrinelli and Proyart to make to those beneficiaries indicated in letters dating back to February 1959 had not yet been carried out. He wrote an angry letter to Feltrinelli on November 18 (Mancosu 2013, 342–46) asking for an explanation, which Feltrinelli provided in his reply dated December 8, 1959 (Mancosu 2013, 350–52). Pasternak and Ivinskaya were confused about their financial situation, partly because money was arriving from different sources and partly because Feltrinelli had not yet sent them an accurate accounting of the royalties.

Ivinskaya sent a warrant for $10,000 on d'Angelo's behalf (published in Mancosu 2013, 348–49; see document 16) dated November 19, 1959, which was meant to help in sending funds until the larger sum could be transferred. On December 6, 1959, Pasternak sent a new warrant in favor of d'Angelo (see document 18), allowing d'Angelo to receive $100,000 from Pasternak's royalties. This document reached d'Angelo, through Mirella Garritano, in March 1960.

D'Angelo sent eye drops (together with 44,000 rubles) in February 1960 through Leo Paladini.

Document 15. Boris Pasternak to Sergio d'Angelo, November 19, 1959

Location: SdAP, HILA
Format: Handwritten, signed. Original.
Original language: Russian
Previous publication: Original text and English translation first published in Mancosu and Borokhov 2017

DOCUMENT

Dear Sergio, from the bottom of my heart I thank you for your care and attention, the gifts, the letters. I am struck by the fact that G.F. is impeding my orders regarding monetary gifts. I am writing about this to him personally. When you succeed in obtaining the sum assigned to you, please do not forget about the money that we have promised to your friend J.G. [Giuseppe Garritano] (which is supposed to be received separately, not from your portion). Maybe I have overexerted my heart with something recently. I have begun to feel it sometimes. I hope that this will not interfere with my work or suddenly interrupt it. If it is possible to escape this danger, everything will be fine.

Hugging you, say hello to your wife,
Your B. Pasternak

Commentary. Pasternak mentions his annoyance with Feltrinelli for not having carried out his request concerning the monetary gifts. However, by this time both d'Angelo and Garritano—and many other beneficiaries—had already received their gifts. Pasternak was later informed and apologized to Feltrinelli by means of a note sent by Ivinskaya (see Mancosu 2013, 348).

Document 16. Warrant in favor of Sergio d'Angelo, dated November 19, 1959

Location: AGFE, CP, Busta 1; Fascicolo 2-Feltrinelli-Pasternak
Format: Typewritten, signed. Original.
Original language: Russian
Previous publication: Russian text and English translation in Mancosu 2013, 348–49. Original text and English translation also published in Mancosu and Borokhov 2017.

DOCUMENT

WARRANT

I ask to give to the bearer of this [letter] Sergio D'Angelo ten thousand dollars (10,000) for purposes that he will describe to you personally.

With deepest respect to you,

and grateful in advance,

November 19, 1959,

B. Pasternak.

Commentary. This amount was meant to help with small deliveries of money until the delivery of $100,000 could be set in motion.

Document 17. Olga Ivinskaya to Sergio d'Angelo, end of 1959

Location: SdAP, HILA

Format: Handwritten, signed. Original.

Original language: Russian

Previous publication: Original text and English translation first published in Mancosu and Borokhov 2017

DOCUMENT

Dear Serezha!

I am sending you the power of attorney. Keep in mind that G.F. sometimes sends B.L. some money from the royalties. As I understand it, your transfers will be complementary, rather than against his. M-me J.P. has also sent some money (small sums). This is difficult for them to do for technical reasons, and we think that doing it from three different sources is more reliable and convenient than from one. Anyway, everything is easier for you to see from over there. My personal idea is to sufficiently provide for B.L. for now so that he will only translate for formality's sake and work on his piece. I think that this coincides with your plan.

Waiting for news,

Big kisses,

Olga.

Commentary. The letter can be dated to December 6, 1959, which is the date of the warrant for $100,000 published next.

Document 18. Warrant in favor of Sergio d'Angelo, December 6, 1959

Location: AGFE, CP, Busta 1, Fascicolo 1-Feltrinelli-Pasternak
Format: Handwritten, signed. Original. Also photographically reproduced in d'Angelo 1961b, 35.
Original language: French
Previous publication: Previously translated into Italian: d'Angelo 2006, 156–57; d'Angelo 1961b, 35. Published in original French and English translation in Mancosu 2013, 349. Original text and English translation also published in Mancosu and Borokhov 2017.

DOCUMENT

Peredelkino, near Moscow
December 6, 1959

With the present letter I, the undersigned, give Mr. Sergio d'Angelo the authority to take possession of one hundred thousand dollars ($100,000) of my royalties for the goals and use that he will communicate and explain to two other persons in whom I place my confidence, Mrs. Jacqueline de Proyart and Mr. Giangiacomo Feltrinelli.

B. Pasternak.

[*Added later by Sergio d'Angelo*: Milan, March 9, 1960; Sergio d'Angelo]

Commentary. While talks with de Proyart and Feltrinelli about this sum of money, to be drawn on Pasternak's behalf, went back to the spring of 1959 (see previous commentaries), d'Angelo received the sum in March 1960 (see Mancosu 2013, section 3.56), and soon afterward he began the transfer operation to Pasternak. As already mentioned, this operation was ill-fated and led to the arrest of Olga Ivinskaya and Irina Emelianova after Pasternak's death. D'Angelo 2006 provides a reconstruction of the events, and we have complemented this account in chapter 1. However, while much of the blame has been heaped on d'Angelo's transfers (and in particular the last one, in July 1960 through the Benedettis), it is fair to point out that the formal list of accusations raised against Ivinskaya and Emelianova shows that the Soviet authorities were aware of the various couriers, and of the sums they delivered, from February 1959 to August 1960. Of course, it is possible that one part of such a detailed list could have been obtained during the interrogations of Olga and Irina and not from previous surveillance. But only a part, since, as pointed out in chapter 2, the KGB was already aware in February 1960 that Schewe and Nivat were delivering money to Pasternak. In the indictment against Olga and Irina, the following names and sums were mentioned: Ruge (12,000 rubles), Nivat (6,000 rubles), Schewe (80,000 rubles), Paladini (40,000 rubles), Mirella Garritano (180,000 rubles), and the Benedettis (500,000 rubles). For the full translation of the indictment, see document 50. It is very likely that the authorities had been observing Ivinskaya for a long time and decided to act only after Pasternak's death.

Document 19. Sergio d'Angelo to Olga Ivinskaya, February 2, 1960

Location: AGFE, CP, Busta 1, Fascicolo 7, "Olga Ivinskaya–Sergio d'Angelo (1959–1960)"
Format: Handwritten, signed. Photocopy (originating from Ivinskaya and Emelianova's trial proceedings; see section 2.2).
Original language: Russian
Previous publication: Original text and English translation first published in Mancosu and Borokhov 2017

DOCUMENT

Olga Vsevolodovna, dear, greetings!

The bearer of this letter—Leo Paladini—is a very close and reliable friend of mine, whom you can trust completely. Unfortunately, he knows few Russian words, but his task, so to speak, is limited.

I have asked him to give you a few things, medicines and the like. Giulietta could not find pumps for you in the appropriate size (i.e., length 24.5 and width 11–12) and could not special-order them in time. So I will send them at the next opportunity.

I still have a lot of your money. Therefore I will not only give the agreed-upon sum to our friend as soon as I see him, but will gladly be at your disposal if you write to me about other things that could be useful to you.

You wrote that you have become completely confused about your finances. But I think that after my recent messages, you have sorted things out. However, I repeat: F. instructed me to tell you that he has sent all the gifts and that "over two hundred thousand, about three hundred thousand dollars" remain.

From my side, I can still—safely and quickly—perform the operation that I offered to you. Decide now yourself what to do. No matter what, I particularly recommend that you take advantage of Paladini's trip if you wish to send F., me, or others important letters or documents. To be honest, I do not know when there will be another such convenient opportunity.

Please inform us about B.L.'s state of health in detail; we are sending him the most heartfelt greetings and wish him all the best.

Two years have already passed since our separation, and we very much miss him and all of you. Giulietta and I with all our hearts hope to come visit you during summer tourist trips. It is likely that we will be able to in 1961.

Awaiting your reply (on the typewriter, of course . . .), Giulietta and I send hugs and kisses to you all.

Your
Serezha.

If you have letters for F, me, or others, I ask you to set up a new meeting with Paladini, so you can give them to him. It is better not to talk about your relationship with our friends in Moscow. It is obvious that they want to act very cautiously.

Commentary. Leo Paladini went to Moscow as part of a delegation of journalists and brought Pasternak 44,000 rubles, for which we still have the receipt (see document 20). In addition, he brought eye drops for Pasternak. Notice how d'Angelo at the end of this letter warns Ivinskaya not to reveal her contact with the Garritanos. D'Angelo also says, "I still have a lot of your money. Therefore I will not only give the agreed-upon sum to our friend as soon as I see him, but will gladly be at your disposal if you write to me about other things that could be useful to you." The friend is Garritano, and this passage clearly indicates d'Angelo's intention to send more money through him. D'Angelo has stated, however, in personal correspondence that the Garritanos never brought money inside the Soviet Union, but they received it once they were already inside the Soviet Union. At the same time, d'Angelo cautiously mentions that Paladini could be the right courier for sending the warrant for $100,000. In document 21, Ivinskaya explains to d'Angelo why the document will reach him only in March, although it had been ready since December.

Document 20. Receipt signed by Boris Pasternak, February 8, 1960

Location: SdAP, HILA
Format: Handwritten, signed. Original.
Original language: Russian
Previous publication: Original text and English translation first published in Mancosu and Borokhov 2017

DOCUMENT

Receipt

Received February 8 1960
forty-four thousand rub.
(44 thousand rubl.)

B. Pasternak.

Commentary. This was the receipt for the sum delivered by Leo Paladini on February 8, 1960.

Document 21. Olga Ivinskaya to Sergio d'Angelo, mid-February 1960

Location: SdAP, HILA
Format: Typewritten, signed. Original.
Original language: Russian
Previous publication: Original text and English translation first published in Mancosu and Borokhov 2017
Additional information: According to d'Angelo, this letter was brought to Italy by Leo Paladini.

DOCUMENT

My dear Giulietta and Sergio!

Yesterday, February 8, we met with your friend.

He gave us the money from you, and today we will get the clothes. A big thank-you for everything.

I am happy to tell you that B.L. is feeling well, thank you for the medicines, we received them. He looks marvelous, beaming, he got plump, beautiful. For now, everything is well with his heart.

I am in a rush, so this letter of mine will be short.

I would like to clarify one specific issue. For our friends who are currently in Moscow, we had asked you to set aside money not from the money due to you, but rather completely separately, from the sums that B.L. had set aside for gifts.

The power of attorney in your name about which you write (for one hundred thousand dollars), for the operation to which we agreed, I have already given to Mirella about a month ago. But she wants to personally deliver it to you in March.

She is very cautious, and I decided not to risk it, though I really wanted to take the power of attorney from her and give it to signor Leo P. Our meeting with M[irella] should take place, unfortunately, after the departure of your friend.

Irochka and B.L. send you their warmest regards and gratitude, all of us want to see you very much and hope that everything will be well.

Hugging you,
Your Olga.

My dear friends, regarding shoes and clothes:

For Irochka, summer dresses in size 44, for me size 54–52 (depending on the style).

Irochka is asking for a summer dress, relying entirely on Giulietta's taste, a cute rain jacket, and a petticoat. And just a puffy skirt for the summer. If it's possible, some summer dress, simple and tight. I liked the cream you sent me very much, I want more, and, may Giulietta forgive us for all the trouble we are making, an eye pencil and cosmetic brushes, none of which are good here. I really want perfume. This is just a dream.

If it's not difficult to find summer pumps—(sandals), for me black pumps—all this is very much needed.

My size is our Soviet 37—only I have a wide last. But generally just send us whatever is least difficult for you, we will be very happy with anything. Our sailor Mitia has grown up and really wants to get dressed. His size is 50, third height.[2] He is tall but skinny. He's dreaming of a tie to go with a black suit.

And here we go again coming up with an entire cartload. In a word, we are completely depending on you.

2. In the Soviet era, for clothing sizes, heights were designated in three categories: size 1/2, 3/4, and 5/6. The second category, which includes "third height," corresponds to an average height of 170–176 cm or 5'7"–5'9".

Commentary. The most important thing in this letter is the explanation of how it came about that the warrant for d'Angelo arrived in Italy only in March. Moreover, as will be confirmed by the next letter, this also indicates that the presence of Mirella Garritano in Italy gave d'Angelo the opportunity to arrange delivery of a substantial sum to Pasternak.

Document 22. Sergio d'Angelo to Boris Pasternak and Olga Ivinskaya, March 19, 1960

Location: AGFE, CP, Busta 1, Fascicolo 7, "Olga Ivinskaya–Sergio d'Angelo (1959–1960)"
Format: Handwritten, signed. Photocopy (originating from Ivinskaya and Emelianova's trial proceedings; see section 2.2).
Original language: Russian
Previous publication: Original text and English translation first published in Mancosu and Borokhov 2017

DOCUMENT

Rome, March 19, 1960

Dear friends, greetings!

In a few days, you should receive from me part of what I owe you. And relatively quickly, as I promised you, there will be other transfers.

Verbally, our friend will describe the affair in complete detail. I will tell you only the following:

1. F. requests that you send him just two lines informing him of the revocation of de Proyart's power of attorney.

2. F. completely agrees that only a film outside the polemical political discourse can be made. To accomplish this goal, he is taking on the responsibility, should the need arise, to personally check the script himself.

Hugging you all,
Your S.

Commentary. Sergio d'Angelo has insisted that there were no deliveries of money to Pasternak in March (or April). But I think this letter, which he had not seen since the time it was written, proves unequivocally that d'Angelo intended to transfer a substantial amount of money immediately after writing this letter. Garritano was in charge of explaining the details of the operation, but he was not the person who physically brought the money through customs.

The mention of the revocation of the power of attorney to Proyart concerns a document that Proyart herself had requested from Pasternak, discharging her from her previous responsibilities as Pasternak's representative in the West while approving all her work on his behalf up to that point (see Mancosu 2013, 365). The document was sent to Proyart on April 12, 1960.

Through d'Angelo, Feltrinelli conveyed to Pasternak his resolve to carefully supervise any movie from the novel to avoid political exploitation of the novel.

Document 23. Sergio d'Angelo to Olga Ivinskaya, mid-April or May 1960

Location: AGFE, CP, Busta 1, Fascicolo 7, "Olga Ivinskaya–Sergio d'Angelo (1959–1960)"

Format: Handwritten, signed. Photocopy (originating from Ivinskaya and Emelianova's trial proceedings; see section 2.2).

Original language: Russian

Previous publication: Original text and English translation first published in Mancosu and Borokhov 2017

DOCUMENT

Dear Olga, greetings!

I know that our friends will leave Moscow forever very soon. This circumstance, unfortunately, will complicate our relations, but even going forward, though more rarely, I will cautiously write to you and send necessities when the opportunity arises.

Now, risking reproach from you, I dare to suggest to you a solution that could spare our friends anxiety and difficulties arising from their return to their homeland. I am talking in particular about Mirella, who in my opinion will not be able to obtain a desirable job very soon and who will have difficulties putting her family's affairs in order.

Truthfully, it's possible that it would be completely inappropriate to propose that you make a new gift to Mirella; and I would have refrained from such a proposition if I did not believe that it is very likely that you will not completely deplete that huge sum that has poured out and will continue to pour out of the royalties (F. already has approximately two hundred thousand dollars and another couple of hundred thousand will surely come from the film).

Furthermore, I am completely certain that Mirella has done for you no less than I have; and so to speak, my conscience would be put at ease if you had decided to give a gift to Mirella that was as generous as the one I so undeservedly received.

Do you consider my initiative exceedingly out of place and impudent? In that case, I sincerely apologize. Tear up this letter and say nothing—I implore you—of its contents to either B.L. or Mirella.

I kiss you all fervently.
Your S.

Commentary. The Garritanos were preparing to leave Moscow to go back to Italy at the end of May. As things worked out, they returned to Italy in mid-June. D'Angelo here asks Ivinskaya (and indirectly Pasternak) to consider donating $10,000 to Mirella Garritano for her services. Pasternak agreed with this request, and Feltrinelli was instructed to give d'Angelo another gift for $10,000 (with the understanding that d'Angelo would transfer the money to Mirella Garritano upon her return to Italy). See the letter from Olga Ivinskaya to Giangiacomo Feltrinelli dated May 25, 1960 (Mancosu 2013, 375). The arrangement is further confirmed in a letter from Ivinskaya to Feltrinelli dated June 5, 1960, preserved in the Feltrinelli archives in Milan (document 32).

Document 24. Postcard from Mirella Garritano to Giulietta Pecori, September 3, 1958

Location: SdAP, HILA
Format: Handwritten, signed
Original language: Italian
Previous publication: Original text and English translation first published in Mancosu and Borokhov 2017
Additional information: This postcard and the next four items contain transcriptions of the postcards and letters, written in code, sent between September 1958 and April 1960 from Giuseppe (Pino) Garritano and his wife, Mirella (who were both still in the USSR), to Giulia (Giulietta) Pecori and—obviously—her husband, Sergio d'Angelo (who by then

were back in Italy). In documents 24–28, unsigned annotations in the main text and footnotes signed "–SD" are by Sergio d'Angelo. My additions are marked by "–PM." The explanations for the codes are given by d'Angelo in the main text.

DOCUMENT

Dearest Giulietta,[3]

Adriana [Olga Ivinskaya] has received as scheduled everything that you sent her.[4] She thanks you very much. She is now living somewhat secluded on account of her health:[5] but hopefully she will recover soon. Concerning the plays about which you have asked me, there is only one more left, The Sword of Damocles,[6] still unpublished. The five that are marked with an asterisk have been edited in the people's democracies. I will later send the precise list. (1) The author has promised me the unpublished one as well.

Document 25. Postcard from Pino Garritano to Giulietta Pecori, January 6, 1959

Location: SdAP, HILA
Format: Handwritten, signed
Original language: Italian
Previous publication: Original text and English translation first published in Mancosu and Borokhov 2017

3. "Judging by the handwriting, the postcard could be (but I am not sure) written by Mirella, but the content is not hers. Perhaps, on account of an extreme caution, Pino dictated it to her or to another person? The decision must be made by a graphologist." —SD

4. "She received timely the clothes and the other few objects I [d'Angelo] sent her." —SD

5. "Should one interpret this as referring to the writer's health and also to the mood of both of them in the political climate that precedes by little the award of the Nobel Prize?" —SD

6. These passages are difficult to interpret. I think it is more probable that the reference is to a list of poems, and any reference to *The Blind Beauty* should be excluded, since Pasternak would not start work on this play until after the Nobel Prize, in early 1959. There is a sketch of a play from the twenties that mentions The Sword of Damocles but it is not clear whether there is a connection.

DOCUMENT

Dear Giulia,

I am writing to convey my best wishes for 1959. Please forgive me for being late but I have been unable to do so earlier. For the article you have asked me, the author wants some time to think over the matter: he seems mostly worried about his honorarium.[7] I would like to ask you not to give letters to careless people who call me on your behalf, only after a long time.[8] Do wait in any case for a letter from me. Again I wish you and your family a happy new year.

Document 26. Postcard from Pino Garritano to Giulietta Pecori, erroneously dated March 9, 1958 (but in reality, 1959)

Location: SdAP, HILA
Format: Handwritten, signed
Original language: Italian
Previous publication: Original text and English translation first published in Mancosu and Borokhov 2017

DOCUMENT

Dear Giulia,[9]

Forgive me for these belated good wishes for March 8, Women's International Day. But as compensation, you should soon receive the long-awaited gift:[10] it will however arrive in Milan brought by a Nibelung [Heinz Schewe or Gerd Ruge —PM]. How are you? I hope well. Give my greetings to everybody.

Paolo [Pino]

---

7. "The entire sentence, I suppose, is to inform me [d'Angelo] that Pasternak was very worried because they had destroyed his ability to earn a living." —SD

8. "Did he want to tell me that I had given letters for Pasternak to friends that went to and came back from Moscow? It is not likely, I [d'Angelo] do not recall having done it even a single time. It is much more likely that he wanted to advise me to be extremely cautious (and I was), in Italy not less than in the USSR, with respect to my contacts with Olga." —SD

9. "The date cannot be 1958, as Pino writes, but rather must be 1959. This can be inferred from his references to events that took place, without any doubt, in the year following the one indicated by the sender." —SD

10. "A reference to the monetary gifts, totaling 110,000 dollars, which Pasternak, in a letter dated February 2, 1959, asked Feltrinelli to transfer to seventeen people residing in the West, including me [d'Angelo] and Pino." —SD

Document 27. Mirella Garritano to Giulietta Pecori, November 28, 1959

Location: SdAP, HILA
Format: Handwritten, signed
Original language: Italian
Previous publication: Original text and English translation first published in Mancosu and Borokhov 2017

DOCUMENT

Dear Giulietta,

I received a few days ago news from Olga, who always remembers you with affection. I have explained to her for a second time the reasons that speak in favor of the sending of books [transfer of money] but it seems that Giovanni [Pasternak] at this moment does not deem it necessary because he says he does not need them, they are too many and he would not know where to put them.[11] Recently he received other books from his Paris friends [Proyart] who act very affectionately and desire not to appear inferior to anyone else. The inheritance issue [the controversy between Feltrinelli and Proyart] is still unresolved: it seems that Uncle Giancarlo [Feltrinelli] intends to travel to Belgium [Paris —PM] [to meet, I presume, the de Proyarts] toward the second half of December. This state of affairs worries Giovanni [Pasternak] a little, and it is for this reason that he does not want to make any decisions. Thus, one needs to wait a bit longer.

Meanwhile, Olga will send more books [money], which are quite cute and useful, of which a small part should remain at my disposal, as you know, and as is hinted in one of the letters[12] even if, it seems to me, in somewhat confused terms.[13]

Chiarini received the small present you sent and she was quite happy about it.[14]

---

11. "From me [d'Angelo], he had received in October a first significant transfer. In any case, I waited until February 1960 (the next favorable opportunity) to send a second one." —SD

12. See document 15.

13. Since the letter is dated November 28 and the payment to Giuseppe Garritano of his $2,000 had already taken place in July, it is likely that here Mirella refers to the $10,000 that Pasternak sent to d'Angelo with a warrant dated November 19, 1959 (see document 16, published in Mancosu 2013, 348–49) as a provisional measure to help cover expenses until a resolution of the Feltrinelli-Proyart negotiations would allow for disbursement of the $100,000 to d'Angelo.

14. "Khiarini (Lida) is the name of a young Russian colleague of mine [d'Angelo's] of Italian origin cited in my *Il Caso Pasternak* on account of a curious event. Did I send her a present? Possibly, but frankly I can't recall." —SD

Affectionate greetings and best wishes for Christmas and New Year's Eve to you, Sergio, and the children.

Mi[rella]

Document 28. Mirella Garritano to Giulietta Pecori, April 30, 1960

Location: SdAP, HILA
Format: Handwritten, signed
Original language: Italian
Previous publication: Original text and English translation first published in Mancosu and Borokhov 2017

DOCUMENT

Dear Giulietta,

Please excuse me for not having sent any news about us earlier, but these days we are very busy, for we are very close to our departure. We will come back at the beginning of June and thus we are already in the process of dismantling the camp. Frankly, we are very sad to leave earlier than expected (we were hoping to stay until August) but the magazine has decided so[15] and we can do nothing about it. It is our intention to take a trip in the Soviet Union before coming back to Rome, but taking everything into consideration we will not be able to stay beyond June 15. Keep this date in mind for what concerns the sending of the books [money] I had asked you for and which the comrades [Pasternak and Olga] are waiting for.

The gifts were enthusiastically received and Olga let me know that she intends to reciprocate by sending some souvenirs. If you can, please send her the cream for her face, which seems to be quite good.[16] We had a long chat together, and she spoke to me about her relatives, with whom you are acquainted. Just these past few days, Giovanni [Pasternak] had to halt his work on account of a heart attack, from which, we hope, he will recover soon. The French cousin [Proyart] writes often. She is full of attentions and is determined to be of help: she has not at all given up editorial activity, even if she would like to limit it to the translation, revision, and editing of the Russian

15. "Or the higher Soviet authorities because they knew of the connection to Olga?" —SD
16. "The cream as well as the face" —SD

books [Pasternak's writings] into French with exclusive rights for France. She wrote with the request to support this initiative of hers, and Giovanni [Pasternak] wrote in this sense to the publishing house [Feltrinelli] with the certainty, however, of receiving a denial so that he can elegantly communicate it to the cousin. It would certainly be desirable if one found the way to bring a halt to this "activism," which, among other things, distresses Giovanni, who during this period would need, on the contrary, the most absolute calm. In any case, it is now only a matter of waiting for the editions that have Sergio as intermediary since the recommendation letter has been sent to him.[17]

Everything else is going quite well: Ira is now engaged to a French student [Georges Nivat —PM] and she hopes to marry soon. Marcella [fake name for Boffa's wife[18]] is always involved with book collecting,[19] continues to enrich the library with new books, and misses no occasion to popularize her favorite authors. The problem is that her husband does not understand this obsession of hers, he tries to curb her enthusiasm and often raises his voice.

He is a difficult character and, as we say in Rome, all of a piece. Ignazio[20] has not yet given any sign of life despite our repeated invitations: he must have found a girlfriend, there is no other explanation.

How is life with you? Is the weather good? Here we are still wearing our overcoats but enjoying a magnificent sun. I end this long chat by exonerating you from the need to reply since we will see each other soon.

Affectionate greetings to you, as well as to your husband and children

Mirella

17. "To tell the truth, I [d'Angelo] was not able to exercise any influence in this matter." —SD

18. Giuseppe Boffa, correspondent for *l'Unità*.

19. "Items of luxury clothing, which she often brought in her suitcase from Rome to Moscow and sold at a considerable profit to the wives of the Soviet high officials. Mirella mentioned this to me because one time I said jockingly that the Boffas, in addition to the husband's official role as a correspondent for *L'Unità*, should be considered, on account of the relevant economic gain obtained by the above-mentioned commercial activity, a family of 'magliari,' a term very much in fashion in Italy during the fifties and the title of a movie, if I am not mistaken." —SD

20. "Ignacio, the dear and depressed Spanish friend who is mentioned several times in my [d'Angelo's] *Caso Pasternak*." —SD

Document 29. Gerd Ruge to Kurt Wolff, February 2, 1959

Location: PFP, HILA, Box 107, folder 4
Format: Photocopy
Original language: German
Previous publication: Original text and English translation first published in Mancosu 2018a
Additional information: Excerpt of a letter from Gerd Ruge to Kurt Wolff that Wolff sent to others (for further information on Ruge and Wolff, see Boris Pasternak 2010a)

DOCUMENT

Now to your question about "Lara." Please forgive me if I do not mention the name, B.P. asked me explicitly for discretion. In any case it is a name that cannot mean anything to you and which you probably will not have heard. A few correspondents have drawn false conclusions from Pasternak's intimations, or else by excessive secretiveness created the impression that Lara was an especially influential person with important relationships. This is nonsense. She worked until recently at the publisher "Goslitizdat" and was let go, probably on account of her efforts to help Pasternak. She is the daughter of an officer who fought on different sides in the tumult of the civil war—you know this from Sholokov's "And Quiet Flows the Don." He fell in these battles when his daughter was still too young to retain a memory of him. In other words: Lara is about forty years old, perhaps a little older. She herself had to spend five years in a camp or in prison. That is all the contribution I can make to "Personal Facts." I do not know more myself. But I can describe to you a little how she looks.

For some reason or other, B.P. had the idea one day that I should get to know Lara. She sent her daughter to my street corner—a girl of just about twenty whom I immediately recognized, because she looked for some reason very unusual for Moscow: blond hair bound into a "ponytail," very lively, with somewhat catlike, slanted eyes, very lively and pretty. We began at once a very natural conversation, in which she offered a stream of quite open and oppositional impressions. Her mother's apartment is on the sixth floor, is quite small and—typically Russian—a bit overfilled and not overly organized. (The apartment is appointed in a very bourgeois style, a big sofa with a mirror above and dark wood trim, for example.) Lara is a medium-size, blond woman with a well-proportioned, rather broad face, the Russian bone structure obvious but not overly pronounced, with a touch of a snub nose (nez retroussé) that recurs more distinctively in her daughter. Lara wore a light blue wool jacket, her figure is full but not—as often with Russian women—tending toward fatness, but rather soft and balanced. She reminded me of the blond women that one sometimes finds in Matisse's paintings. Her son was there too, between eighteen and nineteen years old. At the moment he is growing an existentialist beard. I encountered him once more later at an exhibition where Polish painters showed several truly modernist pictures and he argued eagerly with whole groups of astounded and confused visitors.

Before I came, BP had already called and asked if I were there. I arrived many hours too late; they had been waiting for me since five o'clock—the Russian term "evening" is extraordinarily flexible. Then cheese, sausages, ham, fruit, cognac, and red wine were brought, and we began an hours-long conversation in the small living room. Lara herself participated only a little at the beginning. With bemused indulgence she defended the pictures on the walls—good bourgeois Russian taste, slightly antiquated landscapes, etc.—which were mocked by her children. While the boy is very quiet, the girl has what one could call "a sassy mouth"—admittedly with an enormous amount of charm and wit. Her observations about art and politics in the Soviet Union were spot-on, funny, and sharp. (A few times already she had difficulties at the university on account of such remarks.) For B.P. she came up with a fine name: she, and the others now as well, called him "Classic"—so "the Classicist," a little disrespectful but B.P. also likes it. Lara joined the conversation really for the first time when it came to B.P., about whom she worries greatly. Then she spoke indeed very precisely and thoughtfully; she explained what she had already tried and what could still be done. She developed her thoughts with a certain obviousness—as if she seems to deal and live with such obviousness not effortlessly, that would be the wrong word, but yes without any—well, I cannot explain it well, perhaps you understand me anyway. It is nothing forced, nothing deliberate in her.

Document 30. Giangiacomo Feltrinelli to Olga Ivinskaya, June 4, 1960

Location: AGFE, Busta 3, fascicolo 6
Format: Copy
Original language: German
Previous publication: Original text and English translation first published in Mancosu 2018a
Additional information: The transcription of the letter is from the carbon copy preserved at AGFE

DOCUMENT

Milan, June 4, 1960

Dear, honorable Ms. Olga!

Your urgent message not to come to Moscow arrived just before my departure for Bonn (where I intended to submit a request at the consulate for permission to travel). Although everything drew me to yourself, to a last visit to Boris Pasternak, I had to change my travel plans with a heavy heart.

Although unfortunately apart from you, I stood in spirit by Boris Pasternak, by you in all these somber days and hours.

Dear Ms. Olga! I cannot face the idea that the Classic is no more and now lives only in his works, in the memory of those who loved him. His death has not only taken from the world a poet, an artist, a man who was a living example for us all, but also someone who was for [us] a great, humane personality worthy of our love, our entire wonderment.

I stand especially close to you, dear Olga, in this harrowing moment and in the future. Please depend upon me now as ever.

Until soon. May you be embraced

Document 31. Giangiacomo Feltrinelli to Heinz Schewe, June 4, 1960

Location: Heinz Schewe Papers, Berlin
Format: Original
Original language: German
Previous publication: Original text and English translation first published in Mancosu 2018a

DOCUMENT

Dear Heinz Schewe,

The horrible news of Pasternak's death, and the fact that we all lost a friend, a great, wonderful person, is still too raw for us to deal with the entirely new problems that have arisen.

I would only like to ask you to prove our friendship and stand by Olga.

It was very difficult for me to drop my trip to Moscow.

I will write you again in the next days. Heartfelt greetings, also from Inge

Yours, Giangiacomo Feltrinelli

Document 32. Olga Ivinskaya to Giangiacomo Feltrinelli, June 5, 1960

Location: FoGF, Fascicolo "Ivinskaja Olga" (1960–1970), 1.2.1.–b.15, fasc. 150

Format: Original

Original language: Russian

Previous publication: Previously published in German translation, with some cuts, in Schewe 1974, 51–54. Original text and English translation first published in Mancosu 2018a.

DOCUMENT

Dear, dear Giangiacomo!

You already know about our terrible grief. My dear Boryusha is no more. Only two days have passed since his funeral, and yet I am obliged to write to you a letter not just as a friend, but as a business associate. Everyone is hurrying, and it is scary for us to wait.

In April, wishing to occupy himself solely with his play, and feeling a certain weakness, B. wrote me a power of attorney to be given to you. It states that he requests that my signature be trusted as his own—on monetary documents, as well as in any requests coming from him and about him. This power of attorney is written in both Russian and French and has been given [*handwritten*: by me] to friends of Sergio D'Angelo, before Mr. Heinz had returned to Moscow, so that they may personally hand it to you.

If even after Borya's death his will is sacred to you and you still consider me his empowered representative, who has been charged with piously carrying out his will, I ask you to assure me of it. Meanwhile, I will acquaint you with my plans.

First of all, I ask you in turn to consider Mr. Heinz Schewe to be my empowered representative. Through him I will give you, as per Borya's wishes, those manuscripts that he will give to you in due time for publication. This concerns the manuscript of the novel, materials from the archives, which I will put into order without delay, as well as the play. Here, things are more difficult, the utmost care is needed, and in this both you and I will trust Mr. Heinz.

Regarding Mme. P. I have in my hands documents that will help in ending affairs with her as soon as possible.

If you will consider the power of attorney from B. (the last one) [*handwritten*: in my name] to be valid, Mme. P. must agree to its authenticity as well: for this you will suggest the wording of my message to her and I will sign it.

Borya has wishes, which must be carried out after his death with the same precision as if he were alive.

This concerns monetary deductions, which he asks you to make to his friends, who helped him and colored his life. From the money that belongs to him, he wanted to set aside ten thousand dollars to Sergio D'Angelo to give to his friends, who are returning from Moscow. Ten thousand dollars to Mr. Heinz Schewe to his address in Hamburg. Ten thousand to Mr. Georges Nivat to an address in France, Paris (I will confirm the address). Five thousand to Mme. Renata [Renate Schweitzer] (Berlin, Lankwitz Am Gemeindepark 16).

Dear Giangiacomo, I do not need to tell you that the strictest care must be observed: otherwise, I will perish, and so will Borya's manuscripts and archives.

Once I have received your letter, in which you will confirm receipt of the power of attorney in my name (it should be given to you in June of this year by D'Angelo's friends), I can also send you the contract that was signed by Boris Leonidovich while he was still alive, which he had withheld until the peaceful resolution of the conflict with Mme. P. It would be good if you would set aside some area for her to work on. This would coincide with Boris Leonidovich's wishes. Please tell me what you think about this, and I will write to her accordingly. Correspond only with Mr. Heinz, and remember that carelessness can destroy everything. Hurry with your response. I'm here waiting for the remaining sum that should be given to me by D'Angelo's friends in June (the power of attorney was in his name for one hundred thousand dollars, but only a portion has been transferred). After receiving it and settling with them with a receipt as per the agreement, I will ask you to have monetary relationships with me only through Mr. Heinz in the future. After finishing things here, I will do my best to leave for July and put the archive in order. Mr. Heinz, knowing the entire situation that has manifested itself here, approves of my plan.

Until next time, dear friend.
[*handwritten*:] Your O. Ivinskaya

It is entirely possible that relatives of Boris Leonidovich will approach you with claims to the right to take care of his affairs in the West, in particular his sister, whom he supposedly wanted to see before his death. This is actually a lie, it was not his wish, but rather that of his relatives, who wanted to put the power in her hands.

In a potential conflict with her, I will be on your side. They have no official documents to give to their publisher, as they would have liked to. The last official document was the power of attorney about which I wrote to you earlier.

[*handwritten*:] Once again—until next time, Your Olga
[*handwritten*:] Your O. Ivinskaya

Document 33. Heinz Schewe to Giangiacomo Feltrinelli, June 6, 1960

Location: AGFE, Busta 1, fascicolo 5, "Feltrinelli-Schewe" (1959 febbraio 15–1966 dicembre 07)
Format: Original
Original language: German
Previous publication: Published in Schewe 1974, 51–54, with some cuts. Full original text and English translation first published in Mancosu 2018a

DOCUMENT

Editore
Giangiacomo Feltrinelli
Milan
Via Andegari 6
Moscow / Hotel Berlin / 516

June 6, 1960

Dear Mr. Feltrinelli,

I am sitting here now and do not know how to begin. Everything has happened so suddenly. I have still not totally grasped it all. I still cannot believe that he will never again come striding over the little hill to our dacha, will never again enjoyably savor a glass of "Martell" cognac with us, which he called "heaven's nectar," can no longer be excited about our gifts, never more.... It has suddenly become so empty without him. I have never before known this. And I also did not expect that I would miss him so intensely.

Just now I was only able to lay a pretty wreath on his grave. It was a moving funeral. I must still write a report for "STERN" about it. Then I will make you a copy so that you know how it was. I myself took no pictures of the burial. I could not. I went the whole day as if paralyzed and even today am still not quite mobile again.

Now we must all stand together, friendly and fair, so that we only do what he would have wanted. Two things—so it seems to me—should be observed above all:

1) There must be no scandal (trial or civil proceedings or the like) that might harm his memory. A way must be found in all contentious questions to settle things amicably, just as he would have wished it.

2) Nothing must occur that could endanger the freedom, security, and livelihood of Ms. Olga. According to the will of Boris Leonidovich, she is the sole literary heiress

and the only one empowered to act on behalf of his fortune abroad. This I know and can testify to. Boris Leonidovich drew up a correspondent power of attorney for Ms. Olga already on the 15th of April 1960, one week before the beginning of his illness. This power of attorney was prepared in three languages and should be delivered to you by way of Sergio d'Angelo's friends in the course of this month.

With the same mailing I will forward to you a letter from Ms. Olga and a translation that I have prepared of it. You will understand everything by it.

With regard to the drama that was regrettably only half finished, I must additionally tell you the following: the original is with Ms. Olga. She has just prepared a few copies of it. We will try to deposit a copy in a secure location abroad. For the moment, however, nothing may be published in the West yet! The Committee for State Security [KGB] is close on her tail. They recently pressured Ms. Olga even before Boris Leonidovich was under the ground. I advised her to give a copy to these people, since otherwise they will not leave her in peace. This copy will be presented to a high official of the Soviet Committee for State Security in Moscow on Tuesday, the 7th of June, 1960. It was Boris Leonidovich's wish that this new work should first be submitted in Moscow to the state publisher. And so it should happen. We hope that reason wins this time and they decide to publish the fragment. Then nothing would probably stand in the way—after a sufficient interval—of a reprint by yourself, and nobody on this side would be endangered. Be sure that no one in the West except you will receive a copy.

The original should in any case remain in Ms. Olga's hands. I told her that everything else Boris Leonidovich ever wrote during his lifetime has now become an important piece of world literature. She collected everything, all his letters and notes. Hopefully it remains in our possession! We worry, nevertheless, that some authorities in Moscow could potentially tighten their grip. In any case we must now be more careful than ever before. I am convinced that Boris Leonidovich would never forgive us if we, by impatience, carelessness, or self-interest, were to endanger Ms. Olga.

Everything further you will find in Ms. Olga's letter.

With heartfelt greetings, also to Ms. Inge,

Yours, Heinz Schewe

PS: My account at Deutsche Bank in Hamburg: A. 11 27 09. It is, however, perhaps better if we first speak verbally about this—prospectively in September.

Yet another important matter: Ms. Olga asks you most kindly to send her as many foreign newspapers with obituaries for the Classic as possible. Please do so with my courier address. Many thanks!

[Handwritten enclosure] [*In Feltrinelli's hand*: arrived on 15/6 1960]

Dear Mr. Feltrinelli,

This is an important letter from Ms. Olga. I will send the German translation in another envelope with the same mailing.

Your H. Schewe

PS: Your letter to B.P. of the 15th + 20th of May, 1960 unfortunately came too late.

Document 34. Sergio d'Angelo to Giangiacomo Feltrinelli, June 9, 1960

Location: SdAP, HILA
Format: Carbon copy of the original
Original language: Italian
Previous publication: Original text and English translation first published in Mancosu 2018a

DOCUMENT

(copy)

June 9, 1960

Dear Giangiacomo,

The matter about which you speak has been proceeding so far in the most regular way. O.[lga] (who asked me to divide the work in several months) has already received with great satisfaction two large packages. A third one is already in preparation.

I will update you with pleasure on all the work that has been carried out so far but I will not be able to do so before the next month because I find myself in a "fluid" phase and because I am awaiting from O.[lga], by the end of June, indispensable documents (and, I believe, further instructions) about whose imminent arrival I have been informed in the past few days.

Meanwhile, it seems to me that the document dated December 6 and my later receipt should be enough to soften—or at least to deflect in my direction—the possible restlessness of third parties.

Please forgive me for being brief. With very cordial greetings.

Document 35. Heinz Schewe to Giangiacomo Feltrinelli, June 22, 1960

Location: AGFE, Busta 1, fascicolo 5, "Feltrinelli-Schewe" (1959 febbraio 15–1966 dicembre 07)
Format: Original
Original language: German
Previous publication: Original text and English translation first published in Mancosu 2018a

DOCUMENT

Editore
Giangiacomo Feltrinelli
Milan
Via Andegari 6

Moscow / Hotel Berlin / 516
June 22, 1960

Dear Mr. Feltrinelli,

It is once again after midnight and I am very tired. Nonetheless, I absolutely must write you.

As I had expected, the situation after the Classic's death has become quite dramatic and turbulent. Strange things are occurring:

1. The power of attorney that Boris Leonidovich drew up for Ms. Olga before his illness in April of this year has supposedly gone missing. It was given—together with other important papers—to the regional correspondent for "Unita" (friends of Sergio d'Angelo). These people originally wanted to return to Italy in May. I was not in Moscow during this time. Therefore Ms. Olga—at the Classic's wish—handed over these papers to the "Unita" journalists (a married couple). They should have brought the power of attorney to you personally. The "Unita" people, however, did not immediately travel back to Italy, but rather first on vacation to the Caucasus. From this vacation they returned last Sunday (19.6.60) to Moscow—with the horrifying news that they lost all these papers belonging to the Classic on the way!!! Among these papers were: a) the power of attorney (literary and financial) for Ms. Olga, b) a confirmation that the first installment of the $100,000 transfer had reached the Classic, c) the Classic's handwritten wish that you would transfer certain dollar sums to Renate Schweitzer, to the French student Georges, and to myself, as signs of his thankfulness for the friendship we had shown him.

All of this has supposedly gone missing. There were many tears shed by those who lost the documents, as well as by Ms. Olga, who is inconsolable. If the Soviet police find these . . . ? It is inconceivable!

Mirella, that is the first name of the Italian journalist's wife, claims they possibly left these papers in the hotel of one of their resorts in the Caucasus. Well, strange matter. There is something I do not like about it. Ms. Olga also has strong doubts. She believes that the "Unita" people wanted to stash away the power of attorney for other parties' interest. But Mirella, apparently the one who lost them, confirms that she read the papers and knows exactly what was written in them. She says she will also gladly testify as much.

However that may be—a mysterious thing! The only will that existed has, after the Classic's death, disappeared in a most mysterious manner. It was supposed to have been prepared in three languages, says Ms. Olga.

I am also worried sick. Right now I really do not know what I should do. Ms. Olga always asks me for advice. But I am constantly under surveillance! I must still also remain loyal to my company and cannot allow myself to get mixed up in things that could endanger my work here. I also get no rest, which would allow me to consider the whole situation rationally. An unholy mess and most dangerous for everyone involved too!

2. The Pasternak family registered their claims to all of Pasternak's works and honoraria at the local office for authorship rights. As I hear it here, they have a good chance of success. Then nothing would remain for Ms. Olga. That would certainly not be in the spirit of Boris Leonidovich. But what should she do?

3. Ms. Olga fears that she might suddenly lose her freedom of movement. In such a case I could not help at all. I must myself be very careful. With her are stored the handwritten originals of "Dr. Zhivago" and the entire correspondence. Hopefully it will not be confiscated one day! That would be an irreplaceable loss.

All things considered—a very unpleasant, very uncomfortable situation. I will not be in Moscow for the next four weeks. What all could happen in this time, only heaven knows.

I still have not received an answer from you to my letter after Boris Leonidovich's death. Only the letters of condolence that I delivered to their recipients.

I am quite distraught. But perhaps it is because I am once again very tired and overworked. Everything happening to me here in Moscow often overwhelms my abilities.

Friendly greetings, also to Ms. Inge

Your Heinz Schewe

[*handwritten*:] PS: I planted roses on Boris Leonidovich's grave—unfortunately they withered in the heat.

Document 36. Giangiacomo Feltrinelli to Olga Ivinskaya, June 24, 1960

Location: FoGF, Fascicolo "Ivinskaja Olga" (1960–1970), 1.2.1.–b.15, fasc. 150

Format: Carbon copy

Original language: German

Previous publication: Original text and English translation first published in Mancosu 2018a

Additional information: This original letter ended up in the hands of the KGB, as it is cited in one of the Radio Moscow broadcasts about Ivinskaya in January 1961.

DOCUMENT

Milan, 24.6.1960

Dear, honorable Olga!

Thank you for your letter of the 5th of June, which only just now arrived. I waited daily for news from you and was already very uneasy.

Of course I will recognize and honor Boris Pasternak's last will, and am ready to carry out all the instructions he left behind. All the questions and problems that will occur moving forward we will resolve together in the spirit of our dear and beloved Boris. Consciousness of this duty and task will ease our every step.

I am very pleased that you are fully trusting of Heinz Schewe. We could not wish for a better friend who understands the circumstances and problems in both the East and West. But now to your questions individually:

1) In your letter, you task me with paying $10,000 each to d'Angelo, Georges Nivat, Heinz Schewe and $5,000 to Ms. Schweitzer. This will be done in the coming days. I would just like to emphasize that I already sent Ms. Schweitzer $5,000 (at Boris Pasternak's instruction). Is it agreed that I should pay her another $5,000? Please confirm this for me.

2) Madame Proyart. How would it be if I gave her the contract to edit all of B.P.'s works that appear in the West in the original Russian? Would you agree to this?

3) I would think it unwise for you to write to Madame Proyart at this time. It could even be very dangerous, insofar as she is connected with P.'s family in Moscow or London and who knows what kind of initiatives she might take up. Please send me copies of the documents at your disposal; then I can give you concrete advice.

4) Just now Boris's sister Lidya got in touch from London all in a commotion. Wanted to know what assignments I had received from Pasternak and what and whether it would benefit the family. Sent an answer that did not say anything. May

I give some advice? Do not allow it to come to a dispute in Moscow. Be also, when necessary, generous in money matters. They can be dangerous enemies.

5) What do we want to undertake in terms of turning *Dr. Zhivago* into a film? It would probably still be possible now to find concrete interest in this. I have received inquiries in the last weeks.

6) What is the situation with the contract that I sent to Pasternak a few months ago? Is it signed by him on every page? If not—then you can sign it, dated April . . . 1960. You are, after all, according to a power of attorney that I have in hand, authorized to do so. Please ask Heinz Schewe to accompany your signature below the contract with the following words: "I hereby confirm the authenticity of the signature of Olga… Signed Heinz Schewe. I would need to have this document in the near future, as soon as the publication of his remaining works happens.

7) Send me a copy of Boris Pasternak's drama as soon as possible. I will not publish it as long as you tell me not to do so. Should it be published in Moscow, I would strongly recommend that it also be published in the West within 30 days of its appearance. Only thus can we bring it under copyright protection. Such a quick publication requires quite a preparation.

Dear Ms. Olga, I naturally anticipate with suspense the promised documents. Please rest assured that I will avoid every indiscretion. I can imagine the difficulty of your position and am very worried about you. I would also recommend you not leave Moscow at the moment. In Moscow you have been protected until now by Heinz Schewe, and with you the Nachlass of Boris Pasternak!! Do not leave Moscow! Your protection is the threat that the Western world would be informed if something were to happen. Were something to happen to you without it ever becoming known, then *anything* could happen tomorrow.

Dear Olga—in a total rush—this letter must go with the last post, otherwise we will miss a whole week.

I embrace you most affectionately, in complete friendship, with the same reverence that I have for Boris Pasternak.

Document 37. Giangiacomo Feltrinelli to Olga Ivinskaya, July 8, 1960

Location: AGFE, Busta 3, fascicolo 6

Format: Carbon copy and photocopy of the original

Original language: German

Previous publication: Original text and English translation first published in Mancosu 2018a

Additional information: This letter was circulated by the Soviets for the first time in Great Britain in February 1961.

DOCUMENT

Milan, July 8, 1960

Dear Ms. Olga,

Heinz Schewe's letter [dated June 22, 1960] and his report have thrown me into deep despair.

There is no sense in my dwelling at length on the Garritanos. I must just say: why, oh why did you hand over such an important and confidential matter to such people? Why, when our mutual friend H.S. nevertheless stood readily by? In the future do not trust anyone, only Heinz Schewe. And should he one fine day no longer be in Moscow, please trust only those who will show you, as a distinguishing mark, one of the missing halves [of the banknotes].

And now to the core of our matter:

Dear Olga! I will try everything I can to avoid payments to third parties. Should this fail, should I be so forced, I will always do it in such a way that a substantial part of the profits remains for yourself or for Ira.

Now you must, however, be careful of some things:

1) The earlier contract with Boris Pasternak concerning the publication of *Dr. Z.*, as well as the new contract (which I beg you to please send as soon as possible), can never be allowed to come into the hands of the authorities or Pasternak's family. The same goes for my letters to Boris and yourself. All these confidential documents must never be found with you.

2) Send me any other potential documents at your disposal that could be useful to me vis-à-vis Proyart. Everything I receive (I give you my word of honor) will be treated as if sent to me directly by Pasternak.

3) I will protect you in every manner with all my power. Trust me.

4) I will not be at ease until ALL of Pasternak's letters, manuscripts, etc. are in the West.

Dear Olga! Everything that has been undertaken these past years could only have been undertaken on the basis of trust. Difficulties have only arisen when other people, whom I often did not know, got involved in our affairs. Everything that can be undertaken in the future can only be undertaken if you completely trust in me.

With love and friendship I embrace you,

P.S. D'Angelo still has many things here. His route seems too dangerous to me. I would recommend you write to me that he should give everything that is left over back to me. I will communicate it to him when and how you would like.

[*handwritten*:] P.S. If someone shows you his half [of the banknote]—you will also, for your part, show yours.

Document 38. Heinz Schewe to Giangiacomo Feltrinelli, July 15, 1960

Location: AGFE, Busta 1, fascicolo 5, "Feltrinelli-Schewe" (1959 febbraio 15–1966 dicembre 07)
Format: Original
Original language: German
Previous publication: Original text and English translation first published in Mancosu 2018a

DOCUMENT

Hamburg, July 15th, 1960

Dear Mr. Feltrinelli,

On Sunday I will begin my return journey to Moscow. Today I delivered the important package to Mrs. Borgward, as arranged with Dr. Mohr. Because we discussed all the particulars extensively in Vienna, I probably do not need to return to these explicitly. I deliver the manuscript to you by trusted hands.

To all further dispositions, the following is important:

I will return to Germany for a holiday at the end of August / beginning of September. It would therefore be good if the intended package of "loaves" could be sent on time, so that it is in Moscow by the middle of August at the latest.

As arranged with my publishing house, I will probably not return directly to Moscow at the end of my holiday, but rather temporarily stay awhile at home.

I retain the status of Moscow correspondent at WELT, but am relocating my permanent residence from Moscow to Hamburg, and I will only occasionally fly to Russia for shorter stays. I hope that the state of my health will substantially improve with this move. Moreover, with this adjustment I hope to gain a somewhat greater distance from the bleak political developments. Best wishes for now, also to Ms. Inge,

Your [*signed*] Heinz Schewe

Document 39. Heinz Schewe to Giangiacomo Feltrinelli, July 28, 1960

Location: AGFE, Busta 1, fascicolo 5, "Feltrinelli-Schewe" (1959 febbraio 15–1966 dicembre 07)
Format: Original
Original language: German
Previous publication: Original text and English translation first published in Mancosu 2018a

DOCUMENT

Editore
Giangiacomo Feltrinelli
Milan
Via Andegari 6

Moscow / Hotel Berlin / 516
July 28, 1960

Dear Mr. Feltrinelli,

Upon my return to Moscow I encountered Ms. Olga well and in good health again. She enjoyed your letters very much and thanks you dearly. We now want to send the contract in the next days. Also, the order to Sergio d'Angelo to pay back the remaining money will be written up.

In the meantime, I can expressly confirm what I told you in Vienna (you asked me to do so):

1) The two Garritanos delivered the first installment of the $100,000 sum via Sergio d'Angelo. That was in April 1960, when the Classic was still alive. I was not in Moscow at the time.
2) The Garritanos explicitly requested that the Classic write out powers of attorney for Ms. Olga in three languages (Russian, Italian, French) and hand it over to them.
3) The Classic—as Ms. Olga recounted—found the Garritanos unlikable from the beginning.

For weeks an abominable heat has prevailed here. It is 34 degrees in my room! I am already very worn out again. The journey was very pretty—but also exhausting.

Best wishes for now, also to Ms. Inge

[*handwritten*:] Your Heinz Schewe

Document 40. Olga Ivinskaya to Giangiacomo Feltrinelli, July 28, 1960

Location: FoGF, Fascicolo "Ivinskaja Olga" (1960–1970), 1.2.1.–b.15, fasc. 150
Format: Original; draft of the letter in photocopy (the latter originating from Ivinskaya and Emelianova's trial proceedings; see section 2.2)
Original language: Russian and German
Previous publication: Original text and English translation first published in Mancosu 2018a
Additional information: Schewe sent a German translation of the final Russian version. A photocopy of the draft of the Russian letter is in the archives and published here in translation. The order of the documents is as follows: translation into English of the draft and translation into English of the final version.

DOCUMENT
[Draft]

July 28, 1960

Dear, dear signor Giangiacomo!

I received two of your letters through our friend [*handwritten*: Mr. Sch-we]. In the first, you still do not know about our new misfortune, for which Sergio's friends are at fault. About this first letter, about all the activities that you offer in it, and with which I unconditionally agree, we will talk after we fix the mess that took place, if such a thing is even possible.

In your second letter, you express, completely fairly, your bewilderment at why, having at my disposal a true friend in the name of Mr. ~~Heinz~~ Sch-e, I suddenly decided to entrust the most important documents to people who were little known to either me or Boris Leonidovich.

I must explain to you briefly how this happened. You know about the ~~one hundred thousand~~ [*handwritten*: sum] that Sergio was supposed to deliver to B. L. in Moscow per his wishes. These Garritanos, having delivered part of the ~~money~~ [*handwritten*: sum], asked that B.L. renew a power of attorney in my name, ~~so that~~ [*handwritten*: supposedly] for me to be able to write out receipts on the spot for future [*handwritten*: money] transfers. When I relayed this request to B.L., he expressed [*handwritten*: a desire] to give me a general power of attorney for carrying out all of his affairs, so that he would not have to pull himself away from his work on the play. [*handwritten*: He wrote it out right then, and] I delivered this power of attorney to Garritano while

B.L. was still alive, [*handwritten*: as per his wishes], so that they would be accountable before you. Mr. Sch. was not in Moscow at the time. What a pity! He arrived just [*handwritten*: a week] later—but the power of attorney was already in G-o's hands.

I do not have the words to tell you what horror and despair I experienced once again, having just lived through B.'s death.

G-nos told me that all the letters to Sergio, all the letters to you, and all powers of attorney were lost by them during their travels through Georgia. Either lost or stolen. At the beginning, [*handwritten*: after receiving this message,] I did not have a single minute of peace. I was under the threat of practically death, the loss of B.'s archives, the demise of my children—if our government had wanted to publicize the matter. Not just Borya's name—all of us would have been literally crushed by this misfortune—this criminal negligence, or simply a crime, I still cannot understand what forced these people to carry out such a horrific act ~~or if this is truly just negligence~~.

My loyal friend, Mr. Sch-e, helped me live through the first sharp horror, at a moment when the situation seemed to me to be hopeless. [*handwritten*: I had thought that] all that was left for me to do was to simply get ready for anything, for the most terrible thing—for a public court trial, without fulfilling my duty regarding B.'s literary legacy. Mr. Sch-e calmed me down the best he could, his friendly participation helped me, but of course my general state was terrible.

And yet, nothing has happened yet. The fact that these G-nos still have not been to see you, as we know, forces me to suppose that, after all, this was a move on their part, and that they still possess the documents somewhere.

Of course, none of us could have foreseen such baseness on their behalf, but B. did not trust these people on some instinctive level. Everything that they did was somehow tortured; the transfer of letters was drawn out over multiple months, etc.

But, in case of some potential unforeseen event, B. left me the ability to restore his directives, and I have documents, which I have preserved, as well as the ability to restore the text of the lost power of attorney and send you a copy of it signed with Borya's signature.

Of course, I was very upset that the loss of the power of attorney will complicate our relationship, but I was worried more, as you can certainly understand, [*handwritten*: not this but] that this whole package will find its way into hostile, official hands. You are right when you write that everything between us is based on boundless trust. I have already written to you a number of times about how much I valued your behavior regarding Borya during his most difficult days. I always understood, and told him, that you behaved yourself not just as his publisher, but also as a true friend, saving him, protecting him, keeping secrets, etc. Even if after the loss of these documents I would have had no possibility of restoring them, even then I would have believed in your friendship, [*handwritten*: and now,] it is very, very dear to me that you wrote to me so well—after all, you did not know that I had the ability to restore these papers.

Dear, kind Giangiacomo! We will be hoping that the most terrible thing will not happen, that I will be allowed my freedom for now, and I will be able to put in order all of Borya's affairs, and the fate of my children will not be as terrifying as it could have been if this loss was publicized. By good fortune, I have the ability to restore the power of attorney. ~~Observing the strictest secrecy, look at the text of the power of attorney that we – Mr. Schewe and I – are sending to you~~ [*handwritten*: ~~to replace the one that was lost by the Garritanos~~]~~. Is everything there to your complete satisfaction? For now, we can~~ [*handwritten*: ~~still~~] ~~put in some insignificant changes. Please send this text back to us, as soon as possible, and we will send you this power of attorney signed, and send a copy to Mme Proyart~~. Furthermore, I can ~~also~~ send you other documents, such as a power of attorney in my name, notarized by Goslitizdat [*handwritten*: from 1957], for carrying out all activities related to the publication of "D. Zh." [*handwritten*: Currently,] the documents are not at my house. Getting them out of the ~~hidden place~~ secret place is not so easy, and so I will send everything to you at once when I receive from you the text of the proposed power of attorney that [*handwritten*: you] have read. I have also hidden there the contract between you and Boris, signed by B. I will also send it, [*handwritten*: if it is still needed].

For now, I am sending you a letter for Sergio D'Angello [*sic*]. You are absolutely right. Any interactions with people other than those who have been vetted by you are unthinkable for us. The money that D'Angello could not deliver to me I am asking him to return to the address of your notary. If [*handwritten*: you have] an opportunity to make a transfer of a large sum [*handwritten*: at once] [*handwritten*: out of that money], I'm thinking of transferring a stack personally from me to B.'s dacha to arrange for a monument [*handwritten*: dedicated to him].

I would also like to carry out Borya's will regarding the people to whom he wanted to make gifts while he was still alive. These are Mr. George [*sic*] Nivat, Mr. Schewe, and Renata [*sic*] Schweitzer. I know that this will be a second transfer to Renata Schweitzer, but B. wanted this.

Let us talk something else over. After I send you the power of attorney signed by Borya, you can personally talk to Borya's sister, and after telling her that the only thing I want to do in life is to carry out Borya's will, give her a large sum of money—whatever you think is appropriate so that there would be something left over for other needs. But remember that Borya absolutely did not want her to have some sort of priority in the matter of translating and publishing his works. To the contrary, he personally told me that he is afraid his relationship with her could play some sort of negative role. She ~~would~~ [*handwritten*: could] be offered translation rights because she is his sister and [*handwritten*: because of this] someone else more experienced or talented would not be translating his poems. It was [*handwritten*: precisely this] nepotism that Borya was afraid of. [*handwritten*: Borya] completely did not wish to see [*handwritten*: his sister] during the time of [*handwritten*: his] illness. This was a ruse on the part of his relatives. Please, protect Borya's works from the bossiness of dilettantes. [*handwritten*: We should talk to Mme P. about this.]

You ask what method of [*handwritten*: regularly] receiving money is most convenient for me [*handwritten*: personally]. The same as it has always been. Through Mr. Schewe. At certain intervals [*handwritten*: which are convenient for us]. I cannot imagine the time when ~~he~~ [*handwritten*: Mr. Sch-we] will leave here forever without horror. I do not even want to think about it. Well, that is all for now, though this is far from everything. ~~So, please hasten to look at the text of the power of attorney and send it back to us.~~ In the next parcel, I hope to send you everything else.

Do not print anything without a signal from us. I will prepare and send B.'s letters to friends, where he talks about life, about literature. I saved everything when possible and am not calm while all these things are with me.

Thank you for everything. From the bottom of my heart I wish you success in all your dealings, in all your enterprises.

Forever your friend [*unsigned*]

Final Version

July 28, 1960

Dear, dear signor Giangiacomo!

I received two of your letters through our friend Mr. Sch.

In the first, you still do not know about our new misfortune, for which Sergio's friends are at fault. About this first letter, about all the activities which you offer in it, and with which I unconditionally agree, we will talk after we fix up the mess that took place, if such a thing is even possible.

In your second letter, you express, completely fairly, your bewilderment at why, having at my disposal a true friend in the name of Mr. Sch., I suddenly decided to entrust the most important documents to people who were little known to either me or Boris Leonidovich.

I must explain to you briefly how this happened.

You know about the sum that Sergio was supposed to deliver to B.L. in parts in Moscow per his wishes. These Garritanos, having delivered part of the sum, asked that B.L. renew a power of attorney in my name, supposedly so that I would be able to write out receipts on the spot for future transfers. When I relayed this request to

B.L., he expressed a desire to give me a general power of attorney for carrying out all of his affairs so that he would not have to pull himself away from his work on the play. It was then that this power of attorney was written, in both Russian and French, and this same power of attorney I gave to Garritano while B.L. was still alive as per his wishes, so that they would be accountable before you, or before Sergio, I do not know. Mr. Sch. was not in Moscow at the time. What a pity! He arrived just a week later, when the papers and Borya's letters to you, and mine also to you and Sergio, were already in the Garritanos' hands.

I do not have the words to tell you what horror and despair I experienced once again, having just lived through B.'s death.

The Garritanos told me that all letters and powers of attorney were lost by them during their travels through Georgia. Either lost or stolen, by whom they do not know. After such news, I at first did not have a single minute of peace. You understand—I was under the threat of practically death, the loss of B.'s archives, the demise of my children. If our government had wanted to publicize the matter, we would have been literally crushed by this misfortune—this criminal negligence, I still cannot understand what forced these people to carry out such a horrific act.

My loyal friend, Mr. Sch., helped me live through the first sharp pain, at a moment when the situation seemed to me to be hopeless. I had thought that all that was left for me to do was to simply get ready for anything, for the most terrible thing—for a public court trial, without fulfilling my debt regarding B.'s literary legacy. Mr. Sch. calmed me down the best he could, but of course, my general state was terrible.

The fact that these Garritanos have not been to see you still, and evidently Sergio does not know about the disappearance that took place, forces me to suppose that there is something very dark here—a maneuver of some sort. The G-nos gave me their word that they would immediately inform you of what happened, [*handwritten*: but they didn't do it!]

Of course, none of us could have foreseen such baseness on their part. After all, these people are Sergio's friends. Though to be honest, B.L. did not feel particularly friendly toward these people on some instinctive level. Everything they did was somehow tortured, the transfer of letters was always drawn out, etc.

In the case of some hypothetical unforeseen event, which happened to actually take place, B. left me the possibility of restoring his directives, and I have documents, which I have preserved, as well as the possibility to send you the remaining power of attorney. It will not be of much use to me here.

Of course, I was very upset that the loss of that general power of attorney could potentially complicate our relationship, but it was not this that made me despair: you can understand what would have happened to me, what will happen, if this package falls into hostile, official hands. As far as we are concerned, you are right when you write that everything between us is based on mutual trust, on unbounded trust of each other. I have already written to you a number of times how much I valued your behavior toward Borya during his difficult days. I always told him that you behaved yourself not just as his publisher, but also as a true friend, saving him, protecting him, keeping secrets.

Even if the lost power of attorney was the only one that existed, even then I would believe in your friendship—that you would not leave me behind and would tenderly treat me as if I were a part of a living Borya. It is very, very dear to me now that you wrote to me so well—after all, you could not have known that any papers had been saved.

Dear, kind Giangiacomo! We will be hoping that the most terrible thing will not happen, that I will be allowed my freedom for now, and I will be able to put in order all of Borya's affairs, and the fate of my children will not be as terrifying as it could have been if this loss was publicized. By good fortune, I have the ability to send you the power of attorney. I had wanted to hide this one in case it was needed, but what else is there to do, if things turned out so badly. Furthermore, I can send you a power of attorney in my name, notarized at the time by Goslitizdat, for carrying out all activities related to the publication of "D. Zh." I'm sending you now what I have on hand. I'm not keeping papers at home right now, and getting them out of the hiding place is not so easy. But, if you need the latest contract signed by B., I will send it to you.

The question of what to do about the power of attorney that was given by B. in D'Angelo's name can wait for now. You are absolutely correct, I need to make use of your advice and proposal here as well, but for now I should wait—I need to clarify something regarding this matter, and at the moment, it is being clarified. I still cannot understand how Sergio could not know about this misfortune to this day. I received a message from him on the 15th of this month and judge that he does not know based on it.

But before anything else, I would like to carry out Borya's will regarding the people to whom he wanted to make gifts while he was still alive. I even have the saved drafts of letters in which he asked me to do this—simply to rewrite them myself from his directives, sending them under my own name.

These people are Mr. George NIVAT, Mr. SCHEWE, and Renata Schweitzer. I know that this will be a second transfer to Renata Schweitzer, but B. wanted this. The first two should get ten thousand, she should get five. There was also a directive regarding Sergio's friends—but let it remain unfulfilled for now. Let this be clearer first.

You and I need to discuss a very important question, regarding B's relatives there. After receiving the power of attorney, you can personally talk to his sister. You can tell her the following: 1, that I, as B's empowered representative during his life, want to continue fulfilling his will posthumously, and want one thing only—to fulfill that will. It would be possible to set aside for her (the sister, Madame Later [Slater]) a sum of money—whatever you think is appropriate—I do not even know how much money there is in general, if she will express a desire to help the remaining family in Peredelkino from over there. Though this is something I could do myself—Borya's lifelong dream had been that it would be me who would look after that family—"she was stronger than the others"—as he himself said. Please think about how it would be best to organize this, dear Giangiacomo. In any case, in my opinion, some amount of money needs to be set aside for his sister's side of the family, but what amount—we must decide.

But, I want to warn you: Borya absolutely did not want her, as his sister, to have some sort of priority in the matter of translating and publishing his works. To the contrary, he personally told me that he is afraid that his relationship with her would play some sort of negative role. She could be provided with translation rights because she is his sister and because of this, due to ethical considerations, someone else more talented or better known would not translate his poems. I must tell you that Borya absolutely did not express any desire to see his sister before his death. This is an invention by his relatives. I forced him to correspond with her, but he didn't want to see her—he was afraid that he would meet a complete stranger. Of course, it would have played out exactly this way. Her invitation was simply a ruse by his relatives. Please, dear Giangiacomo, protect Borya's works from the bossiness of dilettantes. Here, I believe, Madame de Proyart could help you.

Now, you ask what method of ~~transferring~~ receiving money is most convenient for me personally. The same as it has always been—through Mr. Sch. At certain intervals that are convenient for you and for him. I am afraid to even think about the time when he will no longer be in Moscow. I will save your "halves." You devised this quite well.

Do not print anything new without a signal from us. I will prepare and send copies of B's letters to acquaintances and close friends, where he talks about life, about literature. I save everything when possible, but am not calm while all these valuables are only with me.

Please, send me clippings from all the newspapers and magazines regarding the funeral. We have far from all of them. I do not even have one from L'Unità.

We await news from you. Thank you for everything.

From the bottom of my heart I wish you success in all your dealings, in all your enterprises.

Forever your friend, [*unsigned*]

Document 41. Olga Ivinskaya to Sergio d'Angelo, July 28, 1960

Location: AGFE, CP, Busta 1, Fascicolo 7, "Olga Ivinskaya–Sergio d'Angelo (1959–1960)"
Format: Typewritten, signed. Original.
Original language: Russian
Previous publication: Published in Mancosu and Borokhov 2017; Mancosu 2018a
Additional information: A copy of a German translation of the original Russian, delivered by Heinz Schewe, is also found in AGFE, CP, "Olga Ivinskaya–Sergio D'Angelo (1959–1960)," Busta 1, Fascicolo 7.

DOCUMENT

Dear Sergio!

You probably already know what second misfortune has crashed upon me. Most likely, Mirella has told you what happened to her, but even more likely, willingly or unwillingly, she did with me. After this incident, I do not have a single minute of peace. Just imagine what will happen to me when the lost package with our correspondence finds its way into the hands of officials. I am surprised that I am still alive. I am very surprised that M. did not fulfill her promise and her direct duty to me—why she did not come to you and F. and did not testify before him [*handwritten*: and you], like she was supposed to, about what happened to her. All of this is odd, bitter, surprising.

Dearest Seregia, I am afraid of everything now. Now I am asking you to return all of the money that is left over after currency exchanges, which B.L. expected to receive from you in Moscow but which you were not able to give to him in time, to the address of F-li's notary, sinior [*sic*] Antonio Tesone.

I think, Seregia, that you understand the horror of my situation very well. I am living in constant fear and despair that I will not see the preservation of B.L.'s archive to the end, and in general—I am waiting for the worst.

I wanted to follow your advice and reward your friends for agreeing to be a link in our friendly chain. I wrote about this in a letter that was among those that were addressed to you and F and lost, together with the lost powers of attorney. But the loss of the documents robs me of the opportunity to do as I thought and in general completely unsettles me. I am living under constant torture. I am very hurt and afraid, Seregia.

I would like to hear from you what you think, how you explain what happened, perhaps—I will hear something calming?

Until next time!

I wish you all the best, with the same amity as before,

[*signed*] Olga
28 July 1960

Commentary. This letter expressed Olga's despair at the loss of the documents sent with the Garritanos and their inexplicable behavior after the fact. Olga had been informed that the Garritanos had not contacted Feltrinelli after their return to Italy, and this increased her suspicions, shared also by Feltrinelli and Schewe, that the Garritanos were perhaps in cahoots with the Soviets. Among the documents contained in the package was a letter from Olga mentioning a reward for Mirella Garritano (reference to this letter is also found in a letter from Mirella Garritano to Giulietta Pecori dated April 30, 1960; see document 28).

Ivinskaya began doubting even d'Angelo, and this is reflected in her request to d'Angelo to give the rest of the $100,000 to Feltrinelli's lawyer, Antonio Tesone. On August 1, she would receive the delivery of 500,000 rubles through the Benedettis and then change her mind about this, informing d'Angelo not to give back the remaining part of the money to Tesone but to proceed as he best saw fit.

Document 42. Heinz Schewe to Giangiacomo Feltrinelli, August 1, 1960

Location: AGFE, Busta 1, fascicolo 5, "Feltrinelli-Schewe" (1959 febbraio 15–1966 dicembre 07)

Format: Original

Original language: German

Previous publication: Original text and English translation first published in Mancosu 2018a

DOCUMENT

Editore
Giangiacomo Feltrinelli
Milan
Via Andegari 6

Moscow / Hotel Berlin / 516
August 1, 1960

Dear Mr. Feltrinelli,

I am sending you a few letters with this mailing. At the moment I still cannot say how many it will be altogether. It is a lot of work, and I have, in addition, a great deal to do at the moment.

To begin with, I translated for you a long letter from Ms. Olga in answer to both of your letters from June 1960. Translation and original are in separate envelopes. In addition, there is the letter to Sergio d'Angelo that you proposed in Vienna (return transfer of the remainder of the $100,000 to your notary Antonio Tesone).

I can probably put more in the mail by Thursday. Mind you, I am being harassed myself at the moment and do not know whether everything will come off on time. Please be understanding! I am doing what I can!

Yet another development. The French student Georges Nivat applied for a marriage with Ira at the Moscow registry office. There are great difficulties. First of all, he is perpetually ill, and second, his visa expires on August 8th. The civil ceremony, however, is set for the 20th of August. Well, we will see. There will surely be a big commotion again. Honestly, an exhausting country.

In a hurry, with best wishes also to Ms. Inge

[*signed*] Your Heinz Schewe

Document 43. Heinz Schewe to Giangiacomo Feltrinelli, August 7, 1960

Location: AGFE, Busta 1, fascicolo 5, "Feltrinelli-Schewe" (1959 febbraio 15–1966 dicembre 07)
Format: Original
Original language: German
Previous publication: Original text and English translation first published in Mancosu 2018a

DOCUMENT

Moscow / Hotel Berlin / 516
August 7, 1960

Dear Mr. Feltrinelli,

enclosed two documents

1) a power of attorney (and if you will, a sort of will) from Boris L. Pasternak for Ms. Olga V. Ivinskaya dated April 4, 1960, signed one month before his death.
2) An older power of attorney from July 10, 1958, for Ms. Olga concerning *Dr. Zhivago.*

I unfortunately will not manage to translate it at the moment.

Heartfelt greetings,

[*signed*] Your H. Schewe
2 enclosures

Document 44. Heinz Schewe to Giangiacomo Feltrinelli, August 7, 1960

Location: AGFE, Busta 1, fascicolo 5, "Feltrinelli-Schewe" (1959 febbraio 15–1966 dicembre 07)
Format: Original
Original language: German
Previous publication: Original text and English translation first published in Mancosu 2018a

DOCUMENT

Editore
Giangiacomo Feltrinelli
Milan
Via Andegari 6

Moscow / Hotel Berlin / 516
August 7, 1960

Dear Mr. Feltrinelli,

This now is the original letter from Ms. Olga, which did not arrive by the last courier in time and so meant that, for the time being, you only received its translation. It was on account of Ira's becoming seriously ill. A mysterious story. Something is not right with the blood. Apparently she was infected by Georges.

At the moment, everything is again going haywire. Monsieur Georges should leave on Wednesday, since his visa is expiring. He absolutely wants to stay in order to marry Ira on August 20th. At the same time, he seems dangerously sick (cancer of the blood???). Telegrams to Khrushchev and Mikoyan with pleas for authorization and extension of the visa. I think the thing has little chance of success.

For Ira this is not a matter of love, but simply a wish thereby to get out of this country. The idea came from the Classic. I am skeptical whether it will work. Besides, I have a feeling that this Georges has a deadly illness, ever since that smallpox vaccination here in Moscow in January 1960.

Further: Olga supplemented the end of her letter with the request to send her absolutely all newspapers and magazines with obituaries for the Classic, and reports of his funeral. [cont'd.]

Yet another important matter:

Ms. Olga asks you to regard the letter concerning Sergio d'Angelo as if not written [*underlined by GF*]. I had sent you a translation of the draft, as I am very overworked and have guests at the moment too, and so do not always have time to accomplish everything as quickly as I would like. The rest of the $100,000 will thus not be given back to your notary!

This new situation arose as follows: two tourists showed up from Italy, a married couple. They visited Ms. Olga. I myself did not meet them. Ira interpreted from the French as well as possible. After this conversation, Ms. Olga again decided entirely differently. Apparently the two messengers—they came at d'Angelo's instruction—reported bad things about yourself [*underlined by GF*], so that Ms. Olga became unsure of her earlier decision.

Now it looks as if we might slide into new difficulties and disarray, such as we already know from the earlier double-dealing with Madame Proyart. This time Signor d'Angelo seems to be your antagonist [*underlined by GF*]. To me it is a sure thing that he is intriguing heavily against you. Crush him as quickly as possible! Otherwise, we will have a new mess that is perhaps even a great deal worse than the one with your Parisian competitors. I personally, to speak frankly, would have no interest in partaking of such complicated and unpleasant matters. What does Signor d'Angelo really want anyway? Probably just to earn money. Why does he send people to Moscow to put strange doubts in poor Ms. Olga's ear about your honesty? What an abominable game! Make a stop of it! This Sergio d'Angelo, whom I have always mistrusted, wants to come to Moscow in the spring of 1961 to speak directly with Ms. Olga. More letters to follow.

[*handwritten*:] Heartfelt greetings, Your H. Schewe

Document 45. Heinz Schewe to Giangiacomo Feltrinelli, August 7, 1960

Location: AGFE, Busta 1, fascicolo 5, "Feltrinelli-Schewe" (1959 febbraio 15–1966 dicembre 07)
Format: Original
Original language: German
Previous publication: Original text and English translation first published in Mancosu 2018a

DOCUMENT

Editore
Giangiacomo Feltrinelli
Milan
Via Andegari 6

Moscow / Hotel Berlin / 516
August 7, 1960

Dear Mr. Feltrinelli,

And here at last an important document that you have long awaited: THE CONTRACT!

Unfortunately, it is only signed by the Classic on the third page. I always and again advised that every page must be individually signed. But of course you remember that this contract was heavily disputed during the Classic's lifetime. It just remained unfinished business.

Since the contract is dated June 30th, 1956 (!!!), I could not decide whether to make any additions. I neither induced Ms. Olga to put her signature on pages 1 and 2, nor did I myself sign as a witness. (Indeed, I was not in Moscow until April 1958.) I assume that this contract in its present, honest form (for it was actually, personally signed by the Classic) should be the most valuable to you. After all, it is signed at the end. The Classic was, as is widely known, a man little experienced in business matters. They will have to forgive him the omission of signatures on the first two pages.

So that's all…

With best wishes, also to Ms. Inge

[*handwritten*:] Your H. Schewe

Document 46. Letter from Olga Ivinskaya to Sergio d'Angelo, August 10, 1960

Location: AGFE, CP, Busta 1, Fascicolo 7, "Olga Ivinskaya–Sergio d'Angelo (1959–1960)"
Format: Typewritten, signed. Original.
Original language: Russian
Previous publication: Published in Mancosu and Borokhov 2017; Mancosu 2018a

DOCUMENT

August 10 [*handwritten*: 1960]

Dear Sergio!

I wrote you a letter dated July 28, which, perhaps, will make it into your hands at the same time as this one. I am writing this one after a visit from your friends, who gave me a letter from you, dated July 15.

It still remains unclear to me if you know about the incident with Mirella, and if you can imagine how everything can change now? Please write to me about this matter.

Your friends relayed everything to me ~~verbally~~. The only thing that worries me, in connection to Mirella, are your plans, which would have made me very happy earlier. In my letter from July 28, I write to you about F.'s notary. Now I ask you to not do that, and if there's still something left of the sum designated by B.L. for transferring to him—please do with it as you see fit.

For everything that you have done for B.L. and me—I give you a great big thank-you. Kisses and greetings, the most heartfelt kind, from all of us, to Giulietta and you. I would really like to see you, I am waiting for a letter from you, where you will touch on the matter that worries me—about the lost or stolen documents. Seregia, have you really not heard anything about it from M.?

Once again—thank you so much!

[*handwritten*:] Your Olga

Commentary. Ivinskaya was wondering what d'Angelo thought concerning the events related to Mirella Garritano and the loss of the important documents. D'Angelo had provided no details in a lost letter dated July 15 (probably sequestered during Olga's arrest and now in some KGB archive) that the Benedettis brought to Ivinskaya on August 1, together with 500,000 rubles. The letter we are commenting upon was the last item of correspondence between Sergio d'Angelo and Olga Ivinskaya. D'Angelo did not reply, as he had planned a trip to the Soviet Union with his wife, Giulietta. He arrived in Moscow on September 4 (see d'Angelo 2006, 175–84). This visit to Moscow would have allowed him to speak with Olga directly, but by the time he arrived in the Soviet Union, Olga had already been arrested and Irina was soon to follow her mother to the Lubianka. D'Angelo discovered that Olga had been arrested from Feltrinelli a few days after his return from Moscow on September 9. Feltrinelli accused d'Angelo of having been the cause of Olga's arrest, and this led to d'Angelo's dismissal from the publishing house and a complete breakdown in relations (see d'Angelo 2006, 185; Mancosu 2013, 378).

Document 47. Heinz Schewe to Giangiacomo Feltrinelli, August 15, 1960

Location: AGFE, Busta 1, fascicolo 5, "Feltrinelli-Schewe" (1959 febbraio 15–1966 dicembre 07)
Format: Original
Original language: German
Previous publication: Original text and English translation first published in Mancosu 2018a

DOCUMENT

Editore
Giangiacomo Feltrinelli
Milan
Via Andegari 6

Moscow / Hotel Berlin / 516
August 15, 1960

Dear Mr. Feltrinelli,

I am extremely worried! Something totally unexpected has happened. Angelo sent a very large sum of money to Olga. I think it was around 200,000 rubles! The Italian tourist couple about whom I have already written to you brought the money. This will certainly not remain hidden from the security organs. As I hear it, Olga just made large purchases that will definitely attract attention. Her son Mitia bought himself a motorcycle, etc.

My gut tells me that this will not go well. Illegal transactions of this nature get eight years in a labor camp! Remittances of smaller amounts might have perhaps been accepted. But that much goes beyond the pale. This cannot go well. It was a big mistake by d'Angelo.

I would not be surprised if I were dragged into this. Probably they will suspect that I brought the money. It fits almost perfectly timewise—my return to Moscow and the large sum. This is very unpleasant. I have good reasons to be extremely cautious. I have decided not to visit Olga for a while. D'Angelo botched the whole thing. All the consequences go on his account. I see only the dark side of this!

It is too stupid. I have always recommended the greatest caution because I know the local circumstances quite precisely. I always warned: "They know everything, everything, everything!" Now everything is probably botched.

The last time I saw Ms. Olga, she told me she wanted to travel with Ira to the South, so that Ira could recover from her illness. Georges Nivat left. They did not extend his visa. Besides, he is very sick. Olga asks you to actually please transfer the money that the Classic had earmarked for him. He has need of it now on account of his illness. The transfer to Mrs. Schweitzer, meanwhile, was probably successful.

Enclosed are two more letters from Ms. Olga. The first is the original of that letter to d'Angelo that I already translated for you fourteen days ago. The second is practically the recall and clarification of why she decided differently.

I am now totally occupied with the Powers trial. Afterward I want to go on holiday. Hopefully everything will not become as bad as I fear. But it looks very grim.

Best wishes, also to Ms. Inge

[*handwritten*:] Your H. Schewe

Document 48. Heinz Schewe to Giangiacomo Feltrinelli, August 23, 1960

Location: AGFE, Busta 1, fascicolo 5, "Feltrinelli-Schewe" (1959 febbraio 15–1966 dicembre 07)
Format: Original
Original language: German
Previous publication: Original text and English translation first published in Mancosu 2018a

DOCUMENT

Editore
Giangiacomo Feltrinelli
Milan
Via Andegari 6

Moscow / Hotel Berlin / 516
August 23, 1960

Dear Mr. Feltrinelli,

Ms. Olga has been arrested. She was accused of "smuggling money." For all this we have Mr. Sergio d'Angelo to thank. He wanted to be especially smart and ruined everything. I have myself come into grave danger through this affair. As I hear it, they suspect me of smuggling this large sum of rubles (it is said to have been 200,000!!!) here and giving them to Olga. By chance the date of my return to Moscow coincided with this transaction, with which—as you know—I had absolutely nothing to do.

All the documents have—so far as I hear—been confiscated by the state police. Heaven knows what sorts of unpleasant things are still to come of this! We will surely be found out on all accounts. Ira is still at home. She is still quite sick. She advised me for the time being not to come by and to avoid any contact. Nobody can help. She says they are all in the greatest danger! I myself too! From the confiscated letters etc., my role as "family counselor and facilitator" will be discovered. Well then, thanks a million, Signor d'Angelo!

That is the state of things here. I beg you, dear Mr. Feltrinelli, for the time being do not send anything to Moscow, not even letters or mail orders. Best greetings to Ms. Inge.

Most sincerely, [*signed*] your Heinz Schewe

[*handwritten*:] P.S.: Please also observe the strictest discretion in Milan! Do not say anything to anyone! Moscow has ears everywhere!

Document 49. Giangiacomo Feltrinelli to Heinz Schewe, September 3, 1960

Location: AGFE, Busta 1, fascicolo 5, "Feltrinelli-Schewe" (1959 febbraio 15–1966 dicembre 07)

Format: Copy. The original (which I consulted) is in the Heinz Schewe Papers, Berlin.

Original language: German

Previous publication: Original text and English translation first published in Mancosu 2018a

DOCUMENT

My dear Heinz Schewe! 3.9.60

We read all of your letters at once, as soon as we returned from our holiday, and are absolutely horrified! The progression of events,—the crescendo in your last letter is truly terrible!

The blame unfortunately lies in carelessness and our friend's temporary mistrust in us, which the other party, whose motives are highly suspicious, exploited despite our warnings and premonitions.

With respect to d'A. I am completely in the dark,—either we are dealing with a provocateur or else with an idiot. I hardly believe that anything can be done at the moment? I am most worried about you and your safety. Hopefully the others also know, since they indeed know so much, that you had nothing to do with this matter. —En passant: d'A. applied for a visa for the Soviet Union recently and should have just departed in these past few days.

I am not at ease so long as you are not back here! Can I do anything for you, perhaps through A.[xel] S.[pringer]?

Please write without delay,—the most heartfelt wishes from Inge and me, your

[*signed*] Giangiacomo Feltrinelli

Document 50. Bill of Indictment against Olga Ivinskaya and Irina Emelianova, November 10, 1960[21]

Location: Copy of the original found at GARF (Moscow): Ivinskaya Olga Vsevolodovna. Nadzirnoe proizvodstvo № 13/2799-00. F. 8131, op. 31, № 89398, State Archive of the Russian Federation, 1960 (GARF).

Original language: Russian

Previous publication: Published in German in Schewe 1974; English translation first published in Mancosu 2018a

Additional information: The translation given in Mancosu 2018a was from the German translation in Schewe 1974, 72–86. The translation presented here is from the original Russian text. The reader should keep in mind that this document was never circulated during the Ivinskaya affair and that it was published for the first time (in German) in Schewe

21. Other documents relating to the arrests of Olga Ivinskaya and Irina Emelianova are in the possession of Irina Emelianova. They include the official reports on the daily searches of their apartment in the period August 16 to September 7, 1960 and an inventory, dated December 7, 1960, of the property confiscated in the searches drawn by the Moscow City Court .

1974. The original in Russian is still unpublished. I used the version kept at GARF.

INDICTMENT

In criminal case Nr. 53 are accused:

Ivinskaya, Olga Vsevolodovna, on account of violating paragraph 15 of the law "On penal responsibility for offenses against the state" and

Emelianova, Irina Ivanovna, on account of violating paragraph 17 of the penal code of the Soviet Union and the Soviet Republics, as well as paragraph 15 of the law "On penal responsibility for offenses against the state."

In 1956, the writer B. L. Pasternak transmitted the manuscript of his novel "Doctor Zhivago," unpublished in the Soviet Union, to the Italian publisher Giangiacomo Feltrinelli via an Italian national, Sergio d'Angelo. At the beginning of 1958, this novel was published in many editions in several capitalist countries. Pasternak was later offered a large sum of money via the Soviet "Iniurkollegiia"—a part of the royalties for the publication of his novel abroad. After Pasternak was reprimanded by the Soviet public for his unpatriotic behavior, he declined to accept this money through official means.

In 1959, however, Pasternak and his secretary Olga Vsevolodovna Ivinskaya established conspiratorial connections with foreign publishing houses in Italy, France, and the Federal Republic of Germany.

In 1959–60, Ivinskaya actively developed ways to acquire Pasternak's royalties by illegal means, either in the form of large amounts of money in Soviet currency, or in the form of valuables that were brought across the border of the Soviet Union. She also entangled her daughter—Irina Ivanovna Emelianova—in these illegal connections with foreigners.

As a result of these actions, O. V. Ivinskaya and I. I. Emelianova were detained in August/September 1960 by the Committee for State Security (KGB) of the Council of Ministers of the Soviet Union for carrying out illegal activities, specifically by accepting large sums of money in Soviet currency and valuables that had been imported by foreigners from capitalist countries.

The investigation concluded that Emelianova, in the absence of Ivinskaya and Pasternak, met in her apartment in February 1959 with the journalist Gerd Ruge, a representative of the West German publisher Kurt Wolff, and received 12,000 rubles from him, which she passed on to Ivinskaya. (See volume I of the bill of indictment, pages 320–337; also volume II, pages 146–160)

In December 1959, Ivinskaya received 6,000 rubles at her apartment, which had been brought across the border, by illicit means from a graduate student at Moscow

State University, the Frenchman Georges Nivat. This money originated from the representative of the French publishing house Gallimard, Jacqueline de Proyart. In August 1960, Georges Nivat was apprehended by Soviet customs officers in a smuggling attempt. (See volume I, pages 363–368; volume II, pages 266–271; volume III, pages 290–293) From the beginning of 1959 up to the day of her arrest, Ivinskaya maintained illegal contact with the West German correspondent Heinz Schewe, who emerged as the authorized representative of the Italian publisher Feltrinelli.

From May 1959 until April 1960, Ivinskaya illegally obtained from Schewe 80,000 rubles in Soviet currency. (See volume I, pages 174–186) Contact between Ivinskaya and the West German correspondent Heinz Schewe is established from multiple letters from Feltrinelli, which were delivered to Ivinskaya from abroad illegally.

It is established from an intercepted letter of Feltrinelli's to Ivinskaya of May 20, 1960, that he [Feltrinelli] apologizes that "Heinz Schewe came to Moscow with empty hands."

In another letter from July 8, 1960, which was written after Pasternak's death and addressed to Ivinskaya, Feltrinelli writes:

"In the future do not trust anyone, only Heinz Schewe. . . . I will always do it in such a way that a substantial part of the profits remain for yourself or for Ira. . . . Now you must, however, be careful of some things:

1) The earlier contract with Boris Pasternak concerning the publication of Dr. Z., as well as the new contract (which I beg you to please send as soon as possible), can never be allowed to come into the hands of the authorities or Pasternak's family. . . . All these confidential [mistranslated as "secret" by the Russians] documents must never be found with you.

2) Send me any other potential documents at your disposal that could be useful to me. . . . Everything that I receive . . . will be treated as if sent to me directly by Pasternak. . . .

4) I will not be at ease until ALL of Pasternak's letters, manuscripts, etc. are in the West. . . ." (volume III, pp. 233–238, 257–259)

During the house search at Ivinskaya's apartment, copies of letters were also found that she herself had written to Feltrinelli and sent via Schewe.

In one of these letters, which was likewise written after Pasternak's death, the defendant Ivinskaya informs Feltrinelli:

"First of all, I ask you in turn to consider Mr. Heinz Schewe to be my empowered representative. Through him I will give you, . . . [*omitted*: as per Borya's wishes,] those manuscripts that he will give to you in due time for publication. This concerns the manuscript of the novel, materials from the archives, which I will put into order without delay, as well as the play. Here, things are more difficult, the utmost care is needed and in this both you and I will trust Mr. Heinz." (See Volume III, pages 271–272)

During questioning, defendant Ivinskaya testified that in July 1960, she forwarded to Feltrinelli a manuscript of the play "The Blind Beauty" by Pasternak through Schewe on her own initiative. This play has not been published in the Soviet Union. (See Volume I, pages 174–186)

Per an earlier arrangement, in February 1960, the Italian journalist Leo Paladini visited Ivinskaya in her apartment. He brought her a letter from the Italian Sergio d'Angelo, as well as 40,000 rubles in Soviet currency.

In this letter, d'Angelo informs Ivinskaya:

"The bearer of this letter—Leo Paladini—is a very close and reliable friend of mine, whom you can trust completely. Unfortunately, he knows few Russian words. . . . I still have a lot of your money. Therefore I will not only give the agreed-upon sum to our friend. . . . From my side, I can still—safely and quickly—perform the operation that I offered to you." (See volume I, pages 277–294; volume III, page 244)

Having received the large sum of illegally delivered Soviet currency from Paladini, Ivinskaya and Emelianova arranged to meet with him the next day at the Hotel "Sovetskaya." Paladini informed them that he would give them a number of items that were brought in illegally from abroad. In the Hotel "Sovetskaya," Ivinskaya and Emelianova received from Paladini a number of valuable pieces of clothing. Among other things, Emelianova acquired a nylon winter coat.

In these meetings with Paladini, Emelianova performed the role of interpreter. (See volume I, pages 277–294; volume II, pages 45–53; volume III, pages 204–216)

In March 1960, at Ivinskaya's instruction, Emelianova met secretly at the Moscow post office with the Italian Mirella Garritano, who handed over to her a suitcase with 180,000 rubles. Still at the post office, Emelianova handed off the suitcase to her brother— D. A. Vinogradov.

The witness Vinogradov confirmed, under questioning, the meeting between Mirella Garritano and Emelianova at the post office and the receipt of the suitcase from her. (See volume III, pages 27–30)

At the end of July 1960, the Italian tourist couple the Benedettis came to the apartment of the defendants. They delivered a letter from Sergio d'Angelo to Ivinskaya and asked her to send for Emelianova, who at the time was staying at the dacha.

Once Emelianova had returned to her city apartment, the Italian Benedettis came again. They delivered to the defendants 500,000 rubles in Soviet currency. This money had been illegally brought into the Soviet Union. In this meeting with the Benedettis, Emelianova functioned as interpreter.

This money was delivered from abroad and given to Ivinskaya and Emelianova packaged in parcels.

A criminal-scientific analysis concluded that the paper in which the money was wrapped was produced abroad. (See volume III, pages 168–172)

After Ivinskaya and Emelianova obtained such a large sum of smuggled Soviet money, they deliberated about how they could hide it. The evening before her arrest, Ivinskaya, in mutual agreement with Emelianova, hid the money with her acquaintances Ermakova, A. I., Bogdanova, T. I., and Struchkova, M. E. In addition, they purchased several xxxxxxxxx things (a motorcycle and a wardrobe).

During house searches of the acquaintances of Ivinskaya and Emelianova, the following sums given to them by Ivinskaya were found and confiscated: with Struchkova—88,000 rubles; with Bogdanova—150,000 rubles, and with Ermakova—249,000 rubles. (See volume I, pages 66–67; 71–72; 76–91)

Found and confiscated in Ivinskaya and Emelianova's apartment were: a motorcycle, model "Kovrovets-175," and a new wardrobe. Both items had been purchased on the evening prior to Ivinskaya's arrest. (See volume I, pages 36–37)

Altogether found and confiscated during the house searches of Iviniskaya and Emelianova's apartment and those of their acquaintances: 570,894 rubles. (See volume I, pages 51–52; volume III, pages 180–184)

With the intent of putting to use the illegally received Soviet money, Ivinskaya and Emelianova intended to acquire a house at the station of Peredelkino, Moscow oblast, and purchase furniture for a three-room apartment. (See volume I, pages 393–400; volume II, pages 197–203)

The investigation additionally concluded that Ivinskaya and Emelianova illegally received, from abroad through the foreigners Schewe and Garritano in the period from 1959 to 1960, a number of valuable pieces of clothing and other articles: two nylon winter coats, a jacket, rain jackets, woolen shirts, two-piece dresses and dresses, as well as a typewriter.

During the house search of Ivinskaya's apartment, a letter from Sergio d'Angelo was confiscated dated April 2, 1959, addressed to Ivinskaya. It reads:

"As far as your receipts are concerned, everything is in order. But 5,000 rubles for a typewriter and a pair of shoes is too much. Therefore, and without needing any new receipts, I am sending right now a pair of summer shoes for you and Irochka, a shawl for you, and a summer dress for Irochka; and then I will send you some nylon winter clothes in a few months (which ones I ask you to specify in more detail if possible). You can be certain of my caution." (See volume III, pages 254–256)

In another letter from September 26, 1959, which was likewise confiscated, d'Angelo writes to Ivinskaya:

"I bought for you and Irochka some winter clothes with your money. If you like the fur coat, I will buy another, when our friend goes on another trip (one cannot send two fur coats together)." (See volume III, pages 249–251)

The following were confiscated during the house search of the apartment of the defendants Ivinskaya and Emelianova: two nylon winter coats, two two-piece dresses, three woolen sweaters, two women's suits, three dresses and a typewriter, model "Torpedo," all carrying foreign manufacturer labels. During interrogations, the defendants indicated that they obtained these things from abroad through the foreigners Schewe, Garritano, and Paladini. (See volume I, pages 420–427; volume II, pages 247–255)

In interrogations, the witness Ermakova, A. I., a seamstress by profession, stated that Ivinskaya brought these things to her for small repairs, informing her that she had obtained these things from abroad. (See volume III, pages 145–165)

Additionally, the investigation concluded that to further her illegal activities, Ivinskaya undertook a prolonged correspondence abroad via the foreigners Schewe, Nivat, and Garritano through illegal channels. She arranged occasional secret meetings with foreigners, for which she had created a password consisting of four halved 500-lira bills. These bill halves are added to the case as evidence. (See volume III, page 222)

The investigation additionally concluded that, per Ivinskaya's instructions, Feltrinelli paid for services rendered by the foreigners, who systematically smuggled large sums of Soviet currency across the border illegally. Thus, in June 1960 at her instruction, Feltrinelli disbursed 10,000 dollars each to the foreigners Sergio d'Angelo, Georges Nivat, and Heinz Schewe.

Also in the evidence file is a confiscated letter from Feltrinelli of June 24, 1960. In it, he confirms to Ivinskaya that he disbursed the specified sums to the named persons. (See volume III, 223–231)

The defendants Ivinskaya and Emelianova have pleaded guilty as charged. They are also proven guilty by the eyewitness testimony presented by Bogdanova, T. I. (See volume III, pages 1–8); Struchkova, M. E. (See volume III, pages 9–26, 127–133); Vinogradov, D. A. (See volume III, pages 27–30); Efron, A. S. (See volume III, pages 38–47, 103–118); Malinkovich, I. Z. (See volume III, pages 59–66, 133–144); Shmelëva, P. E. (See volume III, pages 74–87), and Bam, N. I. (See volume III, pages 119–126), as well as the material evidence, written documents, and criminal-scientific analyses (See volume III, pages 171, 219–293).

<u>On the basis of the above:</u>

1. Ivinskaya, Olga Vsevolodovna, born 1912 in Tambov, Russian, no party affiliation, with university education, active as a literary translator until her arrest

is accused of

participating in illicit activities in the years 1959 to 1960, as evidenced by having received large sums of illegally imported Soviet money from capitalist countries and high-value items from foreigners.

obtaining, in February 1959 via her daughter Emelianova, I. I., 12,000 rubles from the West German journalist Gerd Ruge.

receiving, from May 1959 until April 1960, 80,000 rubles via illegal means from the correspondent Heinz Schewe of the Federal Republic of Germany.

receiving, together with Emelianova in February 1960, 40,000 rubles from the Italian journalist Leo Paladini.

In the same month, together with Emelianova, visiting the Hotel "Sovetskaya" where they received a nylon winter coat and other clothes.

instructing, in March 1960, her daughter Emelianova to secretly meet at the Moscow post office with the Italian Mirella Garritano, from whom Emelianova received a suitcase with 180,000 rubles.

receiving, together with Emelianova at the beginning of August 1960, 500,000 rubles in Soviet currency from the Italian tourist couple the Benedettis, which were brought to the USSR illegally.

illegally receiving, in the period from 1959 to 1960, the following valuables and articles from the foreigners Schewe and Garritano: a nylon winter coat, a rain jacket, 3 two-piece dresses, and a typewriter, which is in violation of paragraph 15 of the ordinance "On penal responsibility for offenses against the state."

2. Emelianova, Irina Ivanovna, born 1938 in Moscow, Russian, until her arrest a student in her fifth year at the Maxim Gorky Literature Institute,

is accused of

having taken part, as the accomplice of the defendant O. V. Ivinskaya, in illicit activities as evidenced by the illegal receipt of large sums of Soviet money and valuables from capitalist countries.

having taken delivery, in her apartment in February 1959, of 12,000 rubles from the West German correspondent Gerd Ruge.

having interpreted, in February 1960, the conversation between Ivinskaya and the Italian Leo Paladini, during which they received 40,000 rubles.

having obtained, together with Ivinskaya in the same month at the Hotel "Sovetskaya," a nylon winter coat and other valuables from Paladini, which were brought into the USSR illegally.

having secretly met, in March 1960 at Ivinskaya's instruction, with the Italian Mirella Garritano, and receiving from her a suitcase that contained 180,000 rubles.

having obtained, together with Ivinskaya in the period from 1959 to 1960, valuable pieces of clothing—a coat, two sweaters, two rain jackets, and a dress—illegally brought into the USSR by the foreigners Heinz Schewe and Garritano.

having acquired from the Italian tourist couple the Benedettis, together with Ivinskaya in their apartment at the beginning of August 1960, 500,000 rubles that had been illegally brought from abroad into the Soviet Union.

having served as interpreter in the transfer of this money.

which is a violation of paragraph 17 of the penal legal code of the Soviet Union and the Soviet Republics, as well as of paragraph 15 of the ordinance "On penal responsibility for offenses against the state."

This bill of indictment was prepared on November 10, 1960 in Moscow.

Chief Investigator of the Investigation Department of the KGB at the Council of Ministers of the Soviet Union

sgd: Aleksanochkin, senior lieutenant

Agreed to by:

Chief Prosecutor of the Investigation Department of the KGB at the Council of Ministers of the Soviet Union.

sgd.: Chistiakov, Major General of Justice

Acting Chairperson of the KGB at the Council of Ministers of the Soviet Union
sgd.: Tikunov

Addendum: Ivinskaya, Olga Vsevolodovna, arrested on August 16, 1960
Emelianova, Irina Ivanovna, arrested on September 5, 1960

Names of witnesses:

1. Bogdanova, Tat'iana Ivanovna, Kostianski Pereulok 10a, kv. 10
2. Struchkova, Maria Efremovna, 2nd Ulitsa Stroitelei 4, Korpus 3, kv. 188
3. Ermakova, Aleksandra Ivanovna, Potapovskiĭ Pereulok 9/11, kv. 10
4. Efron, Ariadna Sergeevna, Tarussa, 1-aya Dachnaia Ulitsa 15
5. Shmelëva, Pelageia Egorovna, Potapovskiĭ Pereulok 9/11, kv. 18
6. Vinogradov, Dmitriĭ Aleksandrovich, Potapovskiĭ Pereulok 9/11, kv. 18
7. Bam, Nina Ignatievna, Mal. Gnezdnikovskiĭ Pereulok 9, kv. 40

Document 51. Documents circulated by P.E.N. International to its members in September 1961 containing letters and telegrams by Surkov, Carver, and d'Angelo

Location: Copy of the originals found at MHP, Oxford
Original language: English
Previous publication: A translation into Italian was published under the title "Documenti: Il caso Ivinskaja" in *Tempo Presente*, September–October 1961, 738–45. French and Russian translations (from the Italian) appeared in *Le dossier* 1994, 216–34; and Afiani and Tomilina 2001, 309–25, respectively. Original text in English first published in Mancosu 2018b.

January 19/1961 Press Release:

Following reports in today's press of the trial in camera and subsequent imprisonment of Madame Ivinskaya, and the detention of her daughter, the Executive Committee of the English Centre of the world association of writers, International P.E.N., met today in London and sent the following cable, in association with the Society of Authors, to the Soviet Writers' Union. (Madame Ivinskaya was, of course, the close personal friend of and literary collaborator with the late Boris Pasternak.)

"A.A. Surkov, Soviet Writers' Union, Moscow.

English Centre International P.E.N. and Society of Authors London urgently appeal your intervention secure release Madame Olga Ivinskaya and her daughter. David Carver, General Secretary, English Centre, International P.E.N."

January 24/1961 Press Release:

Following the telegrams sent to A. A. Surkov of the Soviet Writers' Union in Moscow on January 19 and on January 23, by the English Centre of International P.E.N. in association with the Society of Authors, a cable has been received today at P.E.N. headquarters from Mr. Surkov, which reads:

DAVID CARVER INTERNATIONAL PEN GLEBE PLACE LONDON

WRITERS UNION USSR FINDS NEITHER MORAL NOR LEGAL GROUNDS FOR DEMANDING OLGA IVINSKAYA AND HER DAUGHTER TO BE RELASED STOP IVINSKAYA AND HER DAUGHTER ARE KNOWN TO BE CONDEMNED BY MOSCOW CITY COURT IN NORMAL OPEN SESSION FOR CRIMINAL OFFENCE ILLEGAL CURRENCY MACH-

INATIONS COMMA PUNISHABLE ACCORDING LAWS OF OUR COUNTRY STOP WE CONSIDER STRANGE THAT INTERNATIONAL PEN AND LONDON SOCIETY AUTHORS SO HASTILY AND RESOLUTELY SPEAK IN DEFENCE OF ORDINARY ADVENTURERS HAVING NO RELATION WHATSOEVER TO LITERATURE WITHOUT EVEN TAKING TROUBLE TO LEARN WHO THEY ARE AND WHY CONDEMNED RESPECTFULLY ALEXEI SURKOV

On behalf of the English Centre of International P.E.N. and the Society of Authors, the following reply has been cabled this afternoon to Alexei Surkov:

ALEXEI A SURKOV SOVIET WRITERS UNION MOSCOW

APPRECIATE YOUR TELEGRAM STOP PEN AND SOCIETY OF AUTHORS FULLY AWARE IDENTITY OLGA IVINSKAYA AND DAUGHTER STOP INTERNATIONAL PEN INTERESTED IN ALL LITERARY WORKERS IRRESPECTIVE OF STATUS OR FIELD OF ACTIVITY STOP MUST REITERATE REQUEST OUR CABLE YESTERDAY YOU OBTAIN PUBLICATION TRANSCRIPT OF TRIAL AND URGE YOU USE YOUR INFLUENCE OBTAIN ACT OF CLEMENCY DAVID CARVER GENERAL SECRETARY ENGLISH CENTRE INTERNATIONAL PEN

***

Copy of letter from Mr. David Carver to Mr. A. A. Surkov

30th January 1961

Dear Mr. Surkov,

May I refer to the telegrams I have sent you during the last ten days on behalf of the English Centre of International P.E.N. and the Society of Authors regarding the arrest, trial, and imprisonment of Mrs. Olga Ivinskaya and her daughter Irena and also thank you for telegram of the 23rd.

My last telegram will have conveyed to you my surprise that you should have thought that P.E.N. and the Society of Authors should not only be ignorant of the identity of Mrs. Ivinskaya but that either body would have taken the action they did without considerable thought having been given to the matter.

Your telegram stated that the two women were "condemned by Moscow City Court in normal session" but nowhere has it emerged in radio broadcasts or in reports from newspaper correspondents in Moscow, what defence Mrs. Ivinskaya and her daughter made to the charges. Now the news has reached us over Moscow radio that Mrs. Ivinskaya and her daughter have appealed against their sentences unsuccessfully and certain further details of the charges have been given. In order to dispel any illusions that have been created here, could you not, as I have urged in my telegrams, ask the authorities to publish the transcript of the trial or alternatively could you not ask them to make available the reports that appeared in the Moscow press following the trial.

Above all I would urge you to ask the Government for an act of clemency. Those of us who continue to hope for a better rapprochement between Russian writers and writers in the west and elsewhere, cannot help feeling that the events of the past few weeks can only hinder and delay this improvement. The whole matter has aroused the deepest interest in the west especially in literary circles. A merciful gesture by the Soviet authorities would have a profound and lasting effect.

Yours sincerely,
Signed: DAVID CARVER
General Secretary

Alexei A. Surkov, Esq.,
Soviet Writers' Union,
Moscow.

***

Letter to David Carver, General Secretary of International P.E.N., from Alexei Surkov, Secretary of the Soviet Writers' Union, Moscow.

Moscow, April 3, 1961

Dear Mr. Carver,

As soon as I was able to get through with all the urgent matters that awaited me on my return from London, I read the letter you spoke about at the reception in our Embassy.

I deeply regret that I did not have the time and opportunity to talk to you about the so-called 'Ivinskaya case' in a more suitable atmosphere than that of a diplomatic reception.

I cannot turn this letter into a thesis on the moral and legal aspects of the 'Ivinskaya case' and shall therefore be very brief.

After receiving telegrams from Graham Greene, yourself and my Italian friend D. Angioletti, I went to the city court once more and asked them to show me the case proceedings. I studied document after document, every single sheet of the three volume file of this law suit, beginning with the warrant for the search and arrest and ending with the sentence passed by the city court. Since the Western press and Ivinskaya in her testimony insisted that the sums received by her were intended for the allegedly poverty stricken late Boris Pasternak I thought it necessary to find out the size of Pasternak's literary fees in the last months of his life, i.e. after his expulsion from the Writers' Union. In addition, I spoke to his real wife, Zinaida Nikolayevna, and his intimate friends the Ivanovs, Vsevolod and Tamara, in order to clarify this turbid issue.

Everything I have heard and read I shall tell you in concise, telegraphic, form below.

1. WHO IS IVINSKAYA? Ivinskaya is a 48-year-old woman, who since 1946 was known as private secretary of Pasternak and the last mistress of this elderly man who lived until his very last day with his family. In literary circles Ivinskaya was known as an unscrupulous adventuress who advertised her intimacy with Pasternak. Despite her advanced age she did not stop to have many parallel and frequent intimate relations with other men.

When I was editor of the Ogonyok weekly, a group of staff workers was involved in a financial fraud. An investigation showed that Ivinskaya (that was the first time I heard the name) had repeatedly received fees for articles written by somebody else thanks to the fact that she was on intimate terms with M. Osipov, my deputy editor, who in this way compensated her for intimate relations with him. Konstantin Simonov told me that he had to discharge Ivinskaya from her job on the staff of Novi Mir magazine because she was surprised in an office with a man doing far from official things. It is very unpleasant to write all this about a woman, but those who take her under their protection must know what sort of person Ivinskaya is.

Ivinskaya has no direct relation to literature. Out of respect to Pasternak, on his recommendations, some publishers gave Ivinskaya poems to translate which she either very poorly translated herself, or else hired young students for a low price to do the translations which she then passed as her own. And this woman had the nerve to declare in court that she had 'helped Pasternak with his translation work' (!!)

2. WHAT WAS IVINSKAYA TRIED FOR? As the court proceedings reveal, last August the criminal investigations authorities became aware that Ivinskaya had during the past year repeatedly received sums of Soviet money smuggled from abroad, from the publisher Feltrinelli. This money was allegedly intended for Pasternak. According to the documents contained in the files and to Ivinskaya herself, she has received approximately 840 thousand roubles. The money has been smuggled across Italy, and secretly handed over to Ivinskaya, who perfectly well knew how such transactions are treated by the criminal code of our country.

Being aware of the illegal nature of such monetary dealings Ivinskaya received the sums either at the Post Office, or in her country house, or in her flat in the city. The last time, and in order to avoid trouble with the law, she divided the sum among her various women-friends, who later appeared as witnesses in the court. When Ivinskaya was arrested[,] in her flat and in the apartments of her women-friends were found and sequestered 576 thousand roubles in Soviet currency. Besides, according to documents on file and to Ivinskaya's own testimony during the inquest and in court, she had in a contraband way received various articles which had not passed through the customs, and for which no customs' tax had been paid. Among them were articles of men's and women's clothing, a typewriter, etc.

For all these things, which are criminal offences punishable by the laws of any country, Ivinskaya was brought to court and tried in December of last year.

3. FOR THE SAKE OF WHAT DID IVINSKAYA COMMIT THESE OFFENCES? During the inquest and in court she insisted that she did all this on Pasternak's request and in his behalf. But, in the first place, the lion's share of the money was received by her after Pasternak's death. Secondly, Pasternak's wife and his close friends, the Ivanovs, assured me that Pasternak could not have taken this money because till the last day of his life, he lived on his legitimate Soviet earnings. And these legitimate Soviet earnings in only three places where he had his contacts (the Goslitizdat and Iskusstvo Publishing houses, and the Office of Protection of Authors' Rights) for the years 1958, 1959 and 1960 amounted to 496,000 roubles. If we divide this sum per 30 months it will come to a neat 16,500 roubles a month. I must note that such an income is earned by only a few, the most popular of our writers whose works are frequently published.

Apart from this, according to the documents on file and Ivinskaya's testimony, the Injurcollegia, a special office existing in our country, which deals with matters pertaining to money transmittals from abroad to Soviet citizens, had informed Pasternak that sums earmarked for him have been coming in and he could receive them, but Pasternak had refused to receive the money. There is little truth in Ivinskaya's version that Pasternak afterwards had decided to receive the money secretly, in devious ways. Why would Pasternak wish to do this, when he could have received the money in a legitimate way without risking to come into conflict with the laws of the country?

All these established and substantiated facts are repudiating Ivinskaya's version that she had received money for Pasternak. They also refute the lie elaborated in the West that Pasternak was hard up materially after his expulsion from the Writers' Union.

After he was expelled from the Writers' Union, Pasternak continued to live his life in a country cottage that belonged to the Union. His family still lives there. The Literary Fund had spent 27,000 roubles on Pasternak's medical treatment in 1960, on his funeral and the tombstone on his grave.

When Pasternak was still alive Ivinskaya made him sign blank sheets of paper (three such blank sheets with his signature affixed are in the files of the proceedings) which she later, at will, transformed into letters of attorney and used them avariciously to enrich herself.

DID IVINSKAYA, FELTRINELLI AND THEIR AGENTS RESPECT PASTERNAK'S MEMORY? A large batch of original letters by Feltrinelli and his agent D'Angelo, a journalist, which are on file in the proceedings, are graphic proof that both the publisher and the 'most intimate friend' Ivinskaya pursued entirely mercenary ends. Feltrinelli, who was engaged in unlawful machinations of buying Soviet currency abroad and sending it on to Ivinskaya, wanted to buy from Ivinskaya Pasternak archives which she did not possess. And Ivinskaya, being an inborn adventuress and a person without any scruples, used her intimacy with Pasternak to profit in a purely material way by mystifying Feltrinelli with her false assertions that Pasternak's archives were in her possession.

All this is corroborated by the fact that Feltrinelli's letters (Adzhubei offered a photocopy of one of these letters to the London press but they did not want to publish it), and D'Angelo's letters contain frequent warnings that the authorities must not know anything about the transactions with Ivinskaya, neither must Pasternak's family in Moscow and Britain, nor Pasternak himself and his authorised agent the Frenchwoman Prujar [Proyart].

It is disgusting to read Feltrinelli's letter written after Pasternak's death; after the first paragraph of very hurriedly expressed condolences, there follows an elaborate business instruction of how to handle the legacy, how to ship it over, and, in case Pasternak hadn't signed it, how to fake his letter of attorney, entrusting Feltrinelli to handle his publishing affairs, how much money there is still left and how much more is due, etc., etc.

The whole batch of letters written by Feltrinelli and his agent, the international swindler D'Angelo, exposes them, and together with them Ivinskaya, as dirty cynics, profiteers and evil spirits in the life of the outstanding and subjectively honest poet, Boris Pasternak.

To all this I must add that both in the correspondence and among the exhibits of the case there are things entirely in the vein of detective stories, like, for instance, instructions to use the code in letter writing, false addresses, Italian banknotes cut in half which served as identification signs for 'friends'—contact men, etc., etc.

All this taken together convinces us, Soviet writers, that Olga Ivinskaya and her daughter, a former student of the Literary Institute and a Komsomol, an accomplice of her mother, have both received a deserved punishment.

HOW WAS IVINSKAYA TRIED? The inquest and the trial in court were conducted in accordance with strict, and I would add utterly scrupulous, observance of the rules of the Criminal Code of the RSFSR. The case was considered in a regular court session with the participation of both the prosecutor and the counsels for the defence. The defendants were, in due time, handed the indictment and their lawyers (prominent Moscow jurists Kosachevsky and Samsonov, Chairman of the College of Barristers) had been acquainted with the documents of the case. The lawyers visited their clients many times in prison and had talks with them. Ivinskaya and Yemelianova themselves, both when they read their indictment and during the trial distinctly and definitively admitted, under the weight of evidence, their guilt. Their lawyers appealed to the Supreme Court but the latter rejected their appeal and the verdict remained in force.

Since I am not a specialist on judicial procedure, I consulted prominent experts on criminology, who told me that both the inquest and the trial were conducted properly and that the decision of the court and the term of imprisonment are in complete accord with the juridical norms existing in our country.

All this taken together gives me grounds to assure you again that the 'Ivinskaya case' is an ordinary case of swindling which involves smuggling of currency, but presented in an atmosphere of unclean clamour around the name of the deceased poet. It has nothing whatsoever to do with politics or literature and we had all the moral grounds not to soil our hands by touching this evil smelling case or by getting involved in it.

We are quite surprised how could the fastidious advocates of morality and justice have completely overlooked the fact that this clamour and fuss about the unscrupulous mistress whom they elevated to the rank of prototype of Lara, humiliates the memory of Pasternak and deeply insults his wife and children, in whose arms he died, having forbidden during his last illness to let Ivinskaya to his bedside.

It is rather unpleasant for us to know that alongside with the familiar to us well-wisher Edward Crankshaw and other 'objective' experts like him involved in this campaign are respected by us men like Bertrand Russell, Clement Attlee, William Hayter. It was not honest to involve in this campaign people who actually know very little of the case. Neither the French, nor the Italian writers, nor writers from other countries wanted to soil their hands on it.

That is why, Mr. Carver, I cannot do anything that you suggest in your letter. We do not want to urge the government and the court to publish the stenographic record of this ordinary criminal case. Our public would regard it as an insult to Pasternak's family, and to the memory of the poet. Maybe later, some detective story writer will write an ordinary detective story based on the 'Ivinskaya case,' it does not deserve more. We shall not request the government to commute the just sentence passed on Ivinskaya both as far as the substance of the matter is concerned and also because we know the prisoners in our country have many opportunities through honest labour to reduce substantially their prison term, and there are frequent amnesties in our country.

For your information I wish to tell you that last February I have dwelled at length on the 'Ivinskaya case' at the regular session of the Executive Council of the European Community of Writers in Rome. My statement was supported by documentary proof which satisfied the participants of the meeting who represented the literatures of Italy, France, Greece, Spain, FRG, Yugoslavia, Sweden, Denmark, Norway, Hungary, Czechoslovakia, Switzerland and several other European countries and many of whom were approached for signature by Stephen Spender and Ignazio Silone the initiators of the campaign.

Now, a few words about our relations with the International P.E.N. Club.

It seems to us that in view of the present distribution of forces in the world, including that of literary forces, we are hardly more interested in our ties with the P.E.N. Club than it is interested in ties with us. Our literary and historical traditions make us a proud literature, and we expect a gentlemanly minimum of respect from those with whom we enter into contacts. Whether in the capacity of equal members, or as observers, we cannot come to congresses like the last one in Rio de Janeiro, where blinded by class hatred grey-haired demagogues of the de Madariaga type will pour out insults on us while the other participants look on in silence. We are not only puzzled but honestly speaking, indignant by the fact that the tone in the P.E.N. Club is set by the so-called 'writers in exile,' people without a country, people with a past but without a future, people for whom men like de Madariaga are making their speeches in order to satisfy their impotent vindictiveness. We can have contacts with writers of other nations only as equals with equals, on the basis of mutual respect and on the basis of common features that unite us as writers humanists, with due consideration to the difference of opinion that exist among writers on our and your side of the planet.

Two years ago we joined the European Community of Writers which unites writers of the most diverse religious beliefs, philosophical views and political sympathies. We are received there as equals by equals, and within the framework of this community we co-operate with many members of the P.E.N. Club, including its present president Alberto Moravia, and its former president André Chamson.

For many years now we are taking part in the powerful movement of the writers of Asia and Africa, which unites a large circle of talented writers because the membership of our Writers' Union includes not only European writers but a large number of writers that belong to soviet Asiatic literatures.

Thus we have a good feeling of being part of the broad stream of contemporary world literature in which we occupy our modest but definite historical place. In this European and Afro-Asian stream both our colleagues and ourselves try to find that which can unite us in the common feeling of being responsible for the present and future of literature and mankind, and are not hunting for all sorts of insignificant (like the 'Ivinskaya case') pretexts for dissent and disunity. That is why we do not feel, perhaps, such an urgent need to stretch out our hand into emptiness, although we are well aware what an important role in uniting the efforts of writers in our difficult time could be played by the P.E.N. Club with its long-term tradition of international contacts between the writers, and its membership of hundreds of writers respected by us, whose works enjoy a far larger circulation in our country than our works do in the West.

Forgive my long letter. But I wanted, first of all, to 'close' the futile correspondence on the 'Ivinskaya case' and secondly, what is far more important, to outline at least briefly our position as regards further contacts with the organisation of which you are the worthy Secretary General.

In this letter I have expressed my personal point of view on the Ivinskaya case and on our relations with the P.E.N. Club. But, having written the letter, I showed it to my colleagues in the leadership of the Writers' Union. They agreed with its contents.

If you find it possible, I would appreciate it if you would acquaint with this letter your colleagues in the leading Centre of the P.E.N. Club.

I take this opportunity to ask you to tell your wife that I was happy to have made her acquaintance and am sending her my best wishes and regards.

Sincerely yours,
(signed) A. SURKOV.

Mr. David Carver,
General Secretary,
English Centre,
International P.E.N.,
62–63 Glebe Place,
Chelsea, London, S.W.3.,
England.

***

<u>Letter from David Carver to Alexei Surkov.</u> <u>April 26. 1961</u>

Dear Mr. Surkov,

Thank you very much for you letter. I very greatly appreciate your writing to me at such length, and in such detail, and I will certainly bring the contents of your letter to the notice of members of the praesidium of the International P.E.N.

As your letter expressed your personal point of view (which I see you say is endorsed by your colleagues in the leadership of the Soviet Writers' Union), I should like, if I may, to make one or two personal observations in reply.

Whatever may have been the character or behaviour of Madame Ivinskaya during the years preceding Pasternak's death, there seems to be little doubt that she was for upwards of fourteen years the most important single person in the poet's life, and, in any case, alleged or even proven immoralities on the part of an accused person, should not have any bearing on the court's judgment.

Your letter makes no mention of Madame Ivinskaya's daughter, whose sentence has, perhaps, shocked people in the west almost more profoundly.

I would like to express the hope that nothing you say in your letter should be taken to affect the promise you gave while in England that Madame Ivinskaya would be released within a period of months.

With regards to the relations between Soviet writers and International P.E.N., I must reiterate what I said to you when we met at the Soviet Embassy: International P.E.N. offers an open forum, so long as delegates attending its International Executive Committee Meetings and Congresses do not bring purely political issues into their discussions they may express their views—even though their views may be widely at variance with the views held by the greater majority of the members. Don Salvador de Madariaga was, in my view and I think I can say in the view of the majority, gravely wrong in his advocacy, at the Rio Congress last July, of confining membership of P.E.N. to writers of countries with democratic governments only. The policy of P.E.N. has always been to bring writers of all nations together, irrespective of their political or religious views, or the political nature of their countries' governments. But, as I said to you when we met, we felt it best that de Madariaga should be allowed to speak his mind; he must have been under no misapprehension as to the lack of support which his views obtained.

When the P.E.N. International Executive Committee, meeting in London a year ago, decided to ask Soviet writers to attend a P.E.N. Congress in the capacity of observers, the invitation was, of course, from equals to equals on the basis of mutual respect, and, as you say, on the basis of the common views which unite us as writers and humanists. Circumstances over which the Executive Committee had no control (the unfortunate fact that at present no diplomatic relations exist between Brazil and the USSR which would have made it extremely difficult for visas to be obtained from the Brazilian authorities) prevented the fulfillment of this desire, but I know that the P.E.N. International President hopes, as I do myself, that at the next Congress we shall have the pleasure of the company of the Soviet writers, and it would not be, I trust, a question of stretching out their hands 'into emptiness.'

Once again, I would like to emphasize my appreciation of your taking so much time and trouble to write to me. I shall write to you again when I have had an opportunity of discussing your letter with the officers of International P.E.N.

Thank you very much for your kind wishes for my wife, which she warmly reciprocates.

All good wishes to you and your colleagues.

Alexei A. Surkov, Esq.,
Soviet Writers' Union,
52 Vorovsky Street,
Moscow, U.S.S.R.

Yours very sincerely,

(signed) DAVID CARVER
General Secretary, International P.E.N

Open letter from Sergio d'Angelo to Alexei Surkov

Mr. Surkov,

I have only just had the opportunity of reading and commenting on the text of the letter which you sent last April to a representative of the Pen Club with the request that it should be circulated among the members of that organisation.

In that letter (which begins with a series of pornographic inventions intended to defame Ivinskaya) you reject the invitation to intervene on behalf of Pasternak's collaborator and her daughter on the grounds that the heavy sentence of imprisonment imposed on them was 'fully deserved' as it appeared from your careful reading of 'each document' and 'every page' of the three volumes of the record of the case.

In the course of this study you found that the most important element in the case, the fundamental one and the one which excludes every mitigating circumstance for the two persons found guilty by the court, was the fact that the request for money to be sent by illegal channels did not come from Pasternak (who, according to you, was in receipt of a magnificent income in his own country even after the events of 1958), but from Mme. Ivinskaya, who is supposed to have acted without the writer's knowledge and contrary to his interests.

But all this is utterly false, as was demonstrated last May when I caused to be published in certain serious newspapers some letters written in Pasternak's own hand in which the writer, whom you persecuted during his life and pretend to admire after his death, said that he was in a precarious economic state and asked that a part of the income from Dr. Zhivago should be sent to him directly, that is, in the only way he considered possible.

It follows clearly from these letters, which you have found it convenient to ignore, that the whole responsibility of Ivinskaya (who neither planned nor carried out any form of smuggling) is reduced to having received sums of money, already converted into roubles, for the sole purpose of handing them over intact (as the documents prove) into Pasternak's hands. The disinterested and generous nature of Ivinskaya's actions is not lessened by the fact that she was sent a final sum of money on July 31st, 1960, by which time the writer was already dead. The initiative in this was taken by me without my being requested because, although you charge me with being an "international peddler" (taking advantage of the fact that I cannot institute proceedings against you), I preferred to respect Pasternak's explicit wishes rather than to appropriate money which did not belong to me.

You say you are no expert on legal matters. But even if you were an expert, you would not be able to convince anyone, particularly after the publication of Pasternak's letters, that the sentences imposed on Ivinskaya and her daughter are in accordance with your country's legal code. As I have pointed out on another occasion, article 15, which deals with crimes against the State and was applied to the two women, lays down a maximum penalty of 10 years' detention, but concerns only the case of a professional smuggler who personally carries across the frontier 'explosives, drugs, poisons, arms and munitions.' From this it is only too clear that the sentence of 8 years passed on Ivinskaya and that of 3 years passed on her daughter (who played not the smallest part in the affair of the money) are to be explained only by a typical piece of falsification of which you know better than anyone the working and the purpose.

I am perfectly well aware, Mr. Surkov, of your state of mind. You have always hated Pasternak and, dominated by this feeling, you carried out, as first secretary of the Writers' Union, a series of ill-considered acts which did your country a very poor service. In promoting the campaign for the banning of Dr. Zhivago ('a novel written against me,' as you once said, not without presumption) and in pursuing it with methods both mean and childish, you transformed a literary matter, about which Soviet readers could themselves have debated without passion, into an international scandal. Then, when Pasternak was awarded the Nobel Prize, you lost your head completely and, because you have the vice of using coarse language, you said and caused to be said against the author of Dr. Zhivago things which aroused widespread indignation in every country and caused even Communist circles the most profound embarrassment. Still not content, you finally demanded Pasternak's expulsion from the Writers' Union, and who knows how far you would have gone, if the highest authorities in your country, intervening out of love for their country, had not stopped you and later relieved you of your duties as first secretary.

Pasternak's death was not sufficient to satisfy your spite, which you are now venting, with invective and slander, on two defenceless women who are, furthermore, seriously ill.

I have no illusions and I do not think that you will find it possible to change your ways or to show moderation and humanity. But neither should you, on your part, have any illusions about having "closed the futile correspondence on the Ivinskaya affair," as you say in your letter: the conscience of all civilised and honest people will not permit it to be "closed" until justice has been done.

And now one last thing. You assert that among the papers of the trial were numerous letters in which allegedly the publisher Feltrinelli and I suggested to Ivinskaya that she should conceal our transactions from Pasternak's family (both in Moscow and Britain), from Pasternak himself and from his French representative Mme. de Proyart. I may say that, as far as I personally am concerned, you are telling an absolute lie. I have never wished or suggested anything of the kind and I defy you publicly to prove the contrary.

Don't be frightened: produce all the letters, produce all the records of the trial. It will be very interesting to see who has to lose face.

Yours,
Sergio d'Angelo.

Bibliography

Afiani, Vitaliĭ I., and Natal'ia G. Tomilina, eds. 2001. *A za mnoiu shum pogoni: Boris Pasternak i vlast'; dokumenty 1956–1972* [But the hunters are gaining ground: Boris Pasternak and the regime; Documents, 1956–1972]. Moscow: ROSSPĖN.

Barnes, Christopher. 1998. *Boris Pasternak: A Literary Biography*. Vol. 2, *1928–1960*. Cambridge: Cambridge University Press.

Berlin, Isaiah. 2013. *Building: Letters 1960–1975*. Edited by Henry Hardy and Mark Pottle. London: Random House.

Chukovsky, Korney I. 2005. *Diary 1901–1969*. Edited by Victor Erlich. New Haven, CT: Yale University Press.

Conquest, Robert. 1961a. "The Fate of Olga Ivinskaya." *Encounter* (September), 86–92. Also in French as "Le sort d'Olga Ivinskaya," *Preuves* 126 (August 1961), 66–74.

———. 1961b. *Courage of Genius: The Pasternak Affair*. London: Collins and Harvill Press.

Crankshaw, Edward. 1984. *Putting Up with the Russians 1947–1984*. London: Macmillan.

Dalos, György. 1999. *Olga: Pasternaks letzte Liebe*. Hamburg: Europäische Verlagsanstalt.

d'Angelo, Sergio. 1958. "Come riuscii a portare in Italia il manoscritto del 'dottor Zivago' (Intervista di Michele Pellicani)." *Corrispondenza Socialista*, November 2, 1958.

———. 1961a. "Olga è innocente." *Vita*, May 11, 1961, 7–15. Also published in *Paris Jour*, May 7, 1961; and *Sunday Telegraph* (London), May 7, 1961.

———. 1961b. "Giallo a Mosca." *Vita*, May 18, 1961, 33–41.

———. 1961c. "D'Angelo a Surkov: 'Fuori le prove!'" *Vita*, August 3, 1961, 20–21.

———. 1961d. "Il 'mistero' di Pasternak." *Historia* 8, 19–25.

———. 1965. "L'affare Feltrinelli—Pasternak non è finito." *Vita*, December 23–29, 1965, 3–4.

———. 1968. "Der Fall Pasternak—Zehn Jahre danach." *Osteuropa* 7, 489–501.

———. 1972. "I miei rapporti con Feltrinelli." *Vita*, March 25, 1972, 5–6.

———. 1977. "La verità su Pasternak e le nuove bugie della propaganda Sovietica." *Vita*, January 26, 1977, 14.

———. 2006. *Il caso Pasternak*, Milano: Bietti. Translated into Russian as *Delo Pasternaka: vospominaniia ochevidtsa* (Moskva: Novoe literaturnoe obozrenie, 2007). The book can be downloaded in English or Russian from d'Angelo's website, http://www.pasternakbydangelo.com/.

de Mallac, Guy. 1981. *Boris Pasternak. His Life and Art.* Norman: University of Oklahoma Press.

Emelianova, Irina. 1997. *Legendy Potapovskogo pereulka: B. Pasternak, A. Efron, V. Shalamov: Vospominaniia i pis'ma* [Legends of Potapov Alley: B. Pasternak, A. Efron, V. Shalamov: Recollections and letters]. Moskva: Ellis Lak. French translation in Emelianova 2002.

———, ed. 2001. *Pamiati Vadimi Kozovogo: Tvoi Nerasshatann'ii mir: Stichi, Pis'ma, Vospominaniia* [Memories of Vadim Kozovoĭ: Your unshaken world: Poetry, letters, remembrances]. Moskva: Progress-Traditsia.

———. 2002. *Légendes de la rue Potapov.* Paris: Fayard.

———, ed. 2004. *Ariadna Efron: Zhizn' est' zhivotnoe polosatoe: Pis'ma 1955–1975* [Ariadna Efron: Life is a striped animal: Letters 1955–1975]. Moskva: Vigraf.

———. 2005. *Pasternak i Ivinskaya: Provoda pod tokom* [Pasternak and Ivinskaya: Electrified wires]. Moscow: Vagrius.

Feltrinelli, Carlo. 1999. *Senior Service.* Milan: Feltrinelli Editore. Translated into English, with a few cuts, as *Senior Service* (London: Granta Books, 2001). The U.S. edition, published in 2001 by Harcourt, cuts several additional important parts of the book.

Finn, Peter, and Petra Couvée. 2014. *The Zhivago Affair.* New York: Pantheon.

Fleishman, Lazar. 1990. *Boris Pasternak: The Poet and His Politics.* Cambridge, MA: Harvard University Press.

Gibb, Lorna. 2013. *The Extraordinary Life of Rebecca West: A Biography.* London: Macmillan.

Hayward, Max. 1966. *On Trial: The Soviet State vs. Abram Tertz and Nikolai Arzhak.* New York: Harper and Row. Revised and enlarged edition with Leopold Labedz, 1967.

Ivinskaya, Olga. 1978. *A Captive of Time.* New York: Doubleday. Original Russian: *V plenu vremeni.* Paris: Fayard, 1978.

———. 1999. *Zemli raskr'itoe okno: Stichi razn'ik let* [The open window of the world: Poems of different ages]. Moscow: Sinee Iabloko.

Ivinskaya, Olga, and Irina Emelianova. 2007. *God'i c Pasternakom i bez nego* [Years with Pasternak and without him]. Moscow: Vagrius.

Khrushchev, Sergei. 2013. *Memoirs of Nikita Khruschchev. Vol. 2: Reformer.* University Park: Pennsylvania State University Press.

Kosachevskiĭ, Viktor. 1988. "Posleslovie k romany, iz zapisok advokata" [Afterword to the novel: From the lawyer's notes]. *Moskva* 22, 139–47.

Koznova, Anna. 2017. "Vse tesnei kol'tzo oblav'i: Delo 1959 goda na Borisa Pasternaka" [As the dragnet tightens: The Boris Pasternak case of 1959]. *Znamia* 11/17, 1–24.

———. 2018. "'The Pursuit Draws Ever Closer': A Recently Unearthed Dossier on Boris Pasternak." *Russian Literature*, Vol. 100–102, 109–126.

Kudrova, Irma. 1999. *Russkie vstrechi Pitera Normana* [The Russian encounters of Peter Norman]. Saint Petersburg: Zhurnal Neva.

Le dossier de l'Affaire Pasternak: Archives du Comité Central et du Politburo. 1994. Preface by Jacqueline de Proyart. Paris: Gallimard.

Mancosu, Paolo. 2013. *Inside the Zhivago Storm: The Editorial Adventures of Pasternak's Masterpiece*. Milan: Feltrinelli.

———. 2015. *Rebels, Smugglers, Pirates: Itineraries in the Publishing History of Doctor Zhivago*. Stanford, CA: Hoover Press. Russian translation by Azbukovik, Moscow, 2017.

———. 2016. *Zhivago's Secret Journey: From Typescript to Book*. Stanford, CA: Hoover Press.

———. 2018a. "'Moscow Has Ears Everywhere!': From Pasternak's Death to Olga's and Irina's Arrests." *Wiener Slavistisches Jahrbuch / Vienna Slavic Yearbook*, n.s., 6, 35–121.

———. 2018b. "We Need to Help the Russians Save Face": The *Ivinskaya Affair* in the West." *Russian Literature*, Vol. 100-101-102, 127–220.

Mancosu, Paolo, and Paul Borokhov. 2017. "Sergio d'Angelo Correspondence with Olga Ivinskaya and Boris Pasternak." In *Novoe o Pasternakach* [New studies on Pasternak], edited by Lazar Fleishman, 218–309. Moscow: Azbukovnik.

Mansurov, Boris. 2009. *Lara moego romana: Boris Pasternak i Olga Ivinskaya* [My novel's Lara: Boris Pasternak and Olga Ivinskaya]. Moscow: Infomedia Publishers.

Nivat, Georges. 2007. *Vivre en russe*. Lausanne: L'Âge d'Homme.

Pasternak, Anna. 2016. *Lara*. London: William Collins.

Pasternak, Boris. 1957. *Il Dottor Živago: Romanzo*. Milan: Feltrinelli.

———. 1958a. *Essai d'autobiographie*. Paris: Gallimard.

———. 1958b. *Autobiografia e Nuovi Versi*. Milano: Feltrinelli.

———. 1958c. *Le Docteur Jivago*. Paris: Gallimard.

———. 1958d. *Doctor Zhivago*. Translated by Max Hayward and Manya Harari. London: Collins Press.

———. 1958e. *Doctor Zhivago*. With revisions to the English translation. New York: Pantheon.

———. 1994. *Lettres à mes amies françaises: 1956–1960*. Introduction by Jacqueline de Proyart. Paris: Gallimard.

———. 2004. *Pis'ma k roditeliam i sestram 1907–1960* [Letters to his parents and sisters 1907–1960]. Moscow: Novoe Literaturnoe Obozrenie.

———. 2005. *Pis'ma [Letters] 1954–1960*. In *Polnoe Sobranie Sochineniĭ* [Complete works], vol. 10. Moscow: Slovo.

———. 2010a. *Boris Pasternak—Kurt Wolff: Im Meer der Hingabe*. Edited by Evgeniĭ Pasternak and Elena Pasternak with the assistance of Fedor Poljakov. With a preface by Gerd Ruge. Frankfurt am Main: Peter Lang.

———. 2010b. *Family Correspondence 1921–1960*. Stanford, CA: Hoover Press.

Pasternak, Elena V. 2017. "Perekhvachennye pis'ma" [Intercepted letters]. In *Novoe o Pasternakach* [New studies on Pasternak], edited by Lazar Fleishman, 197–217. Moskva: Azbukovnik.

Pasternak, Elena V., and Evgeniĭ Pasternak. 1992. "Boris Pasternak. Pis'ma k Zhaklin de Pruaĭiar" [Letters to Jacqueline de Proyart]. *Novy Mir* 1, 127–89.

———. 1997. "Perepiska Borisa Pasternaka c Ėlen Pel't'e-Zamoĭskoĭ" [Boris Pasternak's Correspondence with Hélène Peltier-Zamoyska]. *Znamia* 1, 107–43.

———. 2001a. "Perepiska Pasternaka s Feltrinelli" [Pasternak's correspondence with Feltrinelli]. *Kontinent* 107, 278–316.

———. 2001b. "Perepiska Pasternaka s Feltrinelli" [Pasternak's correspondence with Feltrinelli]. *Kontinent* 108, 229–74.

———. 2004. *Zhizn' Borisa Pasternaka* [Boris Pasternak's life]. Saint Petersburg: Zvezda.

Pasternak, Evgeniĭ. 1988. *Boris Pasternak: Materialy dlia biografii* [Boris Pasternak: Materials for a biography]. Moscow: Sovietskiĭ pisatel'.

———. 1990. *Boris Pasternak: The Tragic Years, 1930–60*. London: Collins Harvill. A translation of the second part of Evgeniĭ Pasternak 1988.

———. 1997. *Boris Pasternak: Biografiia* [Boris Pasternak: A Biography]. Moscow: Tsitadel'. A second edition of Evgeniĭ Pasternak 1988.

Peltier-Zamoyska, Hélène. 1963. "Pasternak, homme du passé?" *Esprit* 313, no. 1 (January), 16–29.

Roberti, Vero. 1968. *Mosca sotto pelle*. Rome: Volpe.

Ruge, Gerd. 1958. *Pasternak: Eine Bildbiographie*. Munich: Kindler. Translated into English as *Pasternak. A Pictorial Biography* (London: Thames and Hudson, 1959).

Schewe, Heinz. 1974. *Pasternak privat*. Hamburg: Christians Verlag.

Schweitzer, Renate. 1963. *Freundschaft mit Boris Pasternak*. Vienna: Verlag Kurt Desch.

Taubman, William. 2003. *Khrushchev: The Man and His Era*. New York: W. W. Norton.

Toomey, Christine. 1996. "The Spy Who Loved Me." *Sunday Times Magazine*. Available at http://christinetoomey.com/pdfs/The_Spy_Who_Loved_Me.pdf (accessed December 18, 2017).

About the Author

Paolo Mancosu is Willis S. and Marion Slusser Professor of Philosophy at the University of California–Berkeley. He is the author of numerous articles and books on logic and the philosophy of mathematics. He is also the author of *Inside the Zhivago Storm: The Editorial Adventures of Pasternak's Masterpiece* (Milan: Feltrinelli, 2013), *Smugglers, Rebels, Pirates: Itineraries in the Publishing History of Doctor Zhivago* (Stanford: Hoover Press, 2015), *Zhivago's Secret Journey: From Typescript to Book* (Hoover Press, 2016), and the present volume, *Moscow Has Ears Everywhere: New Investigations on Pasternak and Ivinskaya* (Hoover Press, 2019). During his career he has taught at Stanford, Oxford, and Yale. He has been a fellow of the Humboldt Stiftung, the Wissenschaftskolleg zu Berlin, the Institute for Advanced Study at Princeton, and the Institut d'Études Avancées in Paris. He has received grants from the Guggenheim Foundation, the National Science Foundation, and the Centre National de la Recherche Scientifique.

Index